T0314191

DREAMS FOR LESOTHO

RECENT TITLES FROM THE HELEN KELLOGG INSTITUTE
SERIES ON DEMOCRACY AND DEVELOPMENT

Paolo G. Carozza and Aníbal Pérez-Liñan, series editors

The University of Notre Dame Press gratefully thanks the Helen Kellogg Institute for International Studies for its support in the publication of titles in this series.

Barry S. Levitt
Power in the Balance: Presidents, Parties, and Legislatures in Peru and Beyond (2012)

Sérgio Buarque de Holanda
Roots of Brazil (2012)

José Murilo de Carvalho
The Formation of Souls: Imagery of the Republic in Brazil (2012)

Douglas Chalmers and Scott Mainwaring, eds.
Problems Confronting Contemporary Democracies: Essays in Honor of Alfred Stepan (2012)

Peter K. Spink, Peter M. Ward, and Robert H. Wilson, eds.
Metropolitan Governance in the Federalist Americas: Strategies for Equitable and Integrated Development (2012)

Natasha Borges Sugiyama
Diffusion of Good Government: Social Sector Reforms in Brazil (2012)

Ignacio Walker
Democracy in Latin America: Between Hope and Despair (2013)

Laura Gómez-Mera
Power and Regionalism in Latin America: The Politics of MERCOSUR (2013)

Rosario Queirolo
The Success of the Left in Latin America: Untainted Parties, Market Reforms, and Voting Behavior (2013)

Erik Ching
Authoritarian el Salvador: Politics and the Origins of the Military Regimes, 1880–1940 (2013)

Brian Wampler
Activating Democracy in Brazil: Popular Participation, Social Justice, and Interlocking Institutions (2015)

J. Ricardo Tranjan
Participatory Democracy in Brazil: Socioeconomic and Political Origins (2016)

Tracy Beck Fenwick
Avoiding Governors: Federalism, Democracy, and Poverty Alleviation in Brazil and Argentina (2016)

Alexander Wilde
Religious Responses to Violence: Human Rights in Latin America Past and Present (2016)

Pedro Meira Monteiro
The Other Roots: Wandering Origins in Roots of Brazil and the Impasses of Modernity in Ibero-America

For a complete list of titles from the Kellogg Institute Series on Democracy and Development, see http://www.undpress.nd.edu

DREAMS FOR LESOTHO

Independence, Foreign Assistance, and Development

JOHN AERNI-FLESSNER

University of Notre Dame Press
Notre Dame, Indiana

University of Notre Dame Press
Notre Dame, Indiana 46556
undpress.nd.edu

Copyright © 2018 by University of Notre Dame

All Rights Reserved

Published in the United States of America

Library of Congress Cataloging-in-Publication Data

Names: Aerni-Flessner, John, author.
Title: Dreams for Lesotho : independence, foreign assistance, and development /
   John Aerni-Flessner.
Description: Notre Dame, Indiana : University of Notre Dame Press, 2018. |
Series: Helen Kellogg Institute series on democracy and development |
   Identifiers: LCCN 2017055857 (print) | LCCN 2017056758 (ebook) |
   ISBN 9780268103637 (pdf) | ISBN 9780268103644 (epub) |
   ISBN 9780268103613 (hardcover : alk. paper) | ISBN 0268103615
   (hardcover : alk. paper)
Subjects: LCSH: Economic development—Lesotho. | Economic development—
   Lesotho—International cooperation. | Lesotho—Economic conditions—1966- |
   Lesotho—Politics and government—1966-
Classification: LCC HC920 (ebook) | LCC HC920.A56   2018 (print) |
   DDC 338.96885—dc23
LC record available at https://lccn.loc.gov/2017055857

∞ *This paper meets the requirements of ANSI/NISO Z39.48-1992*
(Permanence of Paper).

CONTENTS

FIGURES AND TABLE

FIGURES

TABLE

ACKNOWLEDGMENTS

An author can write a book only by accruing debts, and this book has accrued a large number. So I start with the caveat that while many eyes have looked over this work, any errors of fact and interpretation that remain are mine alone.

The institutions and individuals that have supported this book are located on three continents. In Lesotho, where I accrued my largest debts, the National University of Lesotho (NUL) provided a fruitful home for research in 2008–9 through affiliation with the Institute of Southern African Studies. A stimulating Friday seminar series there allowed me to better understand and grapple with regional politics, history, and economics. I am grateful to the series organizers for allowing me to present the first bit of this research in April 2009. *Ntate* K. C. Maimane and the rest of the faculty in African Languages and Literature were kind enough to tutor me in Sesotho. *Bo-Ntate* Motlatsi Thabane, Tefetso Mothibe, and Munyaradzi Mushonga of the Department of Historical Studies and Jesmael Mataga (now at Sol Plaatje University) were welcoming and supportive as I struggled to gain a fuller understanding of Lesotho's history. *'Me* Tebello at the Lesotho National Archives, *'Me* Mathabo at the NUL Institute of Education, *Ntate* Sekhonyela Molapo at the NUL Library archives, and the staff of the Morija Museum and Archives provided assistance. The staff at *Moeletsi oa Basotho* supported my quest to find, contextualize, and scan images from their photographic collection, and I am grateful for their permission to include some of the images in this book. *Ntate* Stephen Gill of Morija helped to identify interview sources and served as a sounding board for my ideas. Kennedy Matsepe, Leseli Leseli, Motlatsi Thabane, Matt Morley, Kimberley Pal Keeton, and Chris Conz also pointed me to people whom I interviewed for this project. Scott Rosenberg and Richard Weisfelder were helpful in discussing the logistics of research in the Mountain Kingdom.

In Lesotho, I also owe many debts of gratitude to those who took me into their homes and made me feel part of their families since I first arrived to teach high school in 2002. The Sisters of the Good Shepherd welcomed me to St. Rodrigue High School, where my teaching experience was formative, and allowed me to live at their hostel in Roma. *Ntate* Leseli Leseli and '*Me* Maboleba Kolobe have been good friends, and I look forward to many more good memories and visits with their respective families. The Selebalo family from Ha 'Mamathe's lovingly welcomes me with open arms every time I return. Donald Mcmillan and Loretta Houston-Mcmillan were kind enough to allow me to stay with them in Maseru. Finally, I owe a special debt to Sister Armelina Tsiki, who has been a friend, mentor, and interview subject. I strive to emulate her grace and compassion and desire to work for the common good.

My undergraduate institution, Grinnell College, gave me great grounding in the practice of history, and sent me to Lesotho for the first time, and for that I remain grateful. My adviser, and now confidant and friend, George Drake, urged me to apply for the Lesotho teaching program, and I am thankful that I had the wisdom to listen to him. At Washington University in St. Louis, the Department of History and the International and Area Studies Program provided generous support to start the research for this book. My graduate adviser, Timothy Parsons, has been the best mentor an aspiring academic can hope for. He always made time to read my written material and has provided sage counsel through the years. Jean Allman, Lori Watt, Shanti Parikh, Nathan Jensen, and Mary Ann Dzuback served on my committee and have continued to play a mentoring role in my academic life. During graduate school, Iver Bernstein, Elizabeth Borgwardt, Daniel Bornstein, Margaret Garb, Derek Hirst, Christine Johnson, Peter Kastor, Steven Miles, Sloan Mahone, J. Cameron Monroe, Sowande' Mustakeem, Mungai Mutonya, Guy Ortolano, Wilmetta Toliver-Diallo, Sasha Turner, and Robert Vinson were all encouraging. My peers in the graduate program at Washington University were also sources of strength: Kevin Butterfield, Ben Dyer, Rajbir Hazelwood, Sara Jay, Matthew Stewart, Scott Morris, Tanya Roth, Muey Saeteurn, Steve Schrum, and Janek Wasserman. I might not have made it through graduate school without my running buddies: Ryan Chapman, Zac Freudenburg, Jason Holroyd, Dusty Lopez, and Tyler Small. A Fulbright-Hays Doctoral Dissertation Research Abroad Fellowship made my initial research possible. Sheryl Peltz worked wonders to help me navigate the university bureaucracy. Robert Edgar, now retired from Howard University, has been a great champion of this project.

The Department of History at SUNY Cortland also provided funding for my research. I received assistance from the HD-REDI program, as well as the Faculty Research Program. This funding allowed me time to peruse the British National Archives, including the Migrated Archive, which was unearthed by the defendants and lawyers in the Mau Mau torture case, to whom I and many historians are deeply indebted. My SUNY Cortland history colleagues helped me learn the ropes of being a professor. Girish Bhat, Laura Gathagan, Scott Moranda, Gigi Peterson, Amy Schutt, John Shedd, Kevin Sheets, Randi Storch, Brett Troyan, Judy Van Buskirk, Luo Xu, along with Don Wright, are examples of the scholar-educators all of us in academia strive to be. Others in Cortland to whom I am indebted include Seth Asumah, Alex Balas, Genni Birren, Christa Chatfield, Ibipo Johnston-Anumonwo, Deirdre Joyce, Tracy Marvin, Tracy McEvilly, Mechthild Nagel, Elyse Purcell, Sebastian Purcell, Vaughn Randall, Frank Rossi, Sharon Steadman, Chris Tucker, and Jeff Werner.

At Michigan State University (MSU), this book has greatly benefited from the support I received from the Residential College in the Arts and Humanities (RCAH) and Dean Steve Esquith. This support allowed me to travel to Lesotho and to Pretoria for research in the South African National Archives (SANA) and the Department of International Relations and Cooperation (DIRCO). The SANA archivists and Neels Muller at DIRCO were extremely helpful. My colleagues, including Eric Aronoff, Joanna Bosse, Lisa Biggs, Kevin Brooks, Guillermo Delgado, Vincent Delgado, Tama Hamilton-Wray, Donna Rich Kaplowitz, Candace Keller, Carolyn Loeb, Dylan Miner, Terese Monberg, India Plough, Niki Rudolph, Chris Scales, Dave Sheridan, Anita Skeen, Estrella Torrez, Katie Wittenauer, and Scot Yoder have been wonderfully encouraging. Carol Cole, Dawn Janetzke, Pam Newsted, and Lori Lancour have helped me navigate the intricate world that is the bureaucracy of a large institution. The African Studies Center has also been a welcoming home and helped nurture this book. I am thankful for the encouragement I received from MSU's contingent of African history faculty members: Jessica Achberger, Nwando Achebe, Peter Alegi, Laura Fair, Walter Hawthorne, Peter Limb, and Jamie Monson. The MSU Department of History has also been exceptionally welcoming. The summer 2016 interdisciplinary writing group that met in Erickson Hall gave me the needed push to get the first draft of the manuscript out the door.

Portions of this book were presented at a number of venues, including the National University of Lesotho's Faculty of Humanities Seminar Series, SUNY Cortland's Black History Month Sandwich Seminars, the African Studies Association annual meeting, MSU's African Studies Center's Eye on Africa series, the North Eastern Workshop on Southern Africa (NEWSA), and the Race, Resistance, and Reason Conference at SUNY Cortland. I am grateful to the *Journal of African History*, the *International Journal of African Historical Studies*, and *Wagadu: A Journal of Transnational Women's and Gender Studies* for allowing me to use portions of articles that have appeared previously.

The moment at which I realized it was possible for me to write this book for a wider community of scholars came during the Andrew Mellon Foundation/National History Center's Eighth International Seminar on Decolonization, held in Washington, DC, in July 2013. Under the leadership of William Roger Louis, Dane Kennedy, Philippa Levine, Jason Parker, Pillarisetti Sudhir, Lori Watt, and Marilyn Young, I came of age academically and found the confidence to get my "writing legs" under me. My cohort in the seminar was a wonderful audience for exploring ideas (and Washington), and I cherish them: Marc Andre, Isabel Barreto, Ellen Boucher, Nicole Bourbonnais, Leena Dallasheh, Andrew Dilley, Charlie Laderman, Jose Pedro Monteiro, Jessica Pearson, Juan Romero, Devika Sethi, Joanna Tague, Birte Timm, and Annalisa Urbano. The 2016 International Seminar on Decolonization Reunion Conference in Washington, DC, was generative as well, and I am grateful to the American Historical Association for supporting such events.

I received translation assistance from *Ntate* Teboho Mokotjo in Lesotho and from Faith Cranfield. The day Chris Conz wandered into the National Archives in Lesotho while I was working was also fortuitous. I have found myself, somewhat to my surprise, using Twitter to keep in touch with Basotho in Lesotho and beyond to stay up to date with events in the country and to think through my ideas on the intersection of history, culture, development, and politics. Charles Fogelman and Nora Kenworthy have been invaluable sounding boards for aspects of this project. Jane Hooper graciously shared book proposals with me, and Beverley Eikli was kind enough to interview her father, Ted Nettelton, and facilitate the use of photographs that he took while stationed in Mokhotlong in the 1960s.

I owe many thanks to Eli Bortz, Scott Mainwaring, and the entire team at the University of Notre Dame Press for the support and encouragement they have extended. This book is much improved from their suggestions and from the comments of the anonymous readers. I also need to thank the archivists and staff at the U.S. National Archives and Records Administration and the World Bank Archives, both in Washington, DC, and the British National Archives in Kew, London.

Finally, I owe a large debt to my family, immediate and extended. All have been great supporters of this project, even if they do not fully understand my continued fascination with all things pertaining to Lesotho. I received proofreading and emotional support from my parents, Kathy and Dan Aerni, as well as my siblings, Sarah, Katie, and Greg Aerni. Melanie and Bruce Flessner have also been wonderfully supportive and provided child care that facilitated my international research. I know that my late grandparents would have appreciated seeing this book in print. Of course, my biggest debt is to Lauren Aerni-Flessner, who put up with my absences and our many moves across the United States for jobs. This book literally could not have happened without her love and support. While Cameron was only somewhat aware that Dad was writing a book and Charlie had no idea (yet), it is to them that I dedicate all the time and effort that went into this since our move to Michigan.

This book further goes out to the Basotho *ba* Lesotho. I have written it from a place of deep love and respect for the people and institutions at work throughout the country. I hope it provides a much-needed window into an important period in national history. *Likhomo*!

Introduction

> Hope . . . is not the same as joy when things are going well, or
> willingness to invest in enterprises that are obviously headed
> for early successes, but rather an ability to work for something
> to succeed. Hope is definitely not the same thing as optimism.
> It's not the conviction that something will turn out well, but
> the certainty that something makes sense, regardless of how it
> turns out. It is this hope, above all, that gives us strength to live
> and to continually try new things, even in conditions that seem
> hopeless.
> —Vaclav Havel, "Never Hope against Hope"

Strolling down Kingsway, the main commercial and governmental street
in Maseru, one finds that most traffic consists of the ubiquitous taxis cruis-
ing slowly for passengers. These include both large white Toyota Hilux
vans and dilapidated "four-plus-ones"—old taxi cars whose horns inevi-
tably sputter rather than hoot from years of overuse. The sidewalks are
packed with Basotho, many of the women wearing patterned and brightly
colored Seshoeshoe dresses with matching head coverings, the men in
suits or wearing *kobo*, wool blankets, with the occasional older man wearing the *mokorotlo*—the iconic conical grass hat of Lesotho.[1]

Amidst this hubbub, one also sees the luxury sedans and massive *bak-
kies* (pickups) of South African businesspeople, Mercedes-Benz sedans
with red governmental license plates, and a profusion of large four-wheel-
drive vehicles marked with an alphabet soup of acronyms—UN (United

I

Nations), WFP (World Food Programme), CARE (Cooperative for Assistance and Relief Everywhere), UNDP (United Nations Development Programme), GIZ (German Agency for International Cooperation), USAID (United States Agency for International Development), DFID (Department for International Development, U.K.), and more. That these aid organizations are ubiquitous in the capital is not surprising as Lesotho consistently ranks among the world's poorest countries. The organizations have heavy-duty vehicles so they can tackle the dirt and gravel tracks that lead to the majority of villages in the country, suggesting that they are focused on serving all Basotho, regardless of ease of accessibility. The massive vehicles also signal, however, a disconnect between the organizations and ordinary Basotho walking Kingsway—low-level civil servants, the roughly forty thousand people employed in the garment industry, rural villagers in town to access banks or health care, or the large population of urban dwellers who muddle through on a combination of remittances, old-age stipends, the informal economy, and a few odd head of livestock that they manage to keep in periurban Maseru settlements. In climate-controlled comfort, the employees of aid organizations, Basotho and expatriate, cruise through town in a sort of luxury known only to senior governmental officials and a few other well-placed businesspeople.

It is no wonder, then, that Basotho like Thabelo Kebise, a fifty-four-year-old union organizer and former professional driver, hope to find work in the development sector. In Kebise's case, this desire remained even though he had a private sector job in a country where such jobs are scarce. He saw the development sector as providing the best potential to increase his earnings and improve his prestige.[2] The development sector is well entrenched in Lesotho, not just in terms of structures—vehicles, buildings, and programs—but also in the minds of Basotho. It is part of the landscape, part of the fiber of the national community, and still a salient marker of Lesotho's sovereignty from South Africa. Lesotho's independence is reaffirmed daily by the fact that Maseru is an international capital with American and Chinese embassies and an international airport and by the presence of a host of multilateral and bilateral development and aid organizations that have separate Maseru offices rather than just branches of a central office based in Pretoria or Cape Town, as they would if Lesotho were a province of South Africa. This state of affairs came about because of how colonial administrators, Basotho officials, and ordinary Basotho internalized the rhetoric of development in the 1960s and 1970s and how they worked for conceptions of independence that were dependent on economic, social, and political development. The definition of *development* was never static or agreed on by all, but the term became a rhetorical linchpin that guided conversations and actions around what independence should look like in Lesotho. Common to all the conceptions was the idea that independence could not come about without development and that more development would lead to greater independence for individuals, communities, and the country as a whole.

Development and development organizations were not always present in large numbers in Lesotho, however. At independence in 1966, there was only a small British aid program, a handful of private charitable organizations with minimal staff, and no industry or manufacturing in the country. And yet nine years later, in 1975, the government of Lesotho was accepting funding from twenty-seven countries, with seventy-two more "international agencies and non- and quasi-governmental organizations" in the country, bringing in millions per year. By the end of the decade, Lesotho received $64 million per year in development assistance, or $49 per person.[3]

This rapid increase raises questions about why so many organizations came to Lesotho after the transfer of power, how local people felt about their arrival, and how their presence affected local political processes. The phenomenon of the arrival of aid organizations and nongovernmental organizations (NGOs) around independence was certainly not unique to Lesotho, but the country was the setting for Ferguson's analysis of the impact of development on local governance and power structures. He argued persuasively that the net effect of this macro-process of "development" was not improved life outcomes for the population, increased national economic output, or any of the other lofty goals put forth by government planners and development professionals. Rather, it was the entrenchment of "bureaucratic state power" by situating decision making about development projects in technical agencies and bilateral funding agreements rather than in local political processes.[4] This formulation suggests a "gatekeeper state" for aid where those in power in Lesotho welcomed such programs because they solidified government authority, even if this authority came with a gradual loss of sovereign decision making by the national government and an inability of the populace to have substantive input into projects.[5] Thus policy makers were defining development as projects that promised to help centralize government power through the implementation, routinization, and bureaucratization of projects that promised poverty amelioration, increased employment, and/or new infrastructure. The rapid increase in the number of development projects and in funding in the years after independence reflected strong support from government for development, but it does not illuminate how those outside government experienced and made sense of the arrival and subsequent rapid expansion of development in Lesotho.

Development, generally speaking, is used throughout this book to refer to the process through which individuals, state agents, humanitarian organizations, and NGOs attempted to implement projects designed to improve the material conditions of life. This definition was not, however, universally agreed on. As noted above, government planners tended to employ development as a strategy designed to help bureaucratize and centralize state authority. For Basotho outside of government, the term often referred to the desire for projects to enable them to find material prosperity in Lesotho, to gain access to more and better governmental services, and to obtain a meaningful political voice in development projects specifically and governance in general. Painting in these broad strokes, however, should not blind us to the fact that conceptions of development were not static.

The malleability of the idea of development is what made it such a powerful rhetorical device that individuals used to claim the mantles of citizenship and belonging. Basotho of all political persuasions and positions in society adopted the rhetoric of development to argue for particular forms of projects that would bring about the world they envisioned upon achieving independence. Development, independence, and nationalism became intertwined in Lesotho in governmental policy decisions and in the public mind beginning in the 1950s. Development remained the salient language through which Basotho debated the forms and meanings of Lesotho's 1966 independence, and it remained the language of political contestation through the 1970s. The prominent place that rhetoric about development enjoyed among politicians and ordinary Basotho put pressure on political leaders to seek out and accept more foreign aid, even if it worked against the short- and long-term interests of the government, national sovereignty, and the public good. Many of the development projects initiated in the post-independence period were "failures" in that they did not ameliorate poverty, increase GDP, or achieve their objectives. But this was not the metric by which government leaders, bureaucrats, and overseas development planners were evaluating projects. Rather, since these individuals viewed development primarily in terms of its ability to extend the reach and further entrench the power of the state, these projects were only too successful.[6]

Ordinary Basotho, however, also managed to find utility in projects that "failed." In the colonial period there were few development projects operating in Lesotho, and those that existed faced significant resistance from the local population because of heavy-handed implementation. Thus, even if independence-era projects did not deliver promised poverty alleviation, more jobs, or increased popular input in governing processes, the sheer fact that the government was bringing development projects to fruition in the country helped Basotho achieve and maintain some faith that the concept of development still held the long-term key to the fulfillment of their independence dreams. This allowed Basotho to continue to nurture optimism through the years of political turmoil that marked post-1970 Lesotho.

Most Basotho hoped for an independence that would improve their material conditions of life and also allow them to remain as far from the apartheid system as possible. For them, the idea of development just "made sense," as Havel wrote. They knew the history of failed colonial development initiatives in the country, but their faith in development and desire for independence led them to prioritize investing time and energy in personally working to help build infrastructure like communal water taps, school buildings, and roads. This physical labor—the literal building of the nation—was a way to surmount the shortcomings of prior development projects that did not live up to their expectations, as well as a way to act out their own visions for independence and build community in Lesotho.

This faith in development as the means to transform the country and individual lives was similar to the "nostalgia for the future" that marked post–Cold War Togo. There, in Piot's formulation, people yearned for the possibility of an unknown and uncertain future, because it had to be better than the present.[7] Similarly, Ahearne found twenty-first-century residents of southern Tanzania looking back fondly on the colonial-era Groundnut Scheme, widely considered one of the worst failures of British colonial development efforts, because it provided the only successful example of large-scale local employment in public memory. In addition to employment, the project had given people the language they could deploy with government and international organizations to "express [and demand] a desire for a better future."[8] Basotho likewise deployed the rhetoric of development and utilized small-scale development initiatives to envision and help bring about a better future for themselves and their communities despite the very real limitations of the postcolonial state.

The faith that Basotho placed in the concept of development, thus, was not rooted in prior project success, or even in seeing governmental officials and project managers as trustworthy. Rather, it was rooted in a belief that development was required in order to ensure a better material future for all and in order to bring about a more responsive government. The irony of this stance was that colonial planners, Basotho leaders, and independence-era development consultants all purported to find Basotho afraid of the idea of development and leery about participating in development projects. These officials seemed genuinely confused as to why individuals and communities as a whole might oppose projects that promised to ameliorate poverty or were designed to meet pressing "national interests."[9] This resistance was rooted not in a rejection of the idea of increasing rural incomes but rather in opposition to how administrators initiated and carried out projects without significant local input. Local populations understood that the government's goal was to increase colonial authority, so there were few avenues for local input into project operations. Since they could not reject particular aspects of projects, they had to reject them in their entirety. Similarly, project administrators, politicians, and bureaucrats misread opposition as evidence that Basotho were opposed to development, nationalism, the parliamentary system, and even the idea of the modern nation-state. This misreading of popular sentiment about development continued into the independence era.

Examining development from the perspective of both local people affected by projects and government planners, it becomes clear that the failure of projects to attain their stated antipoverty goals was not the fault of ordinary Basotho rejecting particular development initiatives. Rather, this failure came about because colonial and independence-era officials misunderstood or did not care that Basotho understood development as a multifaceted process that should lead to a broad range of economic and political outcomes. Accusing individuals and communities of resistance to development became a convenient cover for political leaders to proffer to donors to explain why projects failed to meet stated goals. This put the onus of project failure on local noncooperation and exonerated project administrators and governmental officials—thereby protecting their ability to gain future funding.

At the same time politicians claimed legitimacy based on delivering funded projects. These same projects embodied and bolstered the hopes of many Basotho that they could achieve a degree of material and political independence because the post-independence period offered significant new opportunities for the government to solicit and attain foreign funding for more projects. Basotho saw development as a source of employment, patronage, increased government services, and upward mobility and as an opportunity to have a more significant political voice. There was no other comparable pathway to these desired objectives in the anemic postcolonial nation-state. The concept of development, thus, served as the vehicle through which ordinary Basotho hoped to bring to fruition their independence visions. Politicians, likewise, hoped to harness the funds and connections development promised to achieve political legitimacy at home and diplomatic legitimacy abroad. Development became the language and practice of independence in Lesotho.

DEVELOPMENT HISTORY

The entire concept of development represents, in some ways, a lack of faith in the ability of free markets to achieve specific economic and social goals that the state and nongovernmental entities deem important. In Lesotho, as in many places across the African continent, a wide variety of local, national, and international actors contested how development should operate in the local context. All attempted to harness the energy and vision behind the idea of development to push forward agendas ranging from bringing about particular notions of independence to furthering their own political ambitions. These actors also used development in an attempt to bring about macroeconomic changes in line with particular geopolitical orientations, especially around the Cold War and support for or resistance to the South African apartheid system. Cooper defined development as "state projects, channeling resources in ways the market does not, with the goal of improving the conditions that foster economic growth and higher standards of living."[10] This definition encompasses some aspects of development as defined in this book, but it leaves out humanitarian aid and the activities of local organizations, including NGOs. In Lesotho, for instance, food aid the United States provided for drought relief ended up "financing" development work through self-help programs that "paid" people in food to build infrastructure (as seen in the book's cover photograph).

Similarly Basotho youth and community groups invested their own time and resources in projects that included small-scale infrastructure creation and community-building efforts.

State-sponsored and state-sanctioned development efforts played a key role in defining the parameters of debates on nation- and state-building efforts, but focusing only on state efforts is too limiting. In Lesotho young Basotho were acting out their nationalist visions by working to obtain an education and participating in the building of community infrastructure. Participation in youth and community groups was crucial to the enactment of these agendas since the groups provided an organizing space and the material support necessary to carry forward small, local projects. Basotho worked to construct infrastructure like roads and village water supply projects, but they also worked to build connections across religious, political, and even in some cases national lines as a way of living out and forcing recognition of their dreams for independence and decolonization. Basotho were involved in community organizations because they either lacked formal participatory mechanisms in government development activities or found their options to participate in projects too limiting for their developmental visions. More than simply community service, the actions of individuals in these groups provide physical evidence of the hopes and dreams Basotho had for independence.

Basotho were familiar with the idea of performing public politics. They were, of course, not the only group performing politics on the African continent at the end of colonialism. For Malawi and Tanzania, Power and Geiger expanded studies of nationalism beyond a narrow, mostly male political elite, while in Tanzania and Angola, Askew and Moorman, respectively, explored how ordinary people expressed their relations to the state and national communities through public performance.[11] Coplan detailed the wide array of *lifela* (poetry of mine workers) in Lesotho, arguing that when Basotho performed them in public, the "performance was a rich, even indispensible, resource for understanding the role of consciousness and agency in the interplay of southern African forces, structures, processes, and events," including nationalism within Lesotho.[12]

While Coplan detailed this performative consciousness and nationalism in informal spaces, the *pitso*, or public meeting, also had performative aspects and deep roots in Basotho society. Chiefs called these meetings for the purpose of gathering information, hearing public sentiment, and making communal decisions by consensus. Machobane described the historically idealized form of the meeting as being a place where any man could air opinions and grievances "with the greatest freedom and plainness of speech" and where the chief must "bear the most cutting remarks without a frown."[13] The openness in the meetings and whether important decisions were made by consensus, however, was likely somewhat exaggerated in nineteenth-century accounts. Wallman suggested that *pitsos* were more often a space for performance of public politics and community participation, as they were convened largely as a "social, rhetorical and political exercise."[14] This process intensified in the twentieth century as the colonial state co-opted the *pitso* to make it a venue for announcing policy rather than generating discussion. *Lifela* and the *pitso* show that Basotho had a long history of public political participation but that most people in Lesotho were also aware of limitations on their ability to influence change through formal processes designed to be, at least in part, symbolic exercises.

The youth and community groups that were driving many of the grassroots development efforts in Lesotho were popular because they gave participants the opportunity to work for their own conceptions of independence. They also offered a venue for broader national and international imaginings. These groups were self-consciously operating not only against the backdrop of the transfer of political power in Lesotho but also against continental decolonization and efforts to end apartheid in South Africa. As Rosenberg and Honeck argue for transnational youth organizations during the Cold War, "Youth subjects are less empty vessels for the ambitions of adult organizers than they are complex players with their own agendas, interests, and desires."[15] Still, Basotho political leaders, church leaders, and colonial administrators all hoped that by channeling youthful political, spiritual, and economic energies into organizations run by adults they could control the molding and shaping of political sensibilities and harness the energies of youth for their own purposes. In large part, they were wrong. Basotho in organizations as diverse as the Boy Scouts, the Girl Guides, the Homemakers Association, the University Christian Movement, and the Lesotho Workcamps Association used groups to learn about and act on their own ideas about independence and development.

Focusing on the actions of individuals in these groups, rather than just the recollections of young Basotho, also helps surmount the methodological challenge of pinpointing the memories of oral informants in specific periods. People often conflate memories of one failed development project with another because of the long history of project failure in Lesotho. Actions like building infrastructure or service undertaken through school groups are easier to pinpoint in time because of the specificity of the work and the ability to find corroboration in print about the finished products during the independence era. Thus these actions serve as a good proxy for understanding how youthful conceptions of independence emerged and changed over time.[16]

The high rates at which young Basotho were participating in groups and their projects challenge state theorists and political commentators who saw a failure of Africans to embrace the idea of nationalism or feel a part of national communities.[17] Widespread, active participation in Lesotho suggests this was less a failure of Africans to grasp the concept of nationhood, or to embrace nationalism, and more a failure of African institutions at independence to deliver on the promises of citizenship and national belonging in forms that people desired. In the early independence period, from 1965 to 1970, when democratic institutions prevailed, Basotho of all ages embraced the process of building the nation and state, though their visions split along partisan lines. After the coup of 1970 destroyed democratic institutions like Parliament, Basotho still tried to influence state processes, though their avenues for such ventures were more constrained. In all times and places, Basotho participated in development projects that fit their visions for the nation or that promised to bring enough benefits to outweigh the costs. They were certainly not "traditional," afraid of the idea of development, rooted in the past, or unable to look forward, as various official reports from the colonial and independence periods suggested. Rather, people were willing to participate only in projects that aligned with their needs and desires. For many, this meant that they wished to participate only in projects that made room for them to express potentially divergent opinions, gave citizens mechanisms for input into projects, and held out the promise of creating institutions that better served their material and imaginative interests. Basotho in community organizations were willing and able to invest in nationalist efforts, and questions about their desire to do so reflected a failing of the state and international development planners to adequately recognize and be attuned to the rights and desires of a newly independent citizenry.

Despite the differences in what they meant when using the terminology, by the late 1960s and early 1970s a wide swath of Basotho society was communicating their understandings of and dreams for political and economic independence through the language of development. Newly minted citizens found the language of development congenial to making demands on the governments of the day for increased and improved services. Government leaders also utilized the language to press for more funding from abroad, as well as political support at home for delivering development projects.

That Basotho defined independence by reference to development was possible only because of the groundwork laid by colonial officials, Basotho politicians, and the small but steadily increasing number of educated youth. From the 1950s, these actors deployed the rhetoric of development to link citizenship, independence, and nationalism. The widespread acceptance of the conflation of these three ideas is what this book calls the *rhetorical consensus on development*. While the possibility of rapidly increasing and centralizing state power helps explain why colonial-era officials and politicians wholeheartedly embraced the rhetorical consensus on development, its ability to spread so quickly to all levels of society owes much to the grassroots activities of Basotho in community groups. Seeing all segments of society as not merely accepting the ideas of independence and development, but as actively working for them challenges characterizations of African nationalism as "thin," only a "discourse of protest," a "banal" sentiment that people felt "lazily," or a force harnessed only by "militant urban nationalists" for use as the "social and ideological glue" that held together anticolonial coalitions.[18] While Lesotho is often seen as exceptional on the continent for its supposed ethnic homogeneity, the created nature of the Basotho national community (discussed later in this chapter) and the strength of political rivalries that often correlated strongly with religious affiliation mean that the country is no less "African" or representative for having a larger degree of linguistic and cultural homogeneity. Thus this study of independence-era Lesotho suggests that African nationalism was both a deeper and more robust phenomenon than others acknowledge but also that African nationalism took forms that were not necessarily congruent with the interests of the state and government officials.

Previous work on the history of development in Africa has been voluminous, though much of it has simply examined whether development projects succeeded or failed at meeting their own goals. Alternatively, it has looked at the one-way impact of state projects on local communities.[19] A few works, such as those by Moskowitz on Kenya and Ahearne on

Tanzania, write the history of development from the confluence of local experience and the macro-story. This frame better explains how rural Africans experienced development and how they internalized and utilized the political messaging of development for their own purposes.[20] As I argue in this book, histories of independence and decolonization for rural Africans that do not take into account the intertwined nature of independence and development are incomplete.[21] Telling this story in Lesotho necessarily includes tracing how particular projects arrived, which funding bodies the government approached, and why international funding agencies were interested in financing development in Lesotho. It also must include the stories of how individual Basotho decided when to participate in government development efforts and how they executed their own projects.

Reconsidering development from the bottom up also leads to a better understanding of the weakness of African states. Mann's study of West African NGOs highlights that Sahelian states started losing power not in 1980s neoliberal reform efforts and structural adjustment programs but rather at independence, when political leaders who had "worked to establish that sovereignty" almost immediately began to "mortgage" it in order to further the aims of economic development.[22] Similar processes were at work in Lesotho. The first Basotho government almost immediately gave up some of its recently acquired power over internal affairs in exchange for significant development projects, like a World Bank–funded road and a South African–funded expansion of the police force. This Faustian bargain was, in part, a decision that had to be made because of the extreme poverty of the Lesotho government, but the decision to pursue development funding at all costs was, in larger part, the result of deliberate choices made by Basotho politicians in the 1950s and 1960s.

The increasing entrenchment of the rhetorical consensus around development meant that by 1966, when the transfer of power occurred, most Basotho had come to equate the delivery of development projects with independence. But for politicians, the calculus remained that they had to surrender some amount of sovereignty to gain development funding. There was also potentially, however, a high reward for this trade-off as Basotho political leaders realized that they could gain more support for their parties and agendas by delivering aid. The quest for domestic political legitimacy through the delivery of development would continue through the independence period and into the present, and the potential prize of popular legitimacy made politicians willing to mortgage the greatest symbol of national sovereignty—Basotho control over land in Lesotho.

The early independence period saw great political contestation over the issue of development because the stakes of delivering development were so high. This led, in many cases, to some popular rejection of particular development projects as a divided population viewed projects through a partisan lens. This was especially true for the early independence period when electoral concerns weighed heavily on the minds of all Basotho political leaders. After the coup of 1970 that left the government of Lesotho without domestic political opposition, or having to worry about popular legitimacy through elections, leaders and planners were better able to deliver large development projects that helped consolidate their power. The authoritarian turn was, of course, not unique to Lesotho. The story of the arrival of development is also the story of how authoritarianism in postcolonial Africa led to the entrenchment of state power not only through increased governmental control over state security forces but also through bureaucratic institutions and development projects funded with international aid.

Studying development in Lesotho necessarily involves examining types of projects different from those on which most of the literature on colonial and postcolonial Africa has focused. The Lesotho projects could best be termed piecemeal development, as they were of a much smaller scale than most state-sponsored efforts. As Scott noted, large centrally planned projects were not necessarily more efficient or effective at delivering results to local populations, but they were and are more visible and legible to the state (and, in consequence, historians).[23] While the government of Lesotho desired such projects and actively worked to solicit them, few in the 1960s and 1970s saw the potential for such "high modernist" projects in a country like Lesotho that lacked significant deposits of strategic resources. Therefore, the Lesotho government focused mainly on the smallest projects—ones that could be run with volunteer labor, donated food, and a pittance of cash from domestic and foreign sources. Despite the microscale of these projects, the Lesotho government was quite eager to claim credit for them too, as a way of projecting competency and garnering electoral support. Thus, even though the projects lacked the scale of high modernist ventures elsewhere on the continent, the piecemeal development the Lesotho government undertook had political importance similar to larger projects that came with a more robust state presence.

Smaller development initiatives were, in Lesotho and across the continent, where the majority of Africans came into contact with government, multilateral organizations, and NGO-run development efforts. Understanding these contacts more fully offers the opportunity to rethink how Africans interacted with and internalized understandings of development, nationalism, and independence. The colonial government in Lesotho had attempted a handful of projects, both large and small. There is a body of literature examining the degree to which Basotho participated in these endeavors and how they shaped popular perceptions of colonial interventions.[24] The last major colonial development venture in Lesotho folded in 1961. The relative vacuum of projects in the late colonial period provided a space for Basotho to take initiative on projects in their own communities in ways not possible in the shadow of high modernist efforts.

Overshadowing all scholarship on development in Lesotho is the high modernist Lesotho Highlands Water Project (LHWP). Planning for the project started in the 1950s, with discussions between South Africa and Lesotho starting in the 1960s and 1970s, but an agreement between the parties did not occur until 1986. Today the project's dams supply South Africa's industrial and mining heartland with water delivered through a series of lengthy tunnels drilled through Lesotho's mountains.[25] The studies of this project have elucidated flaws in the project planning and implementation, particularly the displacement of ordinary Basotho by project construction. As with much literature on development, however, the LHWP studies have not rigorously interrogated how the project influenced how ordinary Basotho perceived development. Further, these works largely lack significant discussion of how the project's genesis in the late colonial period influenced the forms the project eventually took during the late apartheid era.

There are plenty of works from across Africa that balance top-down project overviews with bottom-up examinations of local response. These include Van Beusekom's analysis of the Office du Niger, Monson's study of the TAZARA railway, and the Isaacmans' examination of the construction of the Cahora Bassa Dam in Mozambique.[26] These works all nicely elucidate the impact of international relations and geopolitical concerns on development efforts while keeping their focus on how local communities understood the impacts of such projects. Similarly, Lal and Schneider have both rewritten the history of Ujamaa in Tanzania to better understand how the global and the local interacted and how development played out in contexts large and small.[27] Tague, similarly, narrated the intertwined story of planners, local experience, and unexpected development results that came out of rural development projects for Mozambican refugees in southern Tanzania.[28] In all of these works, however, the authors focused on capital-intensive, highly centralized projects that attracted overseas funding in large amounts or were, as with Ujamaa, the primary focus of the central government. In looking at much smaller projects, this book examines development on a scale where local people felt they could and should have significant input into the process of project planning and implementation. Thus these projects gave people the opportunity to engage in a way that embodied the possibilities of independence.[29]

That Basotho could continue to actively work for development and independence despite a dismal record of government failure echoes the situation Piot found in Togo. There people were "committed [to] and hopeful" about an integrated development plan that promised to bring paved roads, tourism, electrification, and feeder roads to rural communities, despite years of broken promises. These Togolese villagers in the early twenty-first century were holding onto a hope similar to that of independence-era Basotho: the hope that development could bring about a better future, even when no one could point to successfully completed projects to support it.[30] Basotho continued to "perform" development work through youth and community groups during the 1960s and 1970s despite feeling disillusioned with the government after independence.

The ability of the term *development* to simultaneously hold multiple meanings for different constituencies helped make it the key rhetorical term around which Basotho constructed and understood the idea of independence. Globally, from the mid-twentieth century, the term was intimately tied to notions of progressive change and industrialization.[31] Western support for development was intimately tied, especially by the United States starting in the 1960s, to efforts to stave off communist penetration in newly independent states by pushing free market economics. This came together most influentially in Rostow's writing as "modernization theory," which posited development as a linear process of change over time that societies went through on their way from the "traditional" to the "modern."[32] In his role as an adviser to U.S. president John F. Kennedy, Rostow was instrumental in establishing the United States Agency for International Development (USAID), an organization that saw modernization as "universal, linear, [and] inevitable."[33] Similar thinking also ruled at multilateral institutions like the World Bank, particularly within the ranks of planners at the International Development Association (IDA). This organization was charged with providing project funding to the poorest countries, a grouping that included Lesotho after independence. Officials thus planned similar projects in different settings. In Malawi, for instance, the Lilongwe Land Development Project served as a model for 1970s-era projects in Lesotho. The IDA goals for Lilongwe were to "establish not only a fixed system of commercially-oriented agriculture, but to inculcate new 'modern' attitudes among farmers."[34] Basotho politicians quickly picked up on the language of funding agencies and used it to garner more funding for Lesotho starting in the 1970s. They also infused the rhetoric and ideas into their domestic political speeches and platforms such that by the mid-1960s politicians from all parties equated independence with "modern," "progressive" change in the economic structures of the country.

Basotho who remained outside of the formal political structures came to embrace the rhetoric of development to define independence as well, but they were expressing a desire for a vision of development different from that of their political leaders. It was the "semantic ambiguity" of the term that allowed so many people with divergent interests to utilize and deploy this language for their own purposes.[35] Most Basotho talked about independence bringing about industrialization, the paving of roads, the construction of railways, and having more Basotho involved in cash-crop farming—in short, what could be simply read as a belief in "modernization." Despite a congruence of form with the visions of politicians, however, those outside the political process saw job and infrastructure creation not merely as drivers of macroeconomic growth but also as starting points for expanding popular participation in governance.

The Sesotho word for "development," *tsoela-pele*, translates as "to continue" or "to move forward."[36] To continue something does not necessarily imply that one is moving closer to a goal. Similarly, while "moving forward" implies motion, again there is no guarantee that this movement is in the desired or planned direction.[37] Basotho outside formal politics using *tsoela-pele* to mean "development" broadly thus did not necessarily have the same notions of progress toward a singular goal that modernization theorists envisioned. The mere presence of development projects in rural areas and the international connections that their presence symbolized, however, acted as potent symbols of the potential of independence to bring about desired changes. Thus, as long as projects were running, Basotho could nurture a sense of hope that *tsoela-pele* might eventually arrive in a suitable form to fulfill their visions. This faith helped many Basotho weather the storms of political failure and disappointment in post-independence Lesotho, but these individuals are, in large part, still waiting for development to fully deliver on its promises.

CONTEXTUALIZING DEVELOPMENT IN LESOTHO

The processes of aid and development overriding local concerns seem to be universal, especially in the Global South where overseas funding for development and debt service from prior development projects often make up large portions of government budgets. However, the context in which governments and people came to accept such funding matters. The best-known work about development in Lesotho is James Ferguson's *Anti-Politics Machine*, which details the Thaba Tseka Development Project from the mid-1970s into the 1980s. This book shows how aid and development came to override local political structures and serve primarily as a tool to centralize governmental authority rather than to promote poverty alleviation or macroeconomic growth. The story Ferguson tells is so compelling and familiar globally that it is cited in a wide variety of contexts to illustrate the hegemonic aspects of development.[38] Ferguson's argument is a starting place for interrogating how and why Basotho politicians, as well as individuals who were not directly involved in politics, were so willing to accept the hegemonic tradeoffs that came with increased aid and development funding in Lesotho.

Understanding how the rhetorical consensus on development came to be and how Basotho worked to turn an intellectual consensus into physical projects explains how people could continue to find hope in projects that consistently failed to alleviate poverty to any degree. As funding came from countries and agencies based far from Lesotho, the story of development is by its very nature transnational. In order to capture both the complexity of the interactions around projects and how Basotho perceived these projects, this book is grounded in the stories of how Basotho experienced and helped shape development efforts on the ground.

Without this history of popular reaction, the decision of the Lesotho government to solicit aid for development that entailed compromising aspects of the country's sovereignty seems to be at odds with the government's stated goal of independent action after colonial rule. Further, the hope that ordinary Basotho placed in the eventual ability of development to lead to independence outcomes they desired, despite decades of evidence to the contrary, looks downright ludicrous. However, these positions make more sense when situated in the context of the widely accepted rhetorical consensus on development. The only way to bring about the economic and administrative changes at the heart of that vision was to pursue development funding at all costs. Thus the solicitation of projects brought about both the continued optimism of the populace and the loss of control by the government.

Lesotho's enclave status played a key role in building a national community, structuring the terms of political debate, and determining how much aid for development flowed into the country. Lesotho was and is a geopolitical oddity because it is by far the largest sovereign state entirely surrounded by another.[39] The enclave status, and Lesotho's current national borders, came about through a complex process of diplomatic negotiations, wars, and adjudicated disputes in the nineteenth century. While the borders today are largely congruent with those of 1868 when Basutoland became a British colony, there has been and continues to be contestation over borders between Lesotho and South Africa in the twentieth and twenty-first centuries.[40]

The kernel of the political entity that emerged from colonial rule in 1966 started in the 1820s and 1830s when a group of people came together for protection under the leadership of Moshoeshoe.[41] Moshoeshoe, initially a minor chief from an area of what is today the northern district of Butha Buthe, established in 1824 a new home at the mountain stronghold of Thaba Bosiu (Mountain of the Night). From this location, Moshoeshoe attracted a variety of individuals who joined his growing community in the expectation that they would provide defense when required and seek Moshoeshoe's counsel as the highest authority in their disputes.[42] This community was the nucleus of today's Basotho nation.

Moshoeshoe effectively marshaled a defense against a host of encroachments in the nineteenth century from groups ranging from the Zulu to the British, but the existential conflict for Basotho was with Afrikaners from the Orange Free State. Utilizing his mountain stronghold at Thaba Bosiu as a fortress, Moshoeshoe successfully defended territory from attacks, but the core of Lesotho gradually shrunk from the 1840s to the 1860s as peace settlements moved the boundary closer to today's border, the Caledon or Mohokare River.[43] The last of these wars, in 1865–68, saw Afrikaner forces overrun most Basotho territory. This impending defeat caused the aging Moshoeshoe to petition Britain to annex the territory, which the Colonial Office did in January 1868 as the Crown Colony of Basutoland.

Through the 1840s and 1850s, Moshoeshoe had increased both the amount of territory claimed by his kingdom and the number of people under allegiance to his rule into a coherent community with shared values. Thus, people increasingly identified as Basotho.[44] The rapid expansion of the heterogeneous community led to the creation of a vast and disparate chieftaincy to help maintain some sort of centralized authority. The polity mainly consisted of a series of small, semiautonomous villages situated at an ever-expanding remove from Thaba Bosiu. Moshoeshoe extended his authority either by accepting existing chiefs and their followers under his protective umbrella or by "placing" his sons, relatives, and other trusted associates in outlying areas.[45] In this way, Moshoeshoe built a system Coplan and Quinlan characterize as a "landscape of social and political relations[,] . . . a chiefdom of chiefdoms."[46]

Important to the later story of twentieth-century development, the nineteenth-century focus on control over land remained at the heart of conceptions of Basotho national identity. The chieftaincy system gave an administrative coherence to Moshoeshoe's kingdom, especially when viewed from the outside. The prime force that united people within the territory, however, was resistance to outside incursions, particularly European settlers.[47] Besides resisting the idea of ceding land to European settlers, however, there was little unanimity among Basotho on key issues like the proper role of the chieftaincy or how much say individuals should have in public life. Coplan and Quinlan characterize the late nineteenth and early twentieth centuries as a period of "competing but overlapping notions of nationalisms" with agreement only on the need to defend the borders of the realm.[48]

Governance during the colonial period in Lesotho took the form of "parallel rule," as chiefs and colonial administrators operated largely independently of each other, rather than the "indirect rule" so common in the rest of British colonial Africa.[49] The chieftaincy system worked well enough in the precolonial and colonial periods from an administrative standpoint when a strong leader was at the top, as Moshoeshoe was during his younger years. As he aged, however, the system started to splinter, with chiefs at a remove from Thaba Bosiu at times signing separate peace treaties and negotiating without the knowledge or consent of Moshoeshoe. After Moshoeshoe's death in 1870, further splits within the chieftaincy weakened the legitimacy of the institution. This weakness and the inability of the system to deal with abusive chiefs gave educated commoners within Lesotho and the colonial administration pause as to whether supporting chiefly rule was worth the price.[50] Still, the chieftaincy remained a strong and vibrant institution in Lesotho into the twentieth century, and chiefs today still maintain some authority over local disputes and land claims. Further, maintaining the chieftaincy's rule in rural areas allowed the British colonial administration to run Basutoland "on the cheap," with only a skeletal imperial presence consisting largely of district commissioners and a few police officers.

While the British viewed Lesotho within the empire as a relatively unimportant territory, it was certainly not isolated from regional politics and global trends, as its deep diplomatic and religious ties illustrate. Moshoeshoe inaugurated diplomatic connections with African groups throughout the broader southern African region. Further, he invited European missionaries from the Paris Evangelical Mission Society (PEMS) to Lesotho in 1833.[51] Later he also invited the Catholics, who started operations in the 1860s, with the Anglicans arriving after his death in the 1870s.[52] The missions set up schools, making for a small but vocal educated Basotho middle class beginning in the late nineteenth century. These educated commoners played an important role in building the rhetorical consensus on development in the mid-twentieth century.

By the 1930s, the colonial administration's concerns about parallel rule led to the first in a series of chieftaincy reforms. The "placing system" Moshoeshoe started had expanded to such an extent that some chiefs numbered their followers only in the low hundreds.[53] The profusion of chiefs concerned the colonial state because perceptions of chiefly despotism threatened social stability in the countryside, where the British administration had almost no presence. Also threatening social stability was deepening rural poverty in the 1930s, so as part of the reforms, the colonial administration for the first time promised to bring "development" to the territory.[54] At its core, however, the package of reforms and development projects was designed to centralize state authority by curbing the power of the chieftaincy and increasing the presence of the colonial state. These goals remained central facets of development work by state leaders throughout the colonial period, as well as the efforts set up by Basotho politicians at independence.

Civil society in Lesotho was flourishing by the early twentieth century. Basotho were active in local civic groups as well as regional and international organizations like Marcus Garvey's United Negro Improvement Association (UNIA) and the South African Industrial and Commercial Workers Union (ICU).[55] The relatively high literacy rates of educated commoners (*bahlalefi* in Sesotho) allowed for a thriving newspaper culture and furthered the sense among *bahlalefi* that they should play a larger role in politics in the territory. All the main missions had newspapers, with the PEMS *Leselinyana la Lesotho* dating to 1863, the Catholic *Moeletsi oa Basotho* dating to 1933, and a host of secular papers that started in the early twentieth century as well.[56] The newspapers served as conduits to South African and global news in addition to reporting on local events and developments in the churches. Their coverage beyond Lesotho especially focused on issues affecting Africans and the African diaspora. Finally, they also serialized Sesotho authors like Thomas Mofolo, Azariele Sekese, and Z. D. Mangoaela, helping facilitate the creation of a robust Sesotho literary tradition.[57]

While most people in Lesotho identified themselves as Basotho from the nineteenth century, this term oversimplified the diverse backgrounds of the population. A strong sense of racial and ethnic solidarity existed with other southern Africans, especially those affected directly by European settlement.[58] But there were also great regional migrations stretching from the 1860s to the early twentieth century. These included significant numbers of migrants going to work in the Cape Colony and in the gold and diamond mines, the Anglo-Boer Wars, the rinderpest epidemic of 1897, and evictions of non-Europeans from the Union of South Africa following the South African Land Act of 1913 that ended sharecropping.[59] Some people left Lesotho during these times, but the net impact of migration prior to the 1920s was an increase in the population in Lesotho. While the newcomers often failed to access as much land as long-established families, especially as arable land became increasingly scarce by the early twentieth century, local communities within Lesotho absorbed them with relative ease. This integration suggests that borders and national imaginings in Lesotho were flexible through the early twentieth century and that the supposed "homogeneity" of the Basotho community is a contemporary political argument rather than a historical truth.[60] In reality, what constituted "the Basotho community" has always been part and parcel of wider political contestation, and this was true from the inception of a Basotho identity under Moshoeshoe to the creation of new institutions during the independence era and even into the present.

At least as important to the creation of a shared national identity as the arrival of migrants was the experience of Basotho with South African labor migration. While not every individual migrated, just about every Basotho family had members who left for durations ranging from months to years. The discovery of diamonds and gold in South Africa during the late nineteenth century allowed Basotho farmers to prosper prior to the 1890s arrival of the railroads because Lesotho was the closest reliable source of grain. Basotho with cattle, horses, and wagons also profited from involvement in the teamster trade. These opportunities were in addition, of course, to laboring in the mines, which was another option many Basotho took. By the late nineteenth century, Basotho were well integrated into the regional economy, with the proliferation of household goods and firearms being the most obvious manifestations back home in Lesotho. In addition to a personal or familial desire for income and goods, many Basotho went to the mines at the behest of local chiefs, for whom access to firearms to assist with defense remained a priority.[61]

By the 1920s, however, the combination of poverty, colonial taxation, and increasingly scarce arable land in Lesotho made migrant labor less a choice for Basotho households and more a necessity.[62] Though miners were the single most identifiable category of migrants, other Basotho migrated to live and work informally on the margins of South African cities. Still others went seasonally to work on farms, especially in neighboring districts of the Orange Free State.[63] The experiences of migrants when they were in South Africa, especially with prejudice and discrimination from people of European descent, contributed to the creation of a sense of commonality between individuals from Lesotho. Once Basotho crossed the Caledon/Mohokare River, they found they had more in common with individuals from Lesotho than they did with others around them. After 1948, the formal apartheid system further reinforced this group consciousness by forcing all Sesotho speakers to live in specific areas.[64]

The single biggest driver of national consciousness among Basotho, however, was the threat of the incorporation of Lesotho's territory into the

Union of South Africa. Much like the nineteenth-century threat from Afrikaners in the Orange Free State that contributed to the start of a national consciousness, Basotho quickly united across clan, religious, and political boundaries whenever South Africa threatened territorial sovereignty. The biggest threat since the 1860s came in 1909 when the Union of South Africa emerged from its four constituent territories—the Cape Colony, Natal, the Transvaal, and the Orange Free State. The British attempted to incorporate the three High Commission Territories (Basutoland, Bechuanaland Protectorate, and Swaziland) into the Union as well. The Basotho response, with the chieftaincy in the lead, was the strongest of any of the territories. They sent an eight-chief delegation to London to personally advocate for the continued territorial independence of Lesotho from the Union.[65] They were successful in the short term, but they could not forestall the inclusion of Clause 151 in the Act of Union that created South Africa. This clause stipulated that the South African Parliament could at any time formally request the incorporation of the territories.

Clause 151 proved to be a continued source of tension in Lesotho throughout the colonial period, as chiefs and commoners alike feared secret colonial administrative machinations to incorporate Lesotho into South Africa without Basotho consent. These fears became even more pronounced after the formal implementation of apartheid in 1948, as South African laws became more blatantly discriminatory. The near-constant fear of incorporation pervaded Basotho political discussions and day-to-day affairs within the territory into the 1960s. The silver lining of this fear was that it helped forge a stronger national identity among Basotho by contrasting South African discrimination with local political opportunity, however limited.

The growing strength of national consciousness, however, did not mean that Basotho were focused only on events within Lesotho. Many Basotho were active in groups working for political change in South Africa because of how closely intertwined the two states were. Basotho played key roles in most of the major South African political organizations from the time they were founded, including the African National Congress (ANC) and the Pan-Africanist Congress (PAC), as well as later groups like the National Union of Mineworkers (NUM). Lesotho's paramount chief, Letsie II, sent three representatives to the 1912 founding of the African Native National Congress (the ANC's precursor organization) in Bloemfontein. Similarly, Lesotho-born Potlako Leballo was one of the earliest leaders of the PAC in the 1960s, and because of the leadership's close connections to Lesotho, the PAC core spent the years 1962–65 in exile in Maseru.[66] James Motlatsi, hailing from Lesotho, was elected NUM's first president in 1982, in part because many of the most radical and militant members of the union were Basotho from Lesotho.[67] In these political organizations, Basotho found space to participate in the politics of South Africa, a country many viewed as having been built, at least in part, on the backs of their own labor.[68] For the majority of miners and migrants who eventually returned to Lesotho, however, these organizations also served as incubators for a politicized consciousness that they brought home. Thus, it was no surprise that returned migrants, miners in particular, played key roles in domestic political developments.

Two commoner groups worked diligently in Lesotho from the early twentieth century to force changes in colonial governance. The Basutoland Progressive Association (BPA) and Lekhotla la Bafo (LLB; Council of Commoners) both worked to push commoner political agendas. They had to work with and through the Basutoland National Council, a consultative assembly primarily for the principal chiefs, which was founded in 1903. Mission-educated commoners formed the core membership of the BPA, which was founded in 1907. The organization's primary goal was to secure more seats for nonchiefs in the council. LLB, on the other hand, drew its membership mainly from rural commoners with less education. The organization's primary aim from its inception in 1919 was to reclaim power for chiefs and commoners from the colonial government and return it to Basotho. Both the BPA and LLB had direct ties to politically active South Africans because of the interrelated nature of regional education and employment systems.[69] While neither group was particularly pleased with the forms colonial reforms took in the early decades of the twentieth century, their active and continued presence in Lesotho helped lay the groundwork for the groundswell of Basotho political interest that started in the 1950s.

Though the BPA and LLB were influential at the national level, there were other avenues for organizing and participating in politics at the grassroots level. One major thrust from the 1930s came from Catholic Church programs that helped local communities organize farming and purchasing cooperatives, construct small-scale irrigation dams, and build more schools.[70] Another impetus for rural discontent, protest, and organizing in this decade came from resistance to the colonial anti–soil erosion campaign (see ch. 1). This 1930s-initiated program proved unpopular because it limited the amount of land available to families for cultivation and grazing. By removing arable land from cultivation in the name of soil conservation, this first major development project in Lesotho galvanized rural populations to organize and protest because the centralizing efforts of the colonial state were having a direct impact on their livelihoods and control over the land.[71] Colonial officials, on the other hand, saw local protests against and efforts to sabotage the project as evidence that Basotho were "naturally" resistant to development. This laid the groundwork for future administrations to dismiss local institutions and populations for impeding the implementation of development projects.

So, by the independence period, Basotho were not experiencing development for the first time. Rather, they were drawing on personal and communal experiences with development efforts—both state-run and at the grassroots level—that in many cases stretched back decades. The emphasis that Basotho and colonial officials placed on the rhetoric of development in the years between the 1930s and independence helped development take a place of prominence in national political conversations, as well as in the minds of many Basotho. By the time of independence, it would become the dominant language through which Basotho expressed their personal and national aspirations. Basotho, by and large, internalized the connection between independence and development, which meant that no matter how many projects "failed" to bring results, Basotho could still retain a faith that someday development would change their lives for the better. Since it was so intertwined with conceptions of independence, to give up hope in development would have meant also abdicating a belief in the eventual success of nation- and state-building projects in Lesotho.

THE STRUCTURE OF THIS BOOK

Chapter 1 traces the political and social changes in Lesotho in the decades leading up to independence. Basotho were increasingly excited about independence but also nervous about the pace of change. Independence, therefore, did not gain simple and straightforward acceptance by the time of the transfer of power in 1966. Chapter 2 traces the manner in which the idea of development came to occupy a place of prominence among ordinary Basotho and politicians during the late colonial period. Colonial development efforts, including the anti–soil erosion campaign, prospecting for diamonds, plans for large dams in the mountains to supply South Africa with water, and area-based agricultural projects, proved to be politically contentious. While the projects did not eliminate poverty in Lesotho, provide many new government services, or open new political spaces, the rhetoric and promise of rural prosperity emanating from them allowed Basotho to have faith in the potential of development. This offered the hope that someday, once Basotho were running their own affairs in an independent Lesotho, development might bring about broad economic prosperity and representative political institutions. Young Basotho, especially those with some education, played a key role in nurturing and propagating these sentiments.

Chapter 3 explores the history of political rhetoric and its connection to development. Politicians of all parties deployed the language of development to argue for their own visions of independence in Lesotho. They connected local politics to global conflicts like the Cold War and the struggle against apartheid, rhetorically attacking their opponents for being insufficiently nationalist for proposing to solicit development funding from particular foreign sources. At independence, Basotho largely disapproved of the negative tenor of these attacks. However, increases in the amount of rhetoric connecting development and independence helped cement the connection between these concepts in the public mind. The period 1965–70 was the high-water mark of Basotho engagement with development in the independence period because a lack of large state-run development projects and ample opportunities for youth and community groups to carry out their own projects led to a proliferation of smaller efforts.

Chapter 4 looks at the role of development in the 1970 election campaign, the subsequent coup, and the efforts of the post-coup government to rebuild popular legitimacy through the delivery of development projects. It was after 1970 that Lesotho started to attract significant overseas funding for large development projects, and this was in part because the authoritarian and despotic post-coup government was better positioned to implement larger-scale projects. The Lesotho government also benefited from changes in the international donor climate that encouraged more giving to the world's poorest countries. Centrally run programs lacking popular input mechanisms proved as unpopular and unsuccessful as similar colonial-era projects had been. Still, Basotho did not give up hope in the eventual ability of development to beget their desired visions for independence because they could easily compare their own conditions in Lesotho to that of South Africans living under the apartheid regime.

Chapter 5 traces the newfound ability of Prime Minister Jonathan's regime to solicit and run significant development projects in the post-coup period. These projects were no more successful in alleviating poverty than earlier attempts, but since they came with larger sums of money, the government was able to bureaucratize and formalize its presence in some rural areas. This shows how the rise of the conditions Ferguson describes in *The Anti-Politics Machine* was the result of a series of choices, each logical in its own right, made by Basotho officials dating back to the late colonial period. Younger Basotho who came of age in the independence period managed to maintain their faith in the idea of development, but they often had to reframe and compromise on their previous visions for independence. Some left Lesotho, while those who remained found that avenues for direct participation in politics were closed due to the authoritarian nature of the government. Rather than give up all hope in the ability of development to bring about change, Basotho, like the Lesotho government, reframed their visions for independence to meet the new political, social, and economic realities.

The short concluding chapter 6 brings together the book's main themes and briefly surveys particular development initiatives that have taken place in Lesotho since independence. It reiterates how Basotho utilized development to not only imagine preferred communities but also actively worked for the success of particular projects despite bureaucratic obstacles and the lack of adequate funding.

CHAPTER I

Political Changes and Basotho Responses, 1950s to Independence

The 1950s and 1960s were heady decades in Lesotho. Multiple rapid constitutional changes, expansion to secondary and tertiary education, and increased tensions with the apartheid South African government contributed to a general sense that Lesotho was on the precipice of fundamental societal change that would reverberate beyond its borders. Increased political interest throughout Basotho society was especially pronounced among the younger generation. The political reforms of the late colonial period, however, arrived in fits and starts with no master plan guiding the process and no sure path to independence until 1964. It was an uncertain time that left many people unsure of how much faith to put in colonial administrators or even Basotho politicians who were promising rapid independence.

Colonial administrators in London and Maseru largely controlled the pace of political change, and they made development efforts central to this process. The creation of district councils in the late 1940s, the National Council in 1960, and an elected Parliament in 1965 marked the evolution of local political representation in the territory prior to independence. Although these changes can be packaged, with hindsight, into a neat and tidy narrative, at the time they were haphazard and largely unanticipated.

The district councils came out of wider British efforts to decentralize power in the late empire; conversely the National Council and Parliament came about largely because of the British government's desire to leave the empire ahead of earlier schedules. Also, these changes took place only after protracted and intense political fights with and among Basotho about the best means to gain and maintain power. The inability of the colonial regime to telegraph its long-term intentions led to some confusion among Basotho as to where to put their efforts, particularly with regard to development. Thus decentralized development efforts such as rural agricultural cooperatives that district councils initiated in the 1950s gave way to efforts to secure centralized, large-scale project funding by the 1960s. No matter how confused the reform efforts were, however, the new political spaces allowed and encouraged a wider swath of Basotho society to engage with and participate in governmental processes, particularly through development efforts.

While support for development and independence was not universal by any means, through the 1950s and 1960s more people in Lesotho came to accept the ideas as linked and desirable for the greater good of individuals as well as the country. The experience of newly independent African states, starting in the late 1950s with Ghana, inspired many Basotho to think about what independence might mean and how they could imagine changes in their own society and country. A relatively free and open local press contributed to the increase in political interest and introduced Basotho to new ideas from across Africa and the world. The press also encouraged people in Lesotho to see local action as part of broader continental and global trends by situating local political developments in a larger context. For many Basotho, it confirmed what they wanted to be true: Lesotho was a place that mattered. Expanded interest in development and independence, however, did not result in agreement on what the terms meant or who got to define them. These debates about nationalism, independence, and development were also common in many other places in Africa.[1]

Driving the increasing interest in politics and development in all forms were the new opportunities for popular participation that the colonial administration granted in the 1950s and 1960s. The new democratic institutions in Lesotho were contrasted in the minds of Basotho with the increasingly harsh apartheid system just across the border, a system with which most Basotho had direct, personal experience. Independence was not an inevitable outcome of political reform efforts until after Britain promulgated Lesotho's second constitution in 1964, which contained a schedule for such a declaration. Basotho did, however, see the incremental changes taking place during these decades as leading inexorably in that direction.

Even after the constitutional guarantee, though, it took a concerted effort by chiefs, politicians, and ordinary Basotho for independence to come to fruition. The terms of the debate were constrained by the limits of the imaginations of colonial planners in London and Maseru, by Lesotho's economic dependence on apartheid South Africa, and by political divisions within Basotho society. However, many Basotho began to work for the independence they wanted to see through active engagement in the new political processes and development projects. Despite the belief of many colonial officials that Basotho were disinterested or apathetic, this active participation in political and development work underscored the degree to which Basotho understood their own independence efforts as part of greater processes of decolonization and as a way to gain more economic and political control of their own lives.

CHIEFTAINCY AND ADMINISTRATIVE REFORM, 1935–1965

Colonial Basutoland was never a territory that the British government in London was particularly enthusiastic to have. Britain took on Basutoland as a Crown Colony in 1868 mainly as a counterweight to the growing power of the two Afrikaner republics in the interior of South Africa, and the main goal of the colonial administration was to maintain the peace without expending resources.[2] The discovery of diamonds in Kimberley and gold on the Witwatersrand in the late nineteenth century made the territory more important to colonial administrators because it was located within easy travel distance of both sites. Basotho farmers supplied grain to the mining regions until the arrival of railroads in the late 1880s and early 1890s undercut the price advantages they had previously enjoyed.[3] After this, Basotho increasingly went to the mines to work as migrant laborers. British colonial administrators encouraged this practice because Basotho labor helped ensure a stable workforce for the mines, which were largely capitalized by British investors, and because the wages allowed more Basotho to pay colonial taxes in cash. Migrant labor underwrote the financial stability of Basutoland and its skeletal administrative structure, which, by 1900, included only about thirty British administrators in the entire territory, including police officers.[4] Thus the mining boom was the impetus that pushed the colonial administration to govern Lesotho as a rural labor reserve for South African mines and farms beginning in the nineteenth century.

In practice, this meant that the colonial administration allowed the Basotho chieftaincy to maintain significant control over land allocation and disputes in an administrative system termed parallel rule. In this system, the paramount chief (Morena e moholo) held all of the land in trust for the Basotho people. Stretching back to Moshoeshoe I, the various Marena a moholo (plural) "placed" chiefs in certain areas with the authority to distribute land and settle disputes between individuals in their name. In time this system entrenched a senior chieftaincy (whose members were called district and ward chiefs), which held governing power over all residents in their territories. They presided, in turn, over a hierarchy of minor chiefs and headmen who settled local day-to-day disputes. This chieftaincy system operated for the most part without interference from or reference to the colonial government, hence its name, "parallel rule." In practice this meant that the Morena e moholo saw himself (or herself when the regent 'Mantsebo occupied the office in 1941–60) as the equal of the British resident commissioner.[5] Parallel rule, however, left both the colonial administration and the senior chieftaincy dissatisfied; both wanted more power and control. Ultimate legislative power rested in the hands of the British High Commissioner to South Africa, which he delegated locally to the resident commissioner stationed in Maseru. The legislative authority of the High Commissioner over Basutoland, Swaziland, and the Bechuanaland Protectorate led the three territories to be called the High Commission Territories (HCT).

The creation of the Union of South Africa in the 1909 Act of Union caused much consternation in Lesotho, particularly among the chieftaincy, as Clause 151 promised the eventual incorporation of the High Commission Territories into the Union. This clause ended up in the act despite the efforts of Morena e moholo Letsie II, who organized and sent a delegation of Basotho chiefs to London to lobby against incorporation. The visceral reaction of most Basotho to the idea of incorporation made it the singular issue during the colonial period that could unite chief and commoner, Protestant and Catholic, young and old. Scott Rosenberg dates the coalescence and start of an explicit Basotho national identity to the period around the Act of Union, while Elizabeth Eldredge dates its start to the increased economic and political insecurity of the late nineteenth century.[6] In either case, by the first decades of the twentieth century inhabitants of the territory saw themselves and increasingly referred to themselves as Basotho, largely because of the outsized influence of South Africa politically, economically, and proximally.

An outgrowth of this emerging national consciousness by the 1920s, at least among the relatively small population of educated commoners, was the presence of the first national and nationalist imaginings of an independent nation-state for Basotho. The local newspaper *Naledi*, a mouthpiece for the Basutoland Progressive Association, printed an opinion piece in late 1926 noting, "The history of the Basuto [*sic*] nation . . . proves [that] . . . the Basuto are amenable to unity . . . [and] not very long from now they will be asking the Imperial Government for their sovereign independence."[7] Similarly, Lord Hailey noted in his 1930s survey of British administration in colonial Africa that people in the territory, particularly the chieftaincy, had a "strong sense of nationality, and a firmly fixed ideal of Basutoland as a semi-independent state."[8] While this certainly does not prove or even suggest a widespread nationalist sentiment for independence, the presence of such ideas among chiefs and educated commoners helped lay the groundwork for greater political interest and more widespread acceptance of the dream of independence by the 1950s and 1960s.

Further laying the groundwork for independence-era nationalism were attempts by the colonial administration to curb the power of the chieftaincy and decentralize authority, which led many Basotho to protest what they saw as colonial administrative overreach. These reforms did, however, create the political space in which youth and community groups could implement small-scale development projects by the late 1950s and 1960s. The reforms started in the 1930s with efforts by the colonial administration to convert the system of parallel rule into the indirect rule more common in the British Empire's nonsettler colonies in Africa. The other goal of the reforms, though, was to address the serious economic crisis ravaging the territory as a result of the combination of a three-year drought and the global Great Depression that depressed commodity prices. To find a path forward, the Colonial Office appointed its African financial expert, Sir Alan Pim, to head a committee tasked with investigating the social, economic, and political issues the territory faced. The report's two main recommendations for ensuring social stability and increasing economic prosperity were chieftaincy reforms and a campaign against soil erosion.

Following the publication of the report, the colonial administration started the first explicit development program in the territory by accepting a Colonial Office loan to fund a campaign against soil erosion. While it was the first program in Lesotho, it was not a new initiative; similar efforts were under way across southern Africa. Colonial officials designed these programs with the explicit goal of increasing rural homestead income, but their prime motivation was the consolidation of colonial power through better control over rural areas and African peasant agriculture.[9] The 1930s chieftaincy reforms were part and parcel of these efforts, with the reforms officially framed as efforts to help free local populations from arbitrary and despotic chiefs but with enhanced colonial control over administrative structures as the ultimate goal. The Pim Report–inspired chieftaincy reforms failed to fully break the pattern of parallel rule in Lesotho as the government suspended implementation during World War II, out of fear of social instability. After the war, however, the colonial administration pushed for more reforms. Similarly, the anti–soil erosion campaign generated a lot of resistance among rural populations, and efforts to enforce the terracing of fields were haphazard in their implementation countrywide.[10] Despite this, the mixed record of reforms did not dissuade colonial officials from pushing for more imperial funding for development and reform projects during and after World War II.

After the war, the Colonial Office saw reform efforts and development interventions as a way to reinvigorate colonialism and consequently promoted them even more heavily. The Colonial Office made this strategy clear from 1940 when the British Parliament passed the Colonial Development and Welfare (CDW) Act.[11] For Lesotho, the administration in Maseru made plans for more and better roads to promote trade and tourism, more health care facilities and schools, improved agriculture and livestock breeding programs, large hydroelectric projects, and more cooperative ventures. That these development plans echoed the specifics first set out by the Pim Report is not surprising, for this document and its recommendations for development would reappear almost verbatim in projects during the 1950s, 1960s, and 1970s. They also became the foundation of Basotho political party platforms around independence and continued to influence development efforts after independence. That the recommendations from a 1930s colonial report could form a sizable part of nationalist platforms and popular imaginings suggests the degree to which the rhetoric of development captured elite political discourse and was translated into nationalist ideals in the 1950s and 1960s.

The problem with Basotho politicians embracing the Pim vision of colonial development, however, was that embedded in the report were critiques of ordinary Basotho for their supposed failure to embrace development and of the chieftaincy for supposedly aiding and abetting rural administrative inefficiency. It was the first time the colonial government publicly made such claims. As the embrace of the report by Basotho politicians makes clear, it was colonial administrators as well as Basotho politicians who time and again blamed the lack of development in the territory not only on inadequate colonial funding but also on Basotho intransigence in different forms. So the report claimed rural Basotho were too stubborn to heed the benefits of colonial development initiatives and the chieftaincy was obstinate for failing to properly control land allocation. Pim accused the chieftaincy of having no checks on its behavior: "Control from below has lost its effectiveness, and has not been replaced by any control from above."[12] Thus, in conjunction with the anti–soil erosion development work, the colonial administration pushed the 1938 Khubelu (red) reforms—named after the color of the Pim Report's cover. The administration removed the ability of the Morena e moholo to name chiefs and limited the number of chiefs who could hold court, and thus collect income from the fines levied.[13] A necessary precursor to development, by this logic, was the centralization of administrative control over rural areas because the people who lived there were unable to govern for and by themselves.

The Khubelu reforms marked the start of chieftaincy reform, but colonial officials saw this as merely the first step in finding a way to fill the rural power vacuum that reducing chiefly power would leave. So in the postwar period, various resident commissioners implemented even more reforms. Resident Commissioner Charles Arden-Clark in 1946 created the Basuto National Treasury (BNT), which for the first time made all chiefs salaried employees of the government. By eliminating the ability of chiefs to raise personal revenue through court fines, this effectively ended any vestiges of parallel rule. To persuade the chieftaincy to accept these changes, the colonial government split chiefs into two groups: a senior group that benefited from colonial rule and a junior group that lost power and authority. The British won over the regent 'Mantsebo by placing the administration of chiefs' funds at Matsieng, the royal village and official residence of the Morena e moholo, which allowed her to maintain centralized authority.[14] These reforms left 117 senior chiefs with increased administrative powers but left the 1,348 junior chiefs with diminished powers or none at all. While the reforms finally achieved the administrative goal of bringing Lesotho more in line with the indirect rule of the rest of the empire, it was also a mixed message: the centralization of authority around the chieftaincy happened simultaneously with the creation of decentralized district councils. In addition to sending a mixed message, this created practical problems for development in that it put a recently neutralized chieftaincy in direct competition with local development initiatives for which the district councils were responsible.

The split in the chieftaincy and the loss of power by individual members led to a crisis of authority in rural Lesotho in the 1940s and 1950s that the colonial authorities called the "medicine murder crisis." This outbreak of ritual murders came about as chiefs, reacting fearfully to their loss of power, turned to medicines made from human body parts in an effort to maintain their status and position.[15] The number of murder cases opened by the government climbed rapidly throughout this period, but the execution of two senior chiefs in 1949 so shocked many Basotho that it caused them to start to question the right of the colonial government to be the arbiter of political and administrative changes in the territory. For a period in the mid-1950s, support for the chieftaincy coalesced as Lekhotla la Bafo, the newly formed Basutoland African Congress (BAC) political party, and the chiefs all came together to oppose colonial initiatives.[16] The colonial government, however, signaled a willingness to further embrace the empire-wide push to devolve power by the mid-1950s, and this fragile alliance broke down as groups within Lesotho once again jockeyed for power.

As colonial administrators throughout the British Empire in the late 1950s and 1960s sought to speed up development efforts to justify their continued presence, it was not clear how political devolution or development would happen in Lesotho. Most British administrators were not convinced of the political or economic viability of the territory in a postimperial world because of its dependence on the apartheid state. Despite their misgivings about the long-term viability of the territory, however, the colonial administration was particularly sensitive to unfavorable comparisons with South African development efforts in the Reserves/ Homelands. This was also true of imperial officials in London, up to and including the secretary of state for Commonwealth relations, Patrick Gordon Walker. He visited the region for six weeks in January and February 1951 and afterward called Lesotho and the other HCT the "shop-windows in the midst of the Union [of South Africa]" that must be made "economically strong and progressive" in order to showcase how British colonial efforts compared favorably to the apartheid policies of South Africa. His memo called on the British government to increase its investment because Britain needed to "develop the Territories if we are to hold them." Despite their limited prospects for income-generating development projects, the memo continued, they must still get their "fair share of whatever money we are putting into our Colonies."[17]

In spite of this support for development, Walker's memo mainly reiterated colonial concerns about the difficulties of bringing development to a resource-poor territory and the administrative difficulties that even a marginal increase in funding would entail. Compounding the mixed messaging of the memo for making policy, it claimed both that the chieftaincy was "essential" for development in rural areas and that the government should focus on co-opting an increasingly educated and demanding set of politically active commoners. Without resolving this contradiction, it asked the colonial administration to thread the needle by "prevail[ing] upon the Chiefs to work with elected council and to decentralize [chiefly] authority to local councils."[18] As already noted, the chieftaincy was increasingly distrustful because of the multiple reforms that had stripped their power. How the Maseru administration was supposed to convince these individuals to dutifully and cheerfully carry out colonial development aims while the administration undercut their power through democratic institutions was not explained.

The initial foray into establishing representative institutions in Lesotho was the 1940s creation of the district councils, with the public nominating members at public gatherings, or *pitsos*. These bodies, in conjunction with the formation of the BAC as the territory's first political party in 1952, combined to make more plausible the idea of a local legislative body. Lord Hailey's 1953 survey of administration across the British Empire called for just this, as he noted the territory was ready and able to exercise local legislative and executive functions.[19] The simplest way to do this was to transform the Basutoland National Council into a legislative body, with its members choosing an executive council. The National Council, founded in 1903 as a purely advisory body, was originally composed of the senior chieftaincy along with five commoners appointed by the resident commissioner.[20] The 1940s changes added five members from each of the nine districts and representatives of civil society like traders, former soldiers, and teachers, but hereditary chiefs still held a slim majority in the body.[21] In 1952 and 1953, however, the council passed resolutions calling for the High Commissioner (HC) to devolve legislative powers, and these calls led the HC to appoint the Administrative Reforms Committee in 1954.[22] This six-member body consisting of three British-appointed colonial administrators and three Basotho chiefs, and taking the name of its lead author, Sir Henry Moore, took testimony from over four hundred Basotho. Despite these strong pushes by Basotho and outside experts, the Moore Report called merely for minor changes in local governmental powers and fell far short of advocating for a local legislative body.[23]

The BAC drew strength from a burst of public protest over the lack of a pathway to local legislative authority in the Moore Report. The party newspaper, *Mohlabani*, played a key role in whipping up support for the devolution of more political power to Basotho, and its stringent advocacy drew more young, educated Basotho into political activity, many for the first time. Tšeliso Ramakhula, a twenty-five-year-old teacher in the rural Mafeteng District, was already a BAC supporter, but he remembered the report as a vehicle for galvanizing support for the party and its goal of local self-governance.[24] But it was not only in the political newspapers where reporting on the Moore Report found traction; the religious newspapers *Moeletsi oa Basotho* and *Leselinyana* also dedicated space to its release and analyzed its implications.[25] The wider readership of these newspapers, and the degree to which they circulated in rural areas through the wide network of mission stations, shows the extent to which political news traveled throughout the country.[26] While the report caused a burst of political activity, it was a short-lived phenomenon among the populace at large. It did, however, bring together the chieftaincy and the BAC in an alliance that aimed to secure legislative power for the National Council, and in this it succeeded. Political agitation within the council and by senior chiefs forced the Maseru administration to get Alan Lennox-Boyd, secretary of state for the colonies, to appoint a committee to write a constitution for Lesotho, the first in the HCT.

The 1956 Constitutional Reform Committee, as it was officially called, came into being because of this local pressure, but it was also a result of moves toward political independence across Africa and a response to events in South Africa. Ghanaian independence in 1957 changed the time lines for the independence of British colonies in Africa, but even before this the British found it increasingly hard to criticize South African apartheid policy with development efforts across the HCT so poorly funded. Given long-standing Basotho suspicions that the British government in London cared more about its relations with South Africa than it did for the people of Lesotho, the refusal of the Moore Report to back a local legislature in 1955 looked more sinister in light of a 1954 request from the South African government for the handover of the HCT.[27] While by the 1950s British administrators did not seriously consider South Africa's incorporation requests because of the international opposition to apartheid, Basotho fears were justified given Britain's decades-long neglect of the colonies.

Putting further pressure on the Colonial Office to act on promises of economic development and political reform in the territories was the 1955 Tomlinson Commission in South Africa. The commission's report laid out plans to create ethnic "Homelands," or Bantustans, with calls for increased funding for development in areas reserved for Africans under the apartheid system in order to make these areas viable economically. The apartheid government had little intention of funding all the development proposals in the report, but the renewed focus on development for African communities in the wider region put continued pressure on the British government to more effectively counter charges of colonial neglect.[28]

The Constitutional Reform Committee's recommendation that Lesotho gain a local legislative body led to the first legislative powers for the Basutoland National Council in the 1959 constitution, but it also heightened tension between centralization and decentralization advocates. The constitution mandated that the 1960 elections select only members of the district councils, who, in turn, selected the members of the National Council. In addition, they left the power and the funding for development projects in the hands of the district councils, thereby setting up a two-tiered system of authority whereby legislative power was centralized but control over development funding was decentralized.[29] With the National Council still having half its members as hereditary senior chiefs and colonial government appointees, national-level elected leaders could exercise little actual power. The lack of power for winning the elections made politicians more willing to attempt to wrest control of development funding and projects from the district councils in a centralized system at independence.

THE DEVELOPMENT OF POLITICAL PARTIES IN LESOTHO, 1952–1970

Basotho, male and female, young and old, took to electoral politics with enthusiasm in the late colonial and early independence periods. While formal electoral politics and a legislative body were new in 1960, political participation and interest were not. Earlier organizations like the Basutoland Progressive Association and Lekhotla la Bafo that had played important political roles from the 1920s through the 1940s suggest the degree to which political participation was normalized by that point among many Basotho, not just the educated.[30] While the BPA was largely on the wane by the 1950s, many members of LLB played key roles in the founding and early days of the BAC. The BAC changed its name in the late 1950s to the Basutoland Congress Party (BCP) to contest elections. The Basotho National Party (BNP) and the Marematlou Party, both founded in the late 1950s, also contested the elections.

It was not merely political participation in Lesotho, however, that informed Basotho reactions to political developments. Proximity to and experience with South Africa helped shape the political consciousness of many Basotho. Most Basotho who pursued higher education in the immediate postwar period did so in South Africa because the only university in Lesotho, the Catholic Pius XII University College, was a sectarian institution with a limited degree program until 1964. This meant that many Basotho ended up at institutions like Fort Hare, Lovedale, and Healdtown, where they shared classes and living spaces with future leaders of the ANC, the Pan-Africanist Congress, and other regional political organizations. BAC founder Ntsu Mokhehle, for example, attended Fort Hare simultaneously with future liberation struggle leaders Nelson Mandela, Oliver Tambo, and Robert Sobukwe. So by the time Mokhehle started the BAC in 1952, he had already honed his political philosophies and organizational skills in the ANC Youth Wing in South Africa, as well as in LLB in Lesotho.

Beyond the small handful of Basotho in elite South African schools, an even larger number of Basotho joined groups like the ANC and PAC while on migrant labor contracts in South Africa. The mines in particular were a place of radicalization for those living and working in South Africa, but the politicization of Basotho did not happen only there. Even earlier, Basotho joined groups like the Industrial and Commercial Workers Union and Marcus Garvey's United Negro Improvement Association, which had a strong presence in rural South Africa as well as in Lesotho.[31] Thus the leadership of the BAC developed concurrently with and benefited from the ideas of other local, regional, and international political groups organizing at the time. While all parties in Lesotho attempted to have a cross-border presence among Basotho migrants with chapters in South Africa, only the BAC succeeded to any appreciable degree, with chapters active in most of the Witwatersrand mining communities. The base of the party, however, remained in Lesotho's lowlands, in particular, in towns like Mafeteng, Hlotse (Leribe), and Maseru, because so many returned miners and educated civil servants settled there.[32]

The close ties between Basotho political leaders and their South African counterparts meant that changes on one side of the border often reverberated on the other side. The BAC name change in 1957 to the Basutoland Congress Party reflected a shift to a more direct electoral strategy in response to constitutional changes in Lesotho, but it was also the result of growing ties between BCP leadership and the African Nationalist faction within the ANC. This group soon left the ANC to form the Pan-Africanist Congress (PAC). Ntsu Mokhehle was especially close to the PAC leaders Robert Mangaliso Sobukwe, Potlako Leballo, a Lesotho-born firebrand, and A. P. Mda, who fled into exile in Lesotho in 1963. These close ties are illustrated by Sobukwe's address at the inaugural BCP conference at Fraser's Memorial Hall in Maseru in 1957.[33] The BCP ended up allied with the PAC in part because both ANC and BCP leaders wanted the allegiance of Basotho migrant miners when they were resident in South Africa. The BCP worried that cultivating ties with the ANC would cause Basotho to either stay in South Africa long term without returning home or that their members would lose touch with efforts to effect political change in Lesotho. Mokhehle, ever suspicious, also believed that a 1961 plot to unseat him from his role as party leader emanated from political refugees aligned with the ANC in Lesotho.[34] The links between the BCP and the PAC deepened as this split with the ANC occurred, but the primary driver of these close ties in the early 1960s was the presence in Maseru of most of the leadership of the PAC-in-exile.

It was not only ties with South Africa that Mokhehle and the BCP leadership cultivated. They also looked to Kwame Nkrumah and Ghanaian Pan-Africanism for material and intellectual support starting in the late 1950s. Mokhehle attended the All-Africa People's Conference in 1958 in Accra and was elected to the steering committee, while at the same time the BCP received money from the Ghanaian government.[35] This support from Ghana and, by the mid-1960s, from a wider network that included Egypt and the People's Republic of China gave the BCP the financial ability to hold rallies and develop party structures throughout lowland Lesotho.

The BCP's alliance with Pan-Africanism more broadly led to this international financial support, but it also meant closer scrutiny by the colonial administration and the South African government. The presence of the PAC leadership and worries that the PAC's armed wing, Poqo, was planning strikes from inside Lesotho caused both governments to keep the BCP's activities under close watch.[36] The colonial government had always viewed the BCP as a threat to political stability in Lesotho. Resident Commissioner Edwin Porter Arrowsmith fired three BCP leaders from the government-run Basutoland High School in 1955 because they refused to cease publishing what he deemed antigovernment material in the party newspaper, *Mohlabani*.[37] Similarly, colonial administrators viewed the BCP as being behind every disruption in the country in the early 1960s, for example, blaming a school strike on the BCP. Despite the commission of inquiry's inability to find evidence that party leadership had even met with students beforehand, its report chided the BCP for creating an "atmosphere of indiscipline" that "encouraged" the students.[38]

This view of the BCP as a radical group was not just confined to colonial administrators; many Basotho also saw the group as radically out of step with a rural, conservative populace. Institutionally, the strongest counterweight to the BCP was the Catholic Church, which had the largest number of mission stations and schools scattered throughout the rural areas. These stations still relied heavily on European and Canadian donors to fund operations and French Canadian priests and nuns to staff its churches, schools, and cooperative associations. Their ability to raise funds in North America and Europe made it the best-funded mission entity operating in the country. The Catholic hierarchy, though, worried that

BCP dominance in Lesotho threatened their religious operations, so they played a direct role in the formation of an alternative party in 1958, the Basotho National Party. The BNP's membership drew primarily from junior chiefs and Catholic Basotho, who tended to live in rural areas, and the party was strongly anticommunist because of the influence of the expatriate Catholic hierarchy. The leader of the party, Leabua Jonathan, was himself a minor chief from the rural Leribe District who had worked in South Africa, as well as in the civil service in Lesotho as a judicial adviser under Patrick Duncan in the late 1940s. He had spent much of the 1950s as one of Regent 'Mantsebo's official advisers.[39] Jonathan helped position the BNP as a less radical nationalist alternative to the BCP, arguing that the development potential of Lesotho could not be realized if strident opposition to apartheid damaged the ability of Basotho to migrate for work while the state worked to provide new economic opportunities at home. At the 1960 elections, the BNP, less than two years old, did not fare well, but it grew increasingly strong through the 1960s.[40]

The final major party was the Marematlou Freedom Party (MFP), an amalgamation of disparate interests. It brought together members of the Marematlou Party ("Marematlou" is a Sesotho idiom meaning "the people who come together to push the elephant"), a royalist group founded in 1957 by S. S. Matete to oust the regent 'Mantsebo in favor of her stepson, Constantine Bereng, with the Basutoland Freedom Party. The BFP consisted mainly of disaffected BCP members, led by a former BCP deputy leader, B. M. Khaketla. The Marematlou Party had, by 1960, succeeded in its initial goal of installing Bereng on the throne, but after the amalgamation the party remained a vehicle for the monarch and the senior chieftaincy to have greater influence in electoral politics. Gaining Khaketla's support also meant the party gained the services of the newspaper *Mohlabani*, as he was the publisher.[41]

The MFP positioned itself as a moderate nationalist alternative for those who wished to support the senior chieftaincy and monarchy as defining institutions in Lesotho, but as with all parties, it was also heavily intertwined with regional politics. The MFP came to have close ties with the ANC because the members of the ANC in exile in Lesotho meshed well ideologically with the party but also because the ANC could and did supply funding from abroad that kept the MFP afloat. The vast majority of this funding came via the ANC/South African Communist Party (SACP) organizer and fund-raiser Joe Matthews, who was living in exile in Maseru from 1960 until 1965.[42] The amalgamated nature of the party, and the sometimes-competing interests of the senior chief and monarch with communists, ANC supporters, and discontented BCP members, was awkward at times, but it needed the infusion of cash to compete with its foreign-funded rivals in Lesotho.

During the campaign leading to the January 1960 district council elections, all three political parties agreed on two central tenets: Lesotho should be moving toward political independence, and the British needed to fund more development projects. However, only males over the age of twenty-one who were physically present in the territory were allowed to vote, so, in addition to women, migrant laborers who could not get leave to return were excluded. The exclusive franchise was emblematic of the colonial government's view of popular participation in both governance and development. Administrators in both London and Maseru found it difficult to view colonial subjects as full, equal participants in political processes. All of these factors and the relative newness of electoral politics meant that only about thirty-five thousand Basotho voted in 1960, a participation rate of around 24 percent of the eligible electorate and only about 8.5 percent of the total adult population.[43]

Nevertheless, many Basotho remembered the 1960 campaign as the start of their political consciousness. Alexander Sekoli, a Catholic school-teacher who grew up in the same village as LLB founder, Josiel Lefela, cited this campaign as the start of his political engagement. Previously, he said, "people just continued living their lives like anything," but after the mass rallies and public speeches there was a shift in political engagement.[44] Another young teacher, Moeketsi Lesitsi, identified the campaign and elections as the time when he and others became aware of the importance of politics and first heard about and started to grapple with the idea of independence.[45]

The BCP victory in the 1960 elections put it at the forefront of the push for independence, but at the same time it was a victory that did not allow party leaders to fully exercise their popular mandate because of the shared nature of power under the 1959 constitution. The BCP controlled six of the nine district councils outright and had significant minorities in the other three, which gave them control of rural development programs since development authority was vested in the councils.[46] This control also gave them thirty of the forty seats reserved for district council–elected representatives in the new National Council, but there they remained a minority party because an additional forty seats were reserved for the twenty-two senior chiefs, the paramount chief's nominees, and senior colonial civil servants. The Executive Council, consisting of eight individuals elected from the National Council, controlled central government policy under the 1959 constitution. With the full council selecting these members, the BCP, on account of the threat many chiefs and opposition parties felt from its potential ascension to power, received only one of the eight seats. Even this token representation, however, disappeared in 1961 when that member, Bernard Khaketla, left the BCP for the MFP.[47] This lack of legislative or executive power left the BCP's 1960 victory rather hollow.

Most politically active Basotho saw the 1960 elections and the rapid decolonization of other African territories the same year as a tipping point in the movement toward independence. This contrasted with the vision of Lesotho's colonial administrators. As late as 1959, in fact, the Colonial Office in London was not planning to broach the subject of independence for any of the High Commission Territories in the next ten years.[48] But plans were overtaken by events on the ground and shifts in British government policy. On February 1, 1960, two days before his famous "Winds of Change" speech in the South African Parliament, British Prime Minister Harold Macmillan was in Maseru to meet with local political leaders and government officials. Much of the push for a hastened decolonization time line came from Basotho, however. At the same hour that Macmillan made his famous speech in Cape Town, Basotho chiefs and politicians were gathered in a *pitso* in Maseru to determine when Regent 'Mantsebo would step aside in favor of her stepson. In the culmination of a rancorous debate that stretched back to the 1950s, the chiefs decided that Bereng would replace the regent in March. Bereng took the name Moshoeshoe II on March 12, 1960, when he was installed as constitutional monarch. Through his choice of name, Moshoeshoe II signaled his desire to lead the country to independence by harnessing the reputation of his great-great-great-grandfather as a unifier and nation builder.

While Moshoeshoe II wanted to represent a new flowering of the Basotho nation in the 1960s, the increased public interest in politics and political culture was able to take root, in part, thanks to a vibrant literary culture in Lesotho that allowed for the rapid dissemination of news and opinion. Stretching back to the nineteenth century, Lesotho's literary tradition had blossomed in the pages of the religiously affiliated newspapers *Leselinyana la Lesotho* (Protestant) and *Moeletsi oa Basotho* (Catholic), with writers like Thomas Mofolo, Azariele Sekese, and Z. D. Mangoaela, among others, getting their start by having their work serialized in them.[49] Lesotho had a literacy rate of at least 60 percent by 1950, one of the highest rates in Africa, and this increased in the years preceding independence due to the expansion of education.[50] Mass literacy supported the presence of a highly developed local newspaper culture. The religiously affiliated newspapers were available countrywide, and South African papers were available in major lowland towns. Newspapers were also passed from hand to hand, so that dailies like *The Friend* from Bloemfontein and *The Star* from Johannesburg, as well as periodicals like *The Drum*, *Zonk*, and *New Age*, which focused on fashion and style in addition to politics, circulated widely. These publications accentuated the connections Basotho saw between national aspirations at home and regional and international politics.[51] After 1960, the range of local political publications grew as well. The BCP, after losing *Mohlabani* when Khaketla left the party in 1961, started publishing *Makatolle*, while the BNP founded *Nketu* as their party newspaper.[52]

The connections between Lesotho and South Africa politically, on the state level and in terms of the experiences of individuals, also deepened during the 1960s. A significant number of political refugees arrived in Lesotho in the wake of the March 21, 1960, Sharpeville Massacre. This put many Basotho and the government on the front lines of regional politics.[53] With Portuguese colonialism still entrenched in Angola and Mozambique, white settler rule in the Central African Federation, and South African control over Namibia, the High Commission Territories represented the only safe havens on the border of South Africa for those who needed to flee the apartheid regime in 1960. Lesotho was not the best landing spot for most political refugees, as its location made movement farther north on the continent difficult. Thus most of the top leadership of the ANC avoided Lesotho on their journeys to exile in 1960, yet a few leaders in exile like Joe Matthews and Gilbert Hani made the territory their base. The PAC, on the other hand, saw Lesotho as an ideal place to regroup and set up operations in exile because its leadership had strong roots in both Lesotho and the Transkei, which borders Lesotho to the southwest.[54] The colonial administration worked closely with the South African police, in particular, Special Branch agents, to keep an eye on this group and other newly arrived refugees. Even with this scrutiny, though, the porous borders and the willingness of many Basotho to quietly harbor refugees meant that the colonial administration was unaware of the presence of some liberation leaders. The long, lightly policed frontier between the countries allowed individuals to slip back and forth without detection, as a June 1960 incident illustrates. ANC leader Joe Matthews arranged for a charter flight from Maseru to Swaziland to spirit Wilton Mkwayi, Moses Madhiba, and four other high-profile ANC leaders out of the territory. Prior to the filing of the airplane's manifest, however, the colonial government had "not previously known" that three of the six passengers were in the territory.[55]

The Lesotho border represented an opportunity for South Africans to escape apartheid in the wake of Sharpeville, but even when there was not a direct political crisis, many South Africans attempted to get into Lesotho. As the apartheid regime cracked down on protest through the 1950s, the number of South Africans in Lesotho increased. In 1958, however, due in part to colonial decentralization, the Basutoland government promulgated the Entry and Residency Act. This law created district-level boards consisting of one colonial official and three Basotho to adjudicate and authorize the issuing of residency permits, thereby placing control of legal residency questions in the hands of Basotho.[56] The effect of this was that more South African political refugees were able to secure legal residency in the territory, including well-known leaders like trade union organizer Elizabeth Mafekeng, ANC organizer Gilbert Hani, PAC leader A. P. Mda, and ANC/SACP leader Joe Matthews. Not all refugees utilized this system, preferring to make use of their own local connections to gain asylum. SACP organizer Thabo Mofutsanyana, for example, slipped into Lesotho in 1959 to avoid arrest, without going through official immigration procedures.[57]

Ordinary South Africans and Basotho also made use of the porous border, with Basotho slipping across without going through formal procedures for work and visiting. South African students, in particular, came to Lesotho to attend school in large numbers after the 1955 passage of the reviled Bantu Education Act. In 1958, Leloaleng Technical School in the rural Quthing District enrolled two-thirds of its students from South Africa.[58] Students at the primary and secondary levels often came to live with relatives, however distant, in Lesotho, or they boarded at school hostels. This included students like Motsapi Moorosi, who had residency rights in Lesotho because his Basotho parents were migrant laborers living in South Africa.[59] It also included those who had no birthright claim to the territory like Zakes Mda, who followed his father into exile in Lesotho, and the Mbeki brothers, Moeletsi and Jama, who lived with their aunt in the Roma valley while attending Lesotho schools.[60] While the exact number of South Africans in Lesotho's schools is hard to come by, it was certainly large. By the 1970s, over one thousand South African high school students were enrolled in Lesotho, with even more at the primary level.[61] Since primary and secondary schools were scattered far and wide across the country, most rural communities had South African students in residence. This played a key role in popular support for the anti-apartheid movements and impressed on many the importance of political engagement.

Students who came to Lesotho to attend the university in Roma also played a role in spreading political awareness among Basotho. As the apartheid state cracked down harder on protest and constrained what could be taught in classrooms at all levels, the university became a more attractive option for many students from across southern Africa. In 1964, with funding from the Ford Foundation and USAID, the Catholic Church transferred Pius XII University College to the colonial administration, and it became the University of Basutoland, Bechuanaland Protectorate, and Swaziland (UBBS). Students responded positively to this change; enrollments rose rapidly through the 1960s and 1970s, with individuals coming from South Africa, Zambia, Rhodesia/Zimbabwe, and Nyasaland/Malawi, as well as the three constituent territories.[62] While the direct impact of the students was felt most strongly in the rural community of Roma, the presence of the university meant that there was a cadre of young, politically savvy students in the country. There was also an increasingly international faculty teaching and getting involved with both anti-apartheid efforts and local politics.

Finally, the major religious institutions of Lesotho often had cross-border ties, allowing people to move across the border even if they had no familial connections. Marie Selena, an Anglican nun, was born and raised in the Transkei, but during her novitiate she was sent to the Anglican community at Hlotse (Leribe), Lesotho. She ended up spending most of her career in various parishes across Lesotho.[63] A large number of Catholic clergy and nuns were also expatriates in the 1960s, so religion was a way in which many in Lesotho connected with non-Basotho. Between South African students, the university, a highly developed newspaper culture, and a proliferation of religious institutions, Basotho across the country, even in the most remote mountain villages, were connected to people and ideas from around the region and the world. The political interest that arose in the 1950s and 1960s among Basotho was linked not just to changes in the political structures of late colonial Basutoland but also to the anti-apartheid struggle and the Cold War. Basotho were increasingly aware of changes taking place around them, and they had access to media and networks of people to discuss the ways institutional changes like development and independence in Lesotho would have an impact on and were affected by other changes in the region and the world. While independence was not yet a certainty by the early 1960s, it was an idea that an increasing number of Basotho supported as they dreamed of better economic prospects, more government services in their communities, and the possibility of a more direct say in governance and development projects.

POLITICAL CHANGES, 1960s

Along with the political changes in Lesotho, the colonial administration and Basotho politicians increasingly emphasized development as a rhetorical and political strategy during the 1950s and 1960s. The colonial administration in Maseru had run some large-scale development projects in the 1950s with CDW money. These projects included school expansion and repair, anti–soil erosion efforts, and two large agricultural development projects, the Taung Scheme and the Pilot Project, also known as the Tebetebeng Scheme.[64] These CDW funds represented the first broad infusion of colonial development funding in Lesotho, but compared to other British territories, it was a relatively paltry sum. All of these projects combined garnered only a total of around $23 million worth of assistance from 1944 to 1966 (fig. 1.1).[65]

Despite this limited funding, Basotho politicians increasingly emphasized the linkages between political reform, independence, and development in the 1960s. They promised that independence meant more jobs, more and better infrastructure, and more foreign aid for development from a wider variety of sources. In the pre-independence 1960s, however, there were no large colonial development projects in operation and the only development came from community-level projects run by the district councils, religious institutions, and civic groups. Echoing the growing political divisions within the country and the continued tension between chieftaincy and democratic structures, these local-level projects often

Figure 1.1 Basotho kindergarten class, October 1970. Courtesy of
Moeletsi oa Basotho.

proved controversial. The biggest conflicts centered on who had the authority to allocate and distribute land and control its use. When the project
managers hired by the district council for the Mafeteng FARMECH
Tractor Scheme, for example, tried to get local people to consolidate their
fields into larger plots to allow for more efficient plowing and planting, the
chieftaincy was quick to mobilize local resistance. Some communities
went so far as to refuse to participate because they feared it would mean
the loss of local control over land.[66]

The messy operation of development and local administration, however, did not dampen the enthusiasm of the senior chiefs or leaders of
political parties for independence. They moved as quickly as they could
toward that end, with the National Council passing a resolution calling for
self-government in 1961, the first time it was legal for them to do so under
the constitution. This allowed Moshoeshoe II to appoint the new Constitutional Commission, which completed its work in 1963 with a plan to
devolve even more powers from the colonial government to local bodies.
The commission's report led to formal talks in London in April and May
1964 between National Council representatives and the secretary of state
for the colonies, Duncan Sandys. The outcome of the talks was the first
ever tentative timetable for independence, with elections scheduled for late
1964 or early 1965 to select a parliamentary-style government to jointly

rule with the colonial administration for a year. This positioned Lesotho for independence in late 1965 or 1966.[67]

Basotho, especially the young, were paying close attention to these political developments, largely through the press. Some, like Armelina Tsiki and Chaka Ntsane, noted that they sought out or had access to only one viewpoint in their media consumption, but others, like Selborne Mohlalisi, Mohlalefi Moteane, and Clara Rapholo, tried to get access to as many newspapers as possible to gain a better understanding of the changes.[68] This enthusiasm for political news from multiple perspectives belies the strength of the partisan difference at the national level, where political leaders used fiery rhetoric about other parties in an effort to attract supporters and demonize their opponents. It also speaks to the openness of most Basotho to a variety of meanings and possibilities for what independence would mean. Still, even with the widespread interest, it took persuasion and encouragement for a lot of Basotho to take steps toward political participation. For a few younger Basotho like Raphael Leseli, it was parents who encouraged political participation. In Leseli's case, his parents were BCP members long before he joined the BCP Youth League in 1965, and they encouraged him to attend rallies and events near their rural home.[69] It was the same with Chaka Ntsane, except that his parents were members of the BNP.[70] The parents of many other young Basotho, however, either did not know or did not care about politics, and these young people attributed their political participation to the consciousness-raising environment of schools. Selborne Mohlalisi dated his political engagement to his attendance at the PEMS school in Morija in the late 1950s. He contrasted the enthusiasm of his peers with an older generation that "really was not interested" in the idea of politics and independence until much closer to 1966.[71] In a similar vein, Michael Mateka reported that he learned to avidly read newspapers and follow politics at the Catholic Roma College in the late 1950s rather than because of encouragement from his relatives at home.

The process of gaining and realizing independence for many Basotho did not merely center on October 4, 1966—formal Independence Day. The idea itself was rather abstract, and its meaning to individuals and communities was not always clearly defined. Interestingly, it was an idea that Basotho came to understand both through the promulgation of newly democratic institutions in the late colonial era and through the structures that were significantly less open to popular participation after the 1970 coup and the turn to authoritarian rule. On one extreme were 1950s-era high school students, like Selborne Mohlalisi and Michael Mateka, who had firm ideas about independence even before the implementation of Lesotho's first constitution. On the other extreme was Moeketsi Lesitsi, who finished his secondary education in 1959, the same year as Mateka and only three years after Mohlalisi. Lesitsi was a teacher who had worked for the government on both the 1965 census and the 1966 elections, but at the time of the formal transfer of power, he "didn't even know what independence meant." He identified the years following the 1970 coup as the time when he came to understand independence. For him, the increased possibility of "going to other countries for training and learning" and getting "money from other countries" for development were the outcomes that made the idea of independence for Lesotho real in his mind.[72] These widely divergent experiences, even among those with similar levels of formal education, show how the centering of independence on the formal transfer of power does not take into account the different ways that people experience processes of change in the state.

The differences between Basotho in their views of independence were mirrored in their political divisions, which often broke along generational and religious lines. The BNP tended to garner the support of Catholics, while most Protestant Basotho supported the BCP. At the national level, the rhetoric was harsh, painting political opposition in terms that suggested differences that could not be bridged. Younger Basotho narrated experiences that noted the national political climate, but they had divergent experiences with how this polarization played out on the local level. Raphael Leseli reported that political divides in his home community of Makhalaneng ha Lekota did not greatly hinder social relations between youth. Many attended political rallies and joined the youth wings; afterward "some would go to another political party and some would go to the other one," but everyone came together for "jolling [partying] and cards and anything [relaxing]."[73] Many more Basotho, however, noted that national politics split communities and families. Michael Mateka noted increased rancor as formal independence neared. Divisions between Basotho sharpened "what should have been opposition into enemies . . . : You are against me, you are my enemy. When you are my enemy I bring you down by hook or crook."[74] Young Basotho tended to blame political leaders for this polarization, but this explanation involved some dissembling too, as many also reported being active participants in the youth wings of parties, which were often on the front lines of protest and polarization.[75] It is too much of a generalization, however, to say that all youth political involvement led to polarization, since many sincere young Basotho did not join the youth wings and attempted to build a more inclusive, less partisan version of Lesotho.[76]

Partisanship was felt in the civil service as well, with teachers and other government workers at risk of losing their jobs if they were too open about their political affiliations. Lesitsi was one of many teachers who remembered dressing carefully so as not to inadvertently wear party colors that might cause school managers to accuse him of pursuing a political agenda on school grounds.[77] A female BCP member teaching in the rural Mafeteng District lied to her Anglican school manager about her party membership because, she said, "he could have chased me away from the school [fired her]."[78] These were not idle fears, as the outspoken BCP member Tšeliso Ramakhula found out when he lost his job at the Agricultural College in Maseru in the wake of the BNP victory at the 1965 polls.[79] Schools attempted to keep their students out of politics. Since many of them, especially at the secondary level, were boarding schools, they had a degree of control over their students' lives outside of the classroom. Mohlalefi Moteane, a student at Peka High School at independence, remembered that he and his peers could attend rallies for any party, but they were not allowed to join a party or even to speak at the rallies—just to observe.[80] Motsapi Moorosi said that he never went to the rallies, but many of his peers at St. Monica's high school did. Like Moteane, Moorosi's peers were forbidden from participating in a more active capacity in politics while they were attending school.[81] Although students' actions may have been constrained in the short term, nothing dampened political interest in general among the younger generations. This was especially important in light of the rapid expansion of the education system that took place starting in the 1950s. The colonial administration saw few development opportunities in the territory, so most of the post–World War II CDW money earmarked for Lesotho ended up funding school expansion. The school system had about eleven hundred slots for Basotho students in secondary and postsecondary institutions like teacher training colleges in 1951. By 1966, this number had increased fourfold, and as the enrollments rose with the last of the CDW expansion, there were almost twelve thousand high school students by 1972 (see table 2.1).[82]

Educated youth were at the forefront of efforts to grapple with the concept of independence, and they were the first large group of Basotho, other than politicians, to internalize the connection between independence and development. This happened in large part because of their desire to avoid becoming migrant laborers, but having a large group of mobile, eager individuals thinking about and working for development played an important role in popularizing the linkage between development and independence among the larger population—what this book calls the rhetorical consensus on development. The connections between these concepts existed first in the minds of educated youth, but Basotho youth organizations provided spaces in which these young people could translate ideas into action. Chaka Ntsane was in leadership roles in a number of campus groups at the university around independence, and he remembered his peers talking about "development, development, development."[83] One group in particular was the Lesotho Workcamps Association, which organized students to build infrastructure in villages around the country during school holidays. They received some limited government funding to pay for materials, but the initiative for planning and implementation was the students'. Ntsane remembered students eagerly participating because the work was something tangible young Basotho could do to help improve infrastructure in the country and also because they were able to take the initiative in the organization.[84] Similarly, Mohlalefi Moteane, a high school student at the time, remembered his hopes for independence revolving around the "younger generations [being] able to qualify and become doctors, engineers so that they come back and run their own affairs."[85] Moteane's conception of independence entailed development he defined as the freedom for Basotho to receive sufficient training so that they could stay in Lesotho and find suitable employment. These visions for independence and development—job opportunities in Lesotho, more infrastructure and government services, and a pathway for individuals to contribute expertise and opinion to projects—marked the emerging youth development consensus that spread into the wider population by the late 1960s and early 1970s.

THE 1965 ELECTION AND DEVELOPMENT

The stakes of the election in 1965 were much higher than they had been in 1960 because leading Lesotho to independence would be the main task of the winner. All of the parties were better funded and organized, and the Basotho population at large was better informed and engaged with the political process. There was widespread excitement about what future changes might mean, but there was also anxiety. Politicians and ordinary Basotho alike wanted to see Lesotho emerge as a nation-state with a role on the regional and world stages. Attending rallies, showing up to vote in large numbers, and reading the local papers to stay abreast of changes, Basotho certainly did not have a "pathetic contentment" toward governmental affairs, or their own poverty, as a UNDP consultant named N. Kaul wrote in 1965.[86] Rather, it was a populace that worried about how change would affect individuals, as well as their communities and country.

Over 56 percent of the adult population of Lesotho voted in the 1965 elections, compared to 8.5 percent in 1960. The increased turnout was due to the higher stakes of the elections and the fact that the 1964 constitution extended the franchise to women. Depressing turnout was the lack of provision for absentee voting for workers unable to return to Lesotho for the April elections.[87] Most observers expected the BCP to prevail based on its wide margin of victory in 1960, so the BNP's razor-thin victory was an upset. The BNP received about 40 percent of the vote in the three-way contest, but it swept most of the rural constituencies, especially those in the mountains, while the BCP and MFP split the remainder. The BNP secured thirty-one of the sixty seats up for election in the new Parliament,[88] taking up the reins of shared government with the British colonial regime on May 6, 1965. The British were initially skeptical of the ability of the BNP to govern because of the lack of support the party received from the vast majority of educated Basotho, including most of the civil service. By November, however, British officials were touting BNP leader Leabua Jonathan's abilities to lead Lesotho to independence on October 4, 1966.[89]

In his radio address to the nation at independence, Jonathan laid out his vision for the new Lesotho. He explicitly linked the concepts of development, independence, and individual prosperity, noting that the government needed to assure the people that "land will be used in accordance with their wishes" to "promote economic development and national prosperity."[90] With land having been an emotive issue in Lesotho since the nineteenth-century rule of Moshoeshoe, Jonathan's linkage of land with development and independence was a historical analogy with which his listenership would have readily identified. But it was also part of and the result of a wholesale embrace by Basotho politicians from all parties of the

centrality of development to decolonization. While exactly what independence meant was still open for political debate, and was an open question
for many Basotho, the impact of fifteen years of political rhetoric about
development and independence had started to solidify this linkage in the
minds of many Basotho: independence required development, and development came with independence.

As I discuss in the next chapter, it was Basotho political leaders and
colonial officials who first put forth this formulation, but the answer as to
how and why it succeeded in becoming the dominant way of understanding decolonization among Basotho in general lay in efforts by
younger Basotho. Their embrace of development was rhetorical and political, but it was matched by their actions in youth organizations to bring
projects to fruition that would show significant numbers of people what
development, and hence independence, could look like.

CHAPTER 2

The Colonial Era and the Rhetorical Consensus on Development

Prime Minister Leabua Jonathan was miffed at the £2 million ($5.6 million) that Britain offered at independence for development assistance. He surely knew that the £5.3 million ($14.84 million) he requested at the preindependence negotiations was a pipe dream. He understood as well as anyone the lack of administrative capacity in the Lesotho government and the economic troubles of the sterling area in the mid-1960s weighing on the British Treasury. Still, the £2 million was insulting because Botswana, independent the same week, received £2.5 million ($7.0 million) despite having a smaller population.[1] Comparison with Botswana also highlighted that Jonathan's requests for American aid were falling short, as Botswana at independence had a functioning Peace Corps program while American officials had just discouraged Lesotho from submitting a formal application.[2] In addition to the bruised ego that direct comparison occasioned, Jonathan, like other politicians in Lesotho, had campaigned in 1965 on the ability to produce foreign aid for development as a key marker of independence, so falling short called into question his capacity to succeed as prime minister.

Jonathan presented Lesotho as being better able to garner foreign assistance than colonial Basutoland because the post-independence government could look to sources beyond the United Kingdom to potentially fund development projects. Jonathan and the BNP promised that foreign aid would lead to more and better jobs in Lesotho, infrastructure to improve the quality of life in rural communities, and less overall economic dependence on apartheid South Africa. When Jonathan received significantly less than he had hoped for from the United Kingdom and the United States, the two biggest and best potential sources for a leader positioned as an anticommunist champion, he did not let this dampen his aspirations. Instead, he set off on an ambitious schedule in his first years in office that took him to Austria, the United States, Britain, West Germany, Taiwan, South Africa, and South Korea. On one level, Jonathan's tour highlighted the Lesotho government's ideological stance in the Cold War. Even more importantly, however, it suggested that he felt an urgency to deliver on the promise of significant aid for development because the rhetorical consensus on development had emerged in the middle decades of the twentieth century among Basotho politicians, chiefs, and the rapidly growing student population. This consensus consisted of a widespread belief in the efficacy of development as the means to bring about political and economic independence in Lesotho.

The consensus coalesced first among the chieftaincy and politicians before spreading to younger, educated Basotho and from there further into Basotho society. By independence, development was the dominant rhetoric that Basotho used to make their case for how the state, local institutions, and voluntary groups should be structured. Still, there were vast differences in how various groups thought development should proceed. Politicians largely saw it as a means of consolidating state power and centralizing authority, whereas for Basotho at the grassroots there was a desire to see more economic opportunity, infrastructure, and services but also to link these with opportunities for popular input into governance processes.

The time was right, globally, for Jonathan's efforts to drum up development funding for Lesotho. The developmentalist colonialism of the 1940s through 1960s paved the way by broadening the definition of development from strictly economic projects to include social welfare.[3] It was also the era when modernization theory held sway, in particular in the American administration of John F. Kennedy and, with some modifications, in the Lyndon B. Johnson administration as well. Kennedy administration officials helped popularize the language of development, using it as the "court vernacular" to link implementation of centrally planned development projects to "nation-building."[4] While the language was less explicit in the Johnson administration, USAID and other government agencies primarily viewed aid to Africa in the context of building support for American policies among emerging nation-states.[5] In addition, Cold War concerns undergirded aid-giving strategies. The formation of the Lesotho Communist Party in 1961, funding for Lesotho's opposition parties from the USSR and China, and the presence of South African refugees from the ANC, SACP, and PAC meant that many inside and outside Lesotho saw political events there as being intimately tied to larger Cold War struggles.

Jonathan hoped that by positioning himself as an anticommunist, development assistance from the United States and South Africa would flow freely into Lesotho, but the calculus of donor aid was more complicated. Both the United States and South Africa were loath to fund development efforts in Lesotho that they felt were lingering British colonial obligations. However, both countries wished to meet some of Lesotho's requests but for different reasons. South Africa saw a chance to gain a relatively friendly African state as an ally at a time when few African states would even hold discussions with apartheid officials. The United States saw Lesotho as a site to provide symbolic assistance to an independent African state and thus demonstrate their solidarity against European settler colonial regimes in the region. Rather than provide significant amounts of aid themselves, both countries pressured the United Kingdom to increase its aid contribution to Lesotho in the late colonial period. From 1964 on, the United States provided "nominal or token aid" that showed "humanitarianism and moral support" for Lesotho, Botswana, and Swaziland to help them become "bastions of freedom and non-racialism."[6] South Africa, meanwhile, funneled some aid to Lesotho in the late 1960s because it needed to "do something tangible to prove its goodwill toward Lesotho."[7] Both of these assistance programs helped convince the United Kingdom to give Lesotho more development money and were part of international pressure brought to bear on Britain in the mid-1960s to rethink its southern Africa policy.[8]

By the mid-1960s, the emergence of a robust consensus on the desirability of development was, perhaps, surprising in Lesotho as one and all derided colonial development projects as failures. As a governing strategy and electoral tool, the emergence of the rhetorical consensus on development was less surprising because, as Easterly notes, development was a common "path to power" attractive to both colonial rulers and nationalist politicians.[9] All projects prior to independence faced resistance, mostly because Basotho remained suspicious of the motives of the colonial government. Basotho by and large did not trust that colonial administrators were working in good faith for Lesotho, instead fearing to the last moments that they were planning to facilitate a transfer of the territory to South Africa.

Most Basotho, on the other hand, still strongly favored the expansion of education. They saw schooling as development, since it potentially allowed young Basotho to avoid the most dangerous and low-paying jobs available to migrants in South Africa. But the colonial government kept the number of secondary schools low into the 1950s because they were expensive, and job prospects for graduates were bleak in Lesotho, outside of teaching and the civil service. Thus, with Basotho largely resisting the main colonial anti–soil erosion development initiative and being fatalistic about the prospects of education leading to white-collar employment at home, the emergence of a rhetorical consensus on development from the late 1950s demands more explanation.

The explicit use of the term *development* came to Lesotho, as in much of colonial Africa, in the 1930s with the hesitant programs designed as a response to the Great Depression. In Lesotho, the depression coincided with one of the worst droughts on record, making the mid-1930s an especially tenuous economic time. William Easterly has argued that the rhetorical emphasis on development emerged in the late 1930s as colonial theorists like Lord Hailey were charged with reinventing empire so that its legitimacy was based on the "technical ability to achieve rapid development" rather than explicit racial superiority.[10] But, as Joseph Hodge and Gerald Hödl note, while the language of development was new, it fit within the frame of justifying empire by appealing to the technical and intellectual superiority of Europeans.[11] This rhetorical change did not fully emerge until after World War II when colonial states adopted developmentalist language as their primary vernacular.

In Lesotho, this meant a continued emphasis on education and agricultural improvement, priorities that resulted from the colonial government continuing to view Lesotho as a labor reserve where men migrated to South Africa for work in the mines, factories, and farms, leaving behind women to run rural homesteads.[12] The focus on schools came out of a need for educated Basotho to staff the lower levels of the colonial administration, but it also came about because the missions were influential in Lesotho, and schools were a key site of conversion. The colonial regime had to pay only teachers' salaries because the missions shouldered the burden of constructing and maintaining school buildings. With the three main missions building rural primary schools at a rapid rate, education received a relatively large share of the budget in colonial Basutoland. The agricultural programs focused primarily on halting soil erosion and encouraging more commercial agriculture to increase rural incomes, but these results rarely materialized.[13]

Seeing Lesotho primarily as a labor reserve, the colonial government did not focus on revenue- or employment-generating development projects until very late in the colonial period. After World War II, money from the Colonial Development and Welfare Act allowed the government to fund studies on the viability of activities like mining diamonds and building dams in the mountains in order to sell water and hydroelectric power to South Africa.[14] By the 1950s, the senior chieftaincy in the National Council, whose salaries came from territorial tax revenue, mainly agreed that finding and exploiting resources in the territory was desirable. They echoed the colonial line that these projects helped the financial standing of the territory and better positioned it for independence. National Council member Caswell Molapo noted in 1957 that he needed to listen to proposals for the diamond and water projects because of the macroeconomic shortcomings of the colonial government: "We wonder if we shall be able to manage self-government without adequate finance."[15] Still, there was robust debate on these projects as it was unclear who would benefit from them and how they would affect relations with South Africa.

CDW funds in the 1940s and 1950s helped expand the secondary school system and allowed the government to initiate area-based agricultural projects that focused on mechanization, increased fertilizer use, improving rangelands for grazing, and combating soil erosion. While these funds represented an increase in the amount of colonial funding for development, the total financial outlay was only $23 million over two decades. This figure represented, for Basotho, as well as American and South African administrators, the colonial neglect for which they criticized the British government.[16] On the eve of independence in 1966, even the outgoing British government representative, the highest colonial official, wrote:

> British neglect over the past century has led to Basutoland's complete dependence on the Republic of South Africa, and . . . by granting independence with insufficient aid Britain is in fact 'selling out' the

territory to the Republic. . . . Impecunious independence will not be independence at all, and for this Britain must bear the responsibility.[17]

General dissatisfaction with British development efforts from the 1930s increased Basotho skepticism of colonial rule, and contributed to resistance to CDW projects by the late 1950s. This was especially true for the agricultural projects that dealt with the contentious issues of land allocation and use. At the same time, however, the *idea* of development was gaining support from many Basotho, as ordinary people increasingly saw it as a vital component of independence. Councilor Molapo's 1957 comments were an iteration of this, seeing an impoverished central government as being unable to secure meaningful independence. Tšeliso Ramakhula, an agricultural demonstrator, expressed the idea that economically useful activities were not only possible in Lesotho but also likely to succeed if given a chance. Looking at peach and apple orchards near Ficksburg, South Africa, visible with the naked eye from across the river in Lesotho, he wondered why the colonial government resisted starting similar projects: "That side [fruit farmers] can succeed, this side [colonial agricultural officials] . . . said there would be no orchards. What is that?"[18]

The failure of colonial agricultural projects to meet local expectations led Basotho like Ramakhula to conclude that the idea of development was not at fault; the failure was due to the illegitimacy of the colonial state. Colonial planners and outside consultants of this period, however, read development failures as the result of a "pathetic contentment," in the phrasing of a UNDP consultant, that was at the heart of rural resistance.[19] While many Basotho resisted colonial development efforts, this resistance was rooted not in a blind, superstitious "traditional" view but rather in a refusal to participate in development projects that did not include meaningful popular consultation.[20]

It is an overstatement, though, to claim that all Basotho were in favor of development, even at independence in 1966. Many Basotho noted that older generations were less excited about the prospects of independence and development than younger Basotho because they were not sure that political independence could lead to economic improvement.

Still, by the mid-1960s there was an emerging consensus among politically active Basotho, the senior chieftaincy, and younger, educated Basotho that bringing development to Lesotho had to occur in order for political independence to be meaningful. This consensus was formed through a series of failed development projects in the colonial period that, while not achieving their stated aims, still allowed Basotho of all ages to grapple with what a successful project might entail. The language of development offered Basotho the chance to articulate in concrete terms what independence would or could look like and to have hope for the better life promised by an independent Lesotho run by Basotho. The emerging rhetorical consensus on development played an important role in popularizing the idea of independence. It allowed Basotho to believe that political independence might be feasible, despite Lesotho's dependent economic position vis-à-vis apartheid South Africa.

DEVELOPMENT EFFORTS, 1930s–1940s

Though the World Bank claimed in 1975 that Lesotho maintained a "traditional subsistence peasant society," this had not been true since the late nineteenth century.[21] Rather, since at least the early twentieth century Basotho had been active participants in the regional cash economy, both as agricultural producers and migrant laborers. A combination of land shortages, drought, and the arrival of railways that gave access to the gold and diamond mines in the interior of South Africa meant that by the 1920s and 1930s Lesotho was a permanent net importer of food and exporter of labor (fig. 2.1).[22] Nonetheless, the colonial government believed that Lesotho was an agrarian society, a belief that ensured most colonial development funding was directed to the improvement of subsistence agriculture and the primary education system. This thinking continued into the independence era as bilateral and multilateral agencies continued to replicate colonial ideas about Lesotho and Basotho.

The confluence of the Great Depression and drought in the early 1930s made the colonial government nervous about the potential for a complete collapse of the economy and social system in Lesotho. Thus Sir Alan Pim's committee had a wide remit, which they used to address political as well as economic reform (see ch. 1). The Pim Report tied the idea of economic development to a change in governance in the territory and specifically recommended new checks on the power of the chieftaincy. From a development standpoint, the longest-lasting impact of the Pim Report was its recommendation on combating soil erosion. In addition, the report called for building more and better roads and bridle paths,

Figure 2.1 Young men at Maseru Bridge border post heading to the South African mines. Courtesy of *Moeletsi oa Basotho*.

expanding the health care system, exploring the possibility of building big dams in the mountains, improving the breeding stock of the territory, setting up wool cooperatives, and increasing the number of agricultural demonstrators.[23] In short, it laid out the development agenda for the remainder of the colonial period and much of the post-independence period. Concretely, the report led to the first colonial loan of £160,000 ($779,200) from a fund set up under the 1929 Colonial Development Act to implement the first anti-erosion works. This program built terraces on hillside fields, created grass buffer strips between fields, and put more limits on when livestock could graze on communally held land.[24]

The chieftaincy and some Basotho commoners initially supported these efforts in the late 1930s, but others complained about the loss of already scarce land for plowing and the lack of local input into land selection and demarcation. By the early 1940s, resistance to the project became widespread since it was found that the works could increase erosion in some places by allowing water from summer thunderstorms to pool behind the terraces and buffers before rushing downhill with more velocity, thus carrying off even more topsoil. In response, some Basotho farmers covertly sabotaged anti-erosion works.[25] The connection between these projects and similar Betterment Schemes in South African "Native Reserves" like the Transkei and Ciskei in the 1930s increased skepticism about and resistance to the campaign.[26] Basotho worried that project administrators who came from South Africa were an advance guard in a British–South African plan for the incorporation of Basutoland into the Union of South Africa. They also worried that anti-erosion works, literally, eroded local control over land by removing the power of chiefs and local people from decisions about land use and control.[27] Thus, from the first, Basotho suspicions of development were caused by very real concerns about the efficacy of particular projects and the ramifications of allowing outsiders to have control over land issues in rural Lesotho. The soil erosion projects also failed to recognize Basotho farmers' long history of successfully working the land and did not set up mechanisms to solicit local input in planning and implementing the projects. Again, the patterns established in the 1930s projects in Lesotho were repeated continually in agricultural projects into the 1970s.

SECONDARY EDUCATION EXPANSION, 1950s–1970s

The second major development initiative to receive funding was education. Motlatsi Thabane points out, however, that this was less a coherent development plan for a comprehensive educational system overhaul than a way for the colonial government to haphazardly increase the support for the already existing mission educational efforts.[28] Schools in Lesotho emerged in the nineteenth century as a primary focus of missionary efforts. The two most important were the Paris Evangelical Mission Society and the Catholic Church. The PEMS started schools during the 1830s at its bases of Morija and Thaba Bosiu, while the Catholic arrival in 1862 was centered at Roma. Both groups rapidly expanded their networks to include a series of outstations in the lowlands, foothills, and mountains by the turn of the twentieth century. Although the Anglican Church had a much smaller presence than the PEMS or the Catholic Church, it benefited from being closely aligned with the colonial administration. Subventions from the colonial government to help fund school operations began in the late nineteenth century.[29]

Basotho parents were broadly supportive of schools and schooling by the twentieth century, both because of the rapid spread of Christianity through the Basotho population and because they (and their children) saw education as the only way to avoid the worst aspects of unskilled labor migration. Until the 1950s, mission schools tended to focus on primary education, with a robust network of over 900 primary schools in operation by 1954, enrolling just over 100,000 students. Sixty-two percent of school-aged Basotho (five to eighteen years old) were enrolled, but only 1,461 were attending secondary institutions.[30]

The first high school in the territory, Basutoland High School, opened in 1939. After World War II the demand for more secondary education in the territory grew among Basotho parents and students. When the CDW started funding the expansion of secondary schools in the 1950s, it helped lay the groundwork for the rhetorical consensus on development by rapidly increasing the number of Basotho with post-primary education. Basotho families, who often sacrificed greatly to pay the fees for their children to attend secondary school, also started to demand more employment opportunities at home for their newly educated offspring.

Widespread Basotho support for education was not an anomaly in British colonial Africa, as the strength of the Kikuyu Independent School movement in Kenya from the mid-1930s suggests, but there were distinctive features of the education system in Lesotho.[31] At the primary school level, female students outnumbered their male counterparts. Boys tended to start school later because of their animal herding responsibilities, and they tended to drop out sooner to take up migrant labor in the mines to earn money for the family.[32] Boys who were successful in school, however, tended to get better support from their families. So, despite the preponderance of girls at the lower end of the system, boys finishing secondary school continued to outpace girls until 1970 (table 2.1).[33]

Families valued an education for girls because of how entrenched education was in Basotho society but also because it could increase *bohali* (marriage payment). Catholic Sister Armelina Tsiki recounted growing up in the 1950s in a family with three boys and seven girls. The Tsiki girls all received an education because of the financial support of her miner father, but her older brother also helped support them after he too went to the mines after only a few years of schooling. Tsiki's father was skeptical at first of her decision to attend secondary school and then join a religious order because this would not allow her to help the family financially. However, between having emotional support from her mother and financial support from her older brother, Tsiki was able to pursue further education and her religious vocation despite her father's objections.[34] The Tsiki family experience highlights the value that older Basotho put on education for girls

Table 2.1. Lesotho School Enrollments, 1951–1970

	Primary School	Secondary School	Teacher Training College	Technical/ Vocational School	Tertiary School	Total
1951	83,553	814	248	89	23	84,727
1954	36,144 M 65,745 F	828 M 565 F		90	39 M 11 F +15 in S.A.	37,101 M 66,321 F +15
1959	47,660 M 80,588 F	961 M 660 F	208 M 313 F	185 M 503 F	45 M 7 F	49,059 M 82,071 F
1960	51,631 M 84,480 F	1,044 M 791 F	220 M 316 F	188 M 506 F	34 +14 in U.K.	53,117 M 86,093 F +14
1961	55,235 M 89,460 F	1,067 M 910 F	239 M 333 F	64 M 512 F	29 +45 abroad	56,634 M 91,215 F +45
1962	58,178 M 93,541 F	1,252 M 957 F	208 M 376 F	116 M 427 F	21 M 7 F +61 abroad	59,775 M 95,308 F +61
1963	59,951 M 96,681 F	1,333 M 1,293 F	209 M 365 F	133 M 289 F	30 +87 abroad	61,656 M 98,628 F +87
1964	64,984 M 100,052 F	1,448 M 1,304 F	214 M 360 F	513 M 132 F	53 +119 abroad	67,212 M 101,848 F +119
1965	65,354 M 102,826 F	1,562 M 1,532 F	246 M 377 F	104 M 369 F	49 M 27 F +117 abroad	67,315 M 105,131 F +117
1966	64,315 M 102,854 F	1,443 M 1,499 F	244 M 365 F	153 M 110 F	82 M 25 F +109 abroad	66,237 M 104,853 F +109
1967	65,771 M 102,132 F	1,505 M 1,696 F	237 M 388 F	177 M 212 F	120 +105 abroad	67,810 M 104,428 F +105
1968	71,206 M 108,180 F	1,972 M 2,169 F	242 M 433 F	178 M 533 F	159 +118 abroad	73,757 M 111,315 F +118
1969	73,154 M 107,749 F	2,353 M 2,658 F	476 M 726 F	174 M 340 F	(figures missing) +215 abroad	76,157 M 111,473 F
1970	73,441 M 109,954 F	2,860 M 3,168 F	236 M 459 F	172 M 129 F	No figures	76,709 M 113,710 F

Notes
• All statistics come from Department and Ministry of Education Blue Books for the particular year (cited in selected bibliography).
• Tertiary statistics were reported for the number of Basotho students at the campus in Roma (first Pius XII College, which then changed to the University of Basutoland, Bechuanaland and Swaziland, and then the University of Botswana, Lesotho and Swaziland). The number of students abroad was reported separately, and I have left it as such to better reflect how much tertiary training was available domestically.
• The Technical/Vocational enrollments fluctuate because some of the reports count primarily Catholic-run sewing programs while others do not.
• The table ends with 1970 because 1971 saw the primary curriculum condensed from eight years to seven, making comparisons less germane.

but also shows rifts within families over the appropriate level of education in the 1950s. Her father's desire to have Tsiki marry for the *bohali* so the family could recoup an investment in her education also reflects the gendered nature of these contestations over new educational and developmental opportunities.

Despite strong local support for education, colonial officials were wary of rapidly expanding the educational system within Lesotho. In 1946, Evelyn Baring, British High Commissioner in South Africa, argued against the CDW school expansion because it required a "substantial increase in the money spent annually on education from the general revenues of the Territory." His concern was that there were no new revenue sources to offset spending.[35] This was in keeping with the overall British colonial objective in Lesotho not to burden the British Treasury. Over his objection, however, local officials in Maseru secured CDW funding that led secondary enrollments to go from under a thousand students in 1951 to almost twelve thousand by 1972 (see table 2.1).[36]

Basotho chiefs and politicians in the National Council strongly supported school expansion. The council voted in 1952 to create the Sethabathaba levy, a new tax on all Basotho that funded scholarships to train Basotho in programs not available in the territory's institutions.[37] The CDW school expansion and Sethabathaba ensured that Lesotho did not face as severe a lack of trained locals at independence as did other African colonies such as Congo.[38] The pyramidal nature of the education system, the emphasis by missions on primary schools, and the poverty of most families combined to ensure that most Basotho received only a few years of education. The idea of education, though, was popular and was something to which Basotho students and parents alike aspired. Parents made great sacrifices to send their children to school, as virtually every Basotho interviewed attested.[39]

With some Basotho parents pushing their children to achieve a higher educational level than their generation had, it was not simply individual access to education that was driving the growing rhetorical consensus on development. Rather, education and development were community-wide aspirations that stemmed in part from this newfound access to more education for young Basotho. It also stemmed from community groups that had laid the groundwork for all Basotho to engage with and make claims on the state and other powerful groups like the churches.

WOMEN'S GROUPS, COOPERATIVES, AND COMMUNITY DEVELOPMENT

The idea that rural Basotho, especially women, who were often left to figure out ways to cover daily household expenses in conditions of scarcity,
were skeptical or resistant to development was, in some ways, laughable.
Nothing was further from the truth, but the idea of African resistance to
development and colonial interventions ran deep among colonial administrators. This was, of course, not merely a Lesotho phenomenon. In
nearby Southern Rhodesia, a 1943 government report about resistance to
agricultural campaigns called Africans "'backward' or trapped in tradition," "mired in rural stasis," and unable to "change without compulsion
and control."[40] As in Lesotho, however, this language very likely misconstrued responses to specific programs as a general disposition against development, betterment, agricultural improvement, or whatever names the
government used for programs primarily designed to reshape colonial
economies and societies. The Great Depression pushed even more Basotho into migrant labor in South Africa, with an almost twofold increase
in the number of miners. The increase in migration signaled how far prices
had fallen for Lesotho's primary agricultural exports like wool and mohair,
and it left Basotho women even more dependent on intermittent wage
remittances for basic survival.[41] Thus rural Basotho increasingly desired
alternative sources of income and were open to a wide range of organizations, particularly those run by churches, that focused on ameliorating
women's poverty.

The Catholic Church, in particular, emphasized women's groups,
which were described by the Sesotho term *kopano* (union). The *kopanos*
were essentially prayer societies focused on church work, but the Catholic
hierarchy also mobilized them for other activities. In the 1930s, these included small-scale, local economic development projects. In particular, the
Catholic hierarchy encouraged the formation of local cooperatives, which
included "the development of petty commodity production, co-operative
gardening and marketing, building roads and dams and other forms of
economic 'self-reliance' for women."[42] The Catholic hierarchy, from the
populist Quebecois bishop Bonhomme on down, supported these efforts, but Basotho women embraced the projects because they met wom-
en's spiritual, social, and economic needs. By praying together, providing

volunteer labor for the churches, caring for community members in need, and helping construct small-scale development projects, these women were working for the type of communities in which they desired to live.[43] Colonial officials and political commentators into the 1960s read Basotho women's subordination in the most visible church hierarchies as proof that they were "conservative" and "traditional," words often used to imply that they were also resistant to development (or other "modernization") efforts. Their enthusiastic participation in the *kopanos*, though, suggests again that nonparticipation in later projects was not resistance to the idea of development but a reaction to particular aspects of the projects themselves.[44]

Colonial administrators and Basotho politicians read women's development efforts in light of their own misconstrued notions of women's roles in society. Political leaders like Ntsu Mokhehle of the BCP accused the Catholic *kopano* members of being "a massive gaggle of geese being herded" by political and spiritual leaders.[45] This sentiment, based largely on the BCP belief that rural Catholic women voted only for the BNP, ignored Basotho women's participation in organizations like the *kopanos* and the Homemakers Association. The latter group had the goal of getting Basotho women to raise the "social standard" of communities through "personal exertion with a view to self-improvement."[46] A member of the Homemakers Association, Maleseko Kena, found the group enticing for the same reasons that Catholic women joined *kopanos* in large numbers: it created a support network in villages where many of the men of productive age were off working in South Africa. The chapter meetings became important sites for women to learn skills like sewing and canning vegetables that helped them earn income or stretch household budgets. There were 150 chapters of the Homemakers Association across Lesotho by 1954 and even more by the 1960s, with tens of thousands of active members.[47] While learning handy domestic skills was important, Kena also noted that she and others joined the group in large part simply because it was an organization that Basotho women ran. The leadership "had energy and . . . knew how to get things done" and allowed individual chapters autonomy in terms of their structures and activities.[48] The ability of the groups to make a direct economic impact on women's lives and the spirit of community they fostered made them popular. They also became a model in the minds of Kena and other members for how Basotho women saw development and independence bringing new avenues for political participation. Groups like the Homemakers and the Catholic *kopanos*, thus, helped build the climate in which the rhetorical consensus on development took root among a wider segment of Basotho society.

It was not only in women's groups that Basotho helped lay the groundwork for the emergence of the rhetorical consensus on development, as civic organizations of all forms were popular in the late colonial period. The Catholic Church directly invested in rural schools and health clinics, roads and dams, and programs to teach sewing and handicraft production, all of which served as practical examples of successful development and helped foster the idea that economic conditions could improve in the rural areas. Catholic officials also helped set up popular cooperative wool marketing societies and cooperative buying schemes. Such cooperatives allowed rural Catholics to not just earn more income for their agricultural products by bypassing exploitative traders; they also opened up new avenues to explore popular participation in economic schemes. The colonial government and the BCP built on this foundation in the 1950s and 1960s with their own support for cooperative societies as a strategy for rural development. This support from politically disparate entities led to conflict over who controlled the forms such organizations would take, but their presence in institutions across society normalized the rhetoric and practice of cooperative economic enterprise.[49]

The encouragement of such schemes by these disparate actors and the success of the organizations in providing economic opportunities gave rural Basotho hope that similar projects could continue this trajectory.[50] Cooperatives and district council development efforts like road construction, bridle path maintenance, and irrigation dam construction all helped people see, many of them for the first time, how government support combined with local initiative could bring about positive economic change—development—in areas that were far removed from the center of political life in the territory (fig. 2.2).

Basotho could, and did, operate outside of institutional frameworks to experiment with development. In examining the case of J. J. Machobane, it is clear that these efforts faced strong resistance from the state if they threatened to organize large segments of the population. In the 1940s and 1950s, Machobane developed a system of intercropping that promised to increase the food security and income of subsistence farmers, as well as soil fertility, by planting together a diverse mix of crops that had varied sowing and harvesting times.[51] This system intercropped carbohydrates

Figure 2.2 "Women comprise this work crew which is working on a cross-country road from east to west in Lesotho, ca. 1969." Africa America Institute Records (MS 849). Special Collections and University Archives, University of Massachusetts Amherst Libraries.

and proteins, which meant that soils were never left unplanted and exposed to erosion-causing rains. By making legumes a central component of the mix, the project provided a protein-rich food as well as a nitrogen-fixing crop to keep overtaxed soils healthy and productive.[52] The goal of the program, in Machobane's words, was to make the system simple so that it would be "so self-regulating that the general necessities of life remain in the development and intelligent control of the masses."[53]

Machobane's system interested Basotho as well as colonial agricultural officials during the 1950s, when they were focusing on community development and small-scale programs. In a 1955 visit to Machobane's farm, the senior agricultural and livestock officer remarked that Machobane was "producing several times more foodstuffs on his plot than any Basuto with the same size plots or larger plots," but he also revealed his own perception of Basotho farmers in general, saying that this system was "difficult to propagate amongst the local farmers who generally prefer the easy way."[54] Basotho farmers dispelled the notion that they preferred an "easy way" by signing up for Machobane's Mants'a Tlala (Stamp out Hunger) agricultural college, which he founded in the Nqechane area of the Leribe District. According to A. F. Robertson, the college, which started in 1957 with twelve students learning from Machobane himself, had two hundred instructors and a waiting list of fifteen thousand by 1960.[55] The rapid growth, however, led colonial officials to worry that Machobane was not just building an agricultural system but also a political following that could undermine the limited colonial authority in the rural areas. Thus what had been curiosity from colonial agricultural officials in the mid-1950s turned into increasing hostility to the scheme and the college by the 1960s, as the politicization of Basotho across the territory increased.

The harassment worsened under the first Basotho-run government, which was even more threatened by independent power bases in the rural areas as it worked to consolidate its political control (see ch. 3). The hybrid Basotho-colonial government of 1965 closed down Machobane's college, and he fled his rural homestead in 1966. He moved first to Butha Buthe and from there to Maseru in 1970 where he lived in semi-hiding from 1970 to 1980, as he feared for his personal safety.[56] Perhaps the ultimate indignity of the demise of Machobane's agricultural system was Prime Minister Jonathan co-opting the name of Machobane's college as the name of a donor-sponsored and government-run program that subsidized the seed and fertilizer inputs necessary for monocropping grains—the antithesis of the Machobane program. The fact that so many Basotho took to the Machobane system, which he explicitly designed as an antidote to top-down agricultural programs that left people with little control over projects or outputs, suggests that one of the main problems with development as conceived by colonial and, later, independence authorities was that it did not allow for any significant popular input.

The government interest in Machobane's scheme in the mid-1950s came about in part because there was a growing emphasis on cooperative enterprises and community development by the colonial regime. This interest came out of the influence of the Labour Government in London and the growing strength of trade unions across the empire.[57] While other parts of the empire received well-capitalized, centralized projects like the East African Groundnut Scheme, in smaller territories without obvious resources to tap for development, funds and expertise mainly went to community development. In Lesotho this meant renewed support for agricultural improvement efforts. The idea of community development was left deliberately vague: to "involve people in a community about educating themselves to improve the circumstances of their lives through health, agriculture, civic education, and mass literacy schemes."[58]

The Lesotho district commissioners (DCs) grappled both with the vagueness of the overall remit and the tension inherent in programs that were government run but were supposed to, at least in theory, take their lead from the grassroots. At their 1959 conference, an unnamed DC wanted programs that "start[ed] at the bottom of the social structure, the grass roots, and [were] not imposed from the top." Another noted that this meant government could easily lose control of the process, so "government must be clear on what sort of community should develop."[59] Colonial administrators naturally found it hard to trust local communities enough to cede control of projects, but even if they relinquished this control, it was even harder for them to reconcile decentralized project administration with their need to have a territory-wide strategy for development. This tension remained at the heart of development planning and project implementation in Lesotho through the end of the colonial era and into the independence period.

In addition to worrying that development led to programs spiraling out of the control of government officials, the DCs worried that community development had the potential to disrupt social relations in the villages. Mobilizing women was, in their estimation, a double-edged sword. On the one hand, it offered the best opportunity to stimulate a "latent community development potential" since women were the "best material to work with."[60] On the other hand, it might produce a "class of women entrepreneurs with too great a measure of independence," similar to situations British administrators deemed problematic in West Africa.[61] In the end, the colonial regime had to utilize women extensively in community development projects whether they wanted to or not because labor migration had left most communities with a serious dearth of working-age men.[62] In an attempt to ease some of their concerns, the DCs heard colleagues give examples of Basotho women eagerly participating in development efforts like village water supply projects in Leribe and Quthing and women pooling resources to erect a wind-powered pump for water at Masianokeng in the Maseru District. The early and eager participation of rural Basotho women in development projects suggests that the broad-based rhetorical consensus on development that emerged in the 1960s came about because Basotho had long seen value in a wide variety of projects. Their participation also belied the persistent colonial belief that rural Basotho, and in particular women, were in some way opposed to the idea of development.

ELITE BASOTHO RHETORICAL CONSENSUS ON DEVELOPMENT, 1950s

The rhetorical consensus on development that took root among the general populace by independence emerged first in the late 1950s among the senior chieftaincy, political elite, and educated youth. Debates in the National Council through the decade featured an increasing number of discussions on development projects, and few questioned the desirability of bringing economic development to the territory. On account of these pressures, by the end of the 1950s the government issued a prospecting permit for exploratory diamond mining in the territory, funded feasibility studies for the highlands water project, and operated the first area-based agricultural projects. Among those pushing the elite rhetorical consensus on development, however, there was disagreement on the form development projects should take. The 1950s, with its contentious debates and first forays into project implementation, set the stage for the emergence of a full-blown, nationwide consensus on development by the late 1960s.

The backing of the senior chieftaincy for development efforts in the 1950s was partly a result of the chiefly reforms in 1938 and 1946 that aligned the financial interests of the colonial state with those of senior chiefs. Still, there was no unanimity among senior chiefs as to how specific projects should be implemented. In 1955 the colonial administration, with the assent of Regent 'Mantsebo, awarded Colonel Jack Scott the contract to prospect for diamonds in Lesotho. As a result of Scott's South African citizenship, the entire project became intertwined with worries about incorporation.[63] Further fueling controversy was the provision that all revenue from Scott's operation was to be split equally between the government and the Basuto National Treasury, which the regent controlled. Further, the National Council was not allowed to debate the terms of the contract, which exacerbated the suspicions of certain chiefs who questioned the regent's legitimacy.[64] Chief S. S. Matete's founding of the Marematlou Party two short years after the controversy over the awarding of this contract was no coincidence, and it aptly demonstrates the embedded nature of development and politics even at this early stage.

In an attempt to undercut these criticisms, 'Mantsebo cloaked the project in nationalist rhetoric, implicitly saying that those who opposed it were against "national development." Her 1956 Circular to all chiefs called for them to facilitate the cooperation of all Basotho. They were to assist Scott by telling his representatives where members of local communities found "diamonds, 'Sekama,' garnets, diamond rubies or yellow or blue ground" in order to accrue "the tremendous advantages the nation would derive if diamonds were discovered and worked in this country of our fathers."[65] Diamond mining would "bring advantages to the nation [including] increased revenue in the country, employment in the country and be self-supporting [sic], better communications, and trade with other countries."[66] The clear articulation here in 1956 of the connection between development projects and the prosperity of the state and individuals marks the start of widespread efforts to promote the benefits of development but also to depoliticize development in the name of nation building.

Opposition to diamond mining also came from junior chiefs and educated commoners, highlighting Basotho worries that the benefits of development were not being spread widely. In July 1956, the Standing Committee of the National Council, a six-member advisory board that met when the full council was not in session, did not want to approve an appropriation of £2,000 ($5,560) to fund road construction for Scott. They wanted him to "report on the prospects at a secret session of the [Basutoland] Council" because they had no information on his work and worried "in the end that there were no diamonds." They voted not to fund the road Scott requested.[67] The councilors worried that the secrecy around the project was allowing only those close to the regent and Scott himself to benefit from the prospecting. Butha Buthe councilor Wise Poka raised this issue at the National Council meeting in October 1956. Representing one of the districts where prospecting operations were under way, Poka questioned whether "the nation had been consulted"

about recent changes to the mining contract to allow the mining of wa-
terways.[68] This reflected commoners' worries that the mines disrupted and
endangered their subsistence livelihoods by causing them to lose access
to their summer pastures and river-bottom fields. Concerns over Scott's
operation, thus, foreshadowed the deep politicization of development
projects that marked the early independence period and demonstrated
how representatives employed the rhetoric of nationalism and national
interest in ways that argued for specific development agendas.

The rhetorical consensus on development among the political elite
incorporated the idea that development should be a top-down process designed to maximize macroeconomic benefit for the National Treasury.
The protests over the water surveys in the course of diamond prospecting
had to do with specific details of the projects rather than whether the
government should support them in toto. In the National Council, Sekhonyana Molapo spoke for the majority of the councilors in 1957 when
he asked, "What benefits will the people see from this project?"[69] Despite
differences across the political spectrum in how projects should be implemented and how the benefits would accrue, the consensus was that such
projects were desirable. Both Gabriel Manyeli, who helped found the
BNP, and BCP leader Ntsu Mokhehle argued for centralized state control
of development. The disagreements arose only over who could rightfully
participate in "national" development efforts. Manyeli called for South
African–based experts as advisers, a move that Mokhehle roundly con-
demned as selling out Basotho national interests. Mokhehle argued that
development funds should stay within Lesotho so that the products of the
soil and Basotho labor were not "taken away to foreign countries."[70] But
both couched their arguments in nationalistic terms, helping cement the
popular connection between nationalism and development.

Although it is not possible to gauge how most Basotho felt about
Scott's diamond mining contract, independent miners certainly did not
approve since his exclusive deal threatened their livelihood. The 1956 Circular from Regent 'Mantsebo suggested the obvious: Basotho who lived
near diamond deposits often knew about them and had been mining them
for some time (fig. 2.3). The potentially profitable sites that Scott identified were near Kolo in the lowland Mafeteng District and at mountain
sites at Kao in Butha Buthe and Let'seng-la-Terae in Mokhotlong. Local
people had been surreptitiously mining the Kao deposit since at least the
1930s.[71] It was the death of a female miner at Kao in 1954 that provided
the impetus for the Scott deal, as it brought what had been a mostly

hidden industry out of the shadows and into the view of colonial officials and senior chiefs looking for revenue-generating possibilities.[72] By signing a monopoly contract with Scott, however, these officials made it clear that small-scale, independent diamond mining was not in the national interest. The deal sacrificed the ability of those who lived near or moved to the diggings to make a living for the potential revenue that Scott's prospecting might bring into the National Treasury. For senior chiefs and politicians in the National Council, this seemed a reasonable trade in the national interest, but to the diggers it represented a personal betrayal by those invested in the elite rhetorical consensus on development.

Despite the Scott contract and the National Council prioritization of revenue generation through development, "illegal" diamond mining continued throughout the 1950s and 1960s as the economy of Lesotho failed to generate anything near widespread employment. The chief of Tsikoane, a subdistrict of Leribe bordering South Africa, complained to the district commissioner in 1959 about smugglers who "deal in diamonds and firearms at night," thereby disturbing the peace.[73] According to police files, Elias Monare, a petty criminal, cross-border man of intrigue, and some-

Figure 2.3 Individual diamond digging in Lesotho. Courtesy of Ted Nettelton, former district commissioner, Mokhotlong District.

time political operative for the BCP, made numerous trips to Kao in 1959 and 1960 to purchase illicitly mined diamonds from Basotho diggers.[74] The government was so concerned by the trade in illegally mined diamonds through the two major lowland border crossings, one at Ficksburg Bridge in Leribe and the other at Maseru Bridge, that by 1965 the Basutoland police had forty officers assigned to its diamond unit out of a total force of only eight hundred.[75] The willingness of so many Basotho to flaunt the wishes of the paramount chief by continuing to mine and trade in illegal stones speaks to the poverty that plagued most Basotho and to the sense that the land and its resources should be utilized for ventures that supported the livelihood of individuals and local communities first. The diggers who continued working at Kao and at Let'seng-la-Terae despite the monopoly arrangement were not just challenging the authority of the chieftaincy but also living out the argument that the chiefs had made for over eighty years: the land and resources of Lesotho belonged collectively to Basotho. As a digger Motlatsi Thabane interviewed noted:

> These Basotho, now that it is clear that this country is theirs, and they live on it, with minerals from the soil of their country, now when they are being expelled from here, then where is it being said that they shall live. . . . Is it not an encouragement now that this nation should eat one another and attack one another and eat one another when an act like this is being done.[76]

The 1950s also marked the start of the planning for the highland dams project, and its massive scale and scope meant that politicians and chiefs all jockeyed to reap benefits. The plans called for dams in Lesotho's high mountains to act as catchments with a series of underground supply tunnels to carry the water to South Africa, generating electricity along the way. While project details changed significantly between the 1950s and the 1990s, when construction started, the basic idea was set from this early date, as was the promise of enormous central government revenues. This potential windfall intrigued chiefs and politicians alike in the National Council, but the members were also deeply suspicious of the project because of their general distrust of the colonial administration and outright antipathy to the apartheid government. The extreme secrecy of the Colonial Office with regard to project studies and plans fueled suspicion that the U.K. government was prepared to sacrifice Lesotho's

long-term financial interest in the project to maintain good relations between the United Kingdom and South Africa. A 1951 memo from the
secretary of state for Commonwealth relations declared that the preliminary dam plans were "still confidential," meaning that neither Basotho
nor South African officials were allowed to see them.[77] Once nonsecret
surveys of the upper reaches of the Orange (Senqu) River and its tribu-
taries started in 1954, the project generated an uproar among members of
the council. Similar to the diamond deal, however, controversy arose from
the specific plans for implementation and questions as to who had the
right to be consulted on the project.

The Basotho members of the National Council were correct to suspect that the colonial government knew more than it was telling about
potential water sales. As early as 1935, the South African government
had gained approval from the Basutoland administration to set up water-
monitoring devices on the Caledon River at Ficksburg Bridge.[78] This was
part of 1930s efforts by South Africa to explore options to ease water
shortages throughout the Orange Free State and the Witwatersrand
region. The South African government received permission from Paramount Chief 'Mantsebo in 1942 to drill holes on the Lesotho side of the
river to test the rock formations for their potential viability as dam an-
chors.[79] Simultaneously, South African prime minister Jan Smuts started
corresponding with the British High Commissioner in Pretoria about
whether the British, in principle, supported the handing over and inun-
dation of land in Lesotho should such dams be constructed. The con-
spiratorial tone of the letter, such as when Smuts writes that "the informal
negotiations with your office have, so far, been of a preliminary nature
only," suggested that the colonial administration had not kept Basotho,
including the paramount chief, apprised of the conversations.[80] That the
National Council did not have a discussion about an issue that would
surely have generated an outcry also suggests that the colonial administration kept top Basotho chiefs in the dark.

The worries in the 1950s about the dam plans brought about unanimity from chiefs and other members of the National Council who typically did not agree. Josiel Lefela spoke out against the dam studies in 1954,
calling them a backdoor route to incorporation and arguing that if the
South African government contributed money to the project it "would
be entitled to a share."[81] Despite Lefela's long history of conflict with some
members of the senior chieftaincy as leader of Lekhotla la Bafo, Sloley

Molapo, a pro-government chief, agreed wholeheartedly with his concerns. Molapo noted that once South Africa had a financial interest in the dams they could "become later the property of the Union Government because they are stronger than us."[82] These concerns proved remarkably prescient regarding the impact of significant funding on national sovereignty in light of Ferguson's assessment that large development projects primarily served to heighten uneven power relations between donor and recipients.[83]

That dams could be used to solidify white settler rule and the interests of big capital in southern Africa was not an idle fear in the minds of Basotho chiefs and politicians. Construction on the Kariba Dam in the Central African Federation (CAF) commenced in 1956 with the goal of supplying hydroelectric power to the Northern Rhodesian Copperbelt. The British government's primary goal, however, was to bring the two Rhodesias into closer political alignment, thereby justifying continued European minority rule in the CAF.[84] Similar to the rhetoric deployed by the members of the National Council in Lesotho, African political groups in the CAF objected to the dam as a "cynical device to extend white power."[85]

In a move that showed how Basotho understood the pernicious effect that economic dependence on South Africa could have on a future independence, members of the National Council approached the colonial state for the dam's funding. They preferred funding of the project by the British government and its Colonial Development Corporation rather than forcing them to rely on South African funding. These leaders, most of them vocal anticolonial critics, preferred to tie Lesotho's development future to the British government rather than the apartheid regime as a way to distance Lesotho further from South Africa's politics and economy. The goal of economic independence from South Africa is one that Basotho politicians from all parties nurtured and promised voters throughout the independence period.[86] There were, however, other options, and Basotho leaders knew that, as they solicited funds for the dam project from the World Bank and the UNDP in order to reduce Lesotho's dependency on any one source of funding.[87]

In the late 1950s, however, the project was still too nebulous and Lesotho too far from independence to have a realistic chance of receiving funding from multilateral institutions. So the focus remained on securing more British funding. The pages of *Mohlabani*, the stridently anticolonial BCP newspaper, were rarely a place where readers found positive appeals to the British government. However, a 1958 column written by "Boipuso" (Independence) outright called for "co-operation with Britain" in order to secure funding from the Colonial Development Corporation to "increase the money-earning capacity of the Territory if we are not to forever remain sucklings and tools in the hands of the monied."[88] So while there were reservations about aspects of the project and about who might fund it, support was unanimous among the political elite and chieftaincy.

The elite consensus, however, hid a more complicated local response to the project, especially in the areas where the dams were to be built. Butha Buthe National Council members, in particular, communicated their constituents' concerns. Sekhonyana Molapo reported that worried residents were contacting him when they saw heavy machinery heading into the mountains and they had not been "notified that there were plans for this scheme."[89] Similarly, Kopano Selemo reported that residents feared the loss of scarce and particularly fertile agricultural land in the remote mountain valleys of the district.[90] These comments reflected a general lack of transparency and consultation in the project process.[91] They also reflected a deeper suspicion of colonial-era development projects for being categorically unable to effectively communicate with individuals and local communities.

AGRICULTURAL SCHEMES

Two major area-based agricultural schemes that started in the 1950s aimed at improving rural agriculture and increasing rural household income. These programs represented the biggest colonial development efforts in Lesotho. A 1951 colonial survey that gave impetus to the projects noted that continued erosion and lack of agricultural improvements could lead to the "economic ruin" of the territory.[92] The familiar narrative linking soil erosion and economic deterioration for the majority of Basotho was development gospel for the colonial government, echoing language in the 1935 Pim Report. The immediate precursor to the 1950s schemes was the anti–soil erosion campaign of the 1930s and 1940s. The response of Basotho to the 1950s projects was decidedly mixed, in large part because of the ambiguous legacy of earlier efforts. Basotho in general had suspicions of projects that relied on South African administrators because they worried about incorporation. They also knew about South African Betterment Schemes, projects they perceived as having dispossessed African populations of their most productive land.

The Pilot Project (1956–60) in the Tebetebeng Valley of the Berea District and the Taung Scheme (1956–61) in the Mohale's Hoek District received the majority of colonial development outlays. These were comprehensive schemes designed to do far more than simply ameliorate soil erosion. Both projects promised to increase rural household income by giving Basotho farmers access to improved agricultural services. The Pilot Project constructed small irrigation dams, built community water taps, provided increased amounts of fertilizer to farmers to increase crop yields, and relocated villages situated on steep slopes in an effort to combat erosion. The project was a showpiece for high-profile visitors, but local people struggled to connect with the project as agricultural officials worked primarily through chiefs and headmen rather than directly with them.[93] Even the chiefs who were supposed to act as conduits for information were skeptical of the project at times. Peter Millin, a government agricultural supervisor on the Pilot Project, noted that chiefs' support was uneven, with project officials getting "good cooperation" in some areas and having to "battle" to get support in others.[94] The project ended in 1960; according to official evaluations, it largely failed to arrest soil erosion, improve farming practices, or increase rural incomes.[95]

The Taung Scheme contained the same general programs as the Pilot Project, but it also included an even more controversial plan to cull and limit the number of stock people could hold in an effort to maintain and restore grazing grounds. Further, it encouraged mechanized planting and harvesting by forcing individuals to consolidate their fields, which many Basotho farmers and chiefs saw as an effort to usurp local control of land allocation. The Taung Scheme faced more widespread resistance because of these controversial efforts and because local populations were given "no mechanism for discussing the problems they saw in their fields" with project managers.[96] Thus many Basotho in the project area took "independent action to [sabotage]" project work.[97]

The colonial government saw attempts to sabotage the project as evidence that rural Basotho were resistant to the idea of development, which contributed to the ending of both schemes by 1961. The agricultural department assessment put the onus for project failure squarely on the shoulders of Basotho farmers who were not "receptive to advice [or] prepared to follow approved farming practices."[98] Sandra Wallman, writing in the late 1960s, uncritically adopted the colonial line, arguing that the failure of such schemes was rooted in a "lack of interest and/or understanding" by Basotho. However, her own analysis noted that the project was "out of touch both because there was no effective means of getting opinions from people in the Ward itself and because the administration of the Scheme was concentrated in the District capital."[99] The problem with uncritically accepting the official colonial explanation for project failure is, as Millin noted, that Basotho responses were far more complex than a simple characterization of support/resistance or success/failure captures.

Suspicion of the intentions of colonial reforms was not just confined to areas where showpiece agricultural projects were under way. In the northern Lesotho district of Butha Buthe a shadowy organization called the Ngoajane Political Association came to the attention of the district commissioner in 1951 after "secret" meetings took place in communities on the border with South Africa's Witzieshoek Native Reserve. The reserve, lands the apartheid regime designated for those it classified as ethnically Basotho, had erupted in a major uprising over land issues in 1950–51, and Mopelinyana Mopeli, who was a leader of the uprising, was present at at least one of the Ngoajane meetings.

The apartheid regime's attempts to implement Betterment Schemes was the proximal cause of the uprising, and the fact that Lesotho's anti–soil erosion campaigns and agricultural schemes were modeled on betterment made the colonial authorities especially nervous.[100] They, along with their South African counterparts, also feared Basotho cross-border ethnic solidarity on land and agricultural policy grievances. The fact that they knew so little about Ngoajane worried authorities in Lesotho.[101] While the organization never took root in the subversive ways feared by the colonial government, or to the best of our knowledge coalesced into a long-lasting political group, it is tempting to see the strength of the BCP in the Butha Buthe lowlands as being related, at least in part, to rural organizing and agitating from groups like Ngoajane.

The increasing emphasis that colonial administrators and Basotho chiefs and politicians alike placed on development rhetoric in the 1950s was percolating throughout society. A couple of letters to the editor in the Catholic newspaper *Moeletsi oa Basotho* in 1954 used the term *tsoela-pele* (development) in ways that echoed the language of colonial development planners. In August, D. R. Mochecko argued that the future wealth of individual Basotho depended on their better utilization of the soils and resources of the land, concluding, "Temo ke bona 'm'a Basotho" (Farming is the mother of the Basotho).[102] Responding to Mochecko's letter, S. Lepolesa echoed similar sentiments in September.[103] That readers of *Moeletsi* were starting to speak the language of *tsoela-pele* by the mid-1950s and make connections between development and economic prosperity shows how the rhetorical consensus on development was gaining wider traction in Basotho society.

The Taung Scheme illustrates how Basotho politicians utilized rural organizing to both build support for their political parties and gain more support for the rhetorical consensus on development, even as they opposed this particular project. Efforts by officials to cull stock and place restrictions on livestock in rural areas led to the strongest resistance to agricultural projects in the Transkei, Ciskei, and Witzieshoek.[104] The Betterment Schemes in the Transkei, in particular, were quite close to the Taung Ward, which bordered South Africa just north of the land where the South African administration attempted to implement the Herschel District Betterment Scheme. Many of the Taung administrators came straight from the Herschel project.[105] This confluence of factors, plus the heavy-handed manner in which colonial administrators implemented the Taung project, brought about resistance to the project through an alliance between the BCP, some chiefs in the ward, including Taung Ward Chief Moeketsi, and local people.

Residents of Taung were hungry and poor because soil erosion and drought made the ward one of the least productive agricultural regions in Lesotho. In 1957, the project started badly: agricultural officials, in a breach of popular custom, refused to allow for public input at the *pitsos* called to convey project information to the population.[106] This made local people suspicious of the officials' motives. Political discontent with the project began early. Thus, when the colonial regime implemented the 1959 constitution and held elections in 1960, there was a vein of political discontent in the rural Taung Ward into which the BCP and ambitious chiefs could tap.

The strong outcry against the Taung Scheme also came about because it called for the temporary removal of all livestock from the ward. Cattle played an especially important role in the economy and culture of Lesotho. They plowed many Basotho fields in the spring and were called *molimo o nko e metsi*—the god with the wet nose. Many families kept their savings "on the hoof" in the form of livestock, especially cattle, and bridewealth (*bohali*) was usually calculated in cows. Thus a plan that included moving all district livestock to mountain grazing areas so that local pasture grasses might recover was controversial. The cattle were forcibly removed to mountain outposts, which made them more vulnerable to theft and harder to utilize for spring plowing. The BCP saw an opportunity for organizing rural lowland communities and joined the protests. By February 1958, local outrage combined with BCP organizing acumen meant that project regulations were "only exceptionally obeyed."[107]

Aiding this campaign, some members of the chieftaincy refused to prosecute in their local courts those who disobeyed project managers' orders. So the central administration in Maseru set up a special court to prosecute offenders. This court was separate from local judicial structures. Taung Ward Chief Moeketsi, who reported directly to the paramount chief, saw these courts as a threat to his authority, as did many other members of the chieftaincy because they worried about the precedent of setting up courts run from Maseru. Some chiefs even worked to accentuate the rift between community members and the government by supporting the protesters. With BCP activists also working in the area, there was a three-way alliance between aggrieved local people, political activists, and some local chiefs, which worried the colonial administration greatly. Not only was this, from the colonial perspective, "detrimental to the success of the scheme," but there was a distinct fear that a chiefly alliance with "lawless elements" among the BCP activists could lead to the protests rapidly spiraling out of control and threatening colonial power more broadly.[108] This concern was so grave that colonial officials ended the program in 1961: "Reclamation areas [were] being plowed up and unauthorized grazing [was] occurring everywhere."[109] With the Taung project ending in acrimonious circumstances, the agricultural department decided to switch tactics, working on a smaller scale through individuals rather than in broad, centralized, area-based schemes. It focused on implementing "Progressive Farmer" schemes in the remaining years of the colonial period as a way of limiting the ability of large-scale protest to disrupt development efforts and undermine colonial authority.[110]

The failure of the Taung Scheme, suspicion of diamond prospecting, and popular concerns about surveys for the dam project illustrate how colonial development project failure helped pave the way for the even broader 1960s rhetorical consensus on development. Opposition to these projects was rooted not in popular fear of the idea of development but in the sense that projects were not going to economically benefit particular communities or that Basotho were in fact losing control over their own affairs rather than gaining a say in governance. There was a sense that these projects could, nay, they *had* to, improve when Basotho had the opportunity to run them. Thus, nationalist sentiments grew in 1950s Lesotho because of the failure of these projects, not in spite of it. Basotho could plausibly attribute the tin-eared, lack-of-local-consultation style of project implementation to a colonial regime run by British (and South African) officials rather than Basotho. They could keep alive the hope that an independent, Basotho-run state would do development better.

MOSHOESHOE II AND INTERNATIONAL AID

Even with the scale and scope of colonial development funding for projects increasing, only a relatively small number of Basotho had much contact with the colonial state in the 1950s and early 1960s. The energetic young monarch Moshoeshoe II played an important role in increasing the profile of development efforts both internally and internationally on behalf of the government. His 1960 installation as monarch aided the efforts of Basotho politicians who had been pushing for self-government and development from the colonial state, as he was a strong proponent of both. Educated in Lesotho as well as at Oxford, and being able to claim direct descent from Moshoeshoe, he had a stature on the international scene that no one from Lesotho could match until 1965, when Leabua Jonathan became the elected prime minister. For most of the early 1960s, Moshoeshoe II played a singular public role in pushing for development and independence. His globetrotting attempts to solicit aid from a variety of states and international funding agencies led to contacts that paid off in the form of development funding after independence. They also kept the pressure on the United Kingdom to maintain and even increase development funding.

Moshoeshoe II's first high-profile trip abroad in 1962 took him to the United Kingdom, the United States, Canada, and Ghana. His stated goal was to solicit donations to broaden the funding base for development projects in Lesotho, but the trip was also about staking his claim to the monarchy at home and abroad. Moshoeshoe II never fully accepted that Regent 'Mantsebo, his stepmother, with whom he did not have a particularly warm relationship, had agreed to the 1959 constitution, which considerably diminished the powers of the monarchy. Thus, in addition to working for "the nation" by soliciting development aid, Moshoeshoe II was also looking to establish himself as a major domestic political player by bringing home development funds. He hoped to use these efforts to make the case for the return of an executive monarchy whenever an independence constitution was negotiated.[111]

His timing seemed fortuitous in terms of the international aid environment, but uncertainty about when Lesotho might gain independence and what Britain's role should be in development funding hindered Moshoeshoe II's ability to garner significant project assistance. Until 1958, the U.S. State Department viewed Basotho as a "backward (tradition-oriented)" people, but by 1962 the Kennedy administration, in particular the influential assistant secretary of state for African affairs, G. Mennen Williams, was strongly supportive of aid requests from emerging African countries.[112] The American government was looking to leverage programs like the Peace Corps and USAID to support newly independent and emerging African states to win Cold War allies and as part of a broader strategy to portray the United States as an anticolonial power on the side of African nationalists.[113] In 1961 Kennedy called on the UN to declare the 1960s the "Development Decade," and the General Assembly obliged, calling for more international assistance as a means of increasing economic growth in poor states.[114]

Despite this seemingly favorable environment, Moshoeshoe II came home from his 1962 trip with little aid because the North American governments were loath to fund projects in British colonies. The Canadian government did agree to supply two advisers for the cooperative movement, three lecturers to supplement the instructional staff at the university, and more scholarships for Basotho students at Canadian institutions.[115] In the United States, Moshoeshoe II submitted a detailed plan for over $3.5 million in aid, including a request to hire agricultural experts, expand secondary schooling, build a vocational and trade school, and start an institute of social sciences (law, economics, political science, and philosophy) at the university in Roma. His request employed the language of modernization theory, then in vogue in the Kennedy administration, arguing that aid to

Lesotho would allow for "rapid economic growth and educational advancement" to match "political development."[116]

Despite the positive impression he made on American officials, Moshoeshoe's trip did not net any concrete promises of aid from them. His introductory visits to the offices of USAID, the Peace Corps, and the World Bank, however, laid some of the groundwork for post-independence aid programs to Lesotho. Kennedy administration officials were reluctant to fund projects in Lesotho because they wanted Britain to maintain financial responsibility for its colonies and soon to be former colonies. A 1964 State Department memo noted that "the UK should continue to bear the major share of the responsibility for economic development" in Lesotho as they had "done shockingly little to develop such things as social services, public health, public education, agriculture and communication."[117] This attitude pervaded the thinking of American officials, and Moshoeshoe II came home from Washington empty-handed.

While they were unwilling to commit publicly, especially to an unelected monarch, American aid officials communicating through official channels with British administrators made it known that they were not opposed to quietly assisting with efforts to develop the High Commission Territories. Kennedy and Johnson administration officials wanted these small programs to bolster the anti-apartheid credibility of the United States. These attempts to assist highlighted the relative lack of administrative capacity in Maseru to deal with the planning and implementation of large-scale aid and development projects. The British Colonial Office noted with chagrin that "no applications for American aid have reached London, let alone Washington[,] . . . [and] American offers of help are being wasted because of the delays by British officials in Maseru and Cape Town."[118]

The decades of colonial underinvestment in the bureaucracy in Lesotho meant that when colonial (and global) plans suddenly changed to offer significant amounts of money for development projects the lack of suitable administrative personnel made implementation difficult. Even the resident commissioner wrote that he hoped Moshoeshoe's visits might yield "unexpected results in our search for solutions to the economic challenge we face."[119] The irony, of course, was that the "economic challenge" Lesotho faced was due largely to the long colonial history of scant British government assistance for development because the colonial government was unwilling to treat Lesotho as anything but a labor reserve. By the

1960s, even the colonial administration in Maseru recognized that its own legitimacy was now dependent on successfully providing some sources of development funding for Lesotho and Basotho.

After returning from his 1962 trip, Moshoeshoe II advocated for more British development funding in Lesotho, drafting a lengthy memorandum to the British High Commissioner. In it he spelled out a development philosophy that was notable for its people-first focus, in contrast to the top-down, project-focused, macroeconomic approach favored by the colonial government in the 1960s. He criticized a "lack of clear-cut economic policy and [Britain's] refusal or reluctance to make use of the offers made by various International Agencies" to help improve the "social services—education, health, [and] community development," which have "consequently suffered terribly."[120] He accused the British of "deliberately, but subtly, cutting Basutoland off from the rest of the world willing to render assistance—financial and technical—for the better and rapid economic development of Basutoland" by refusing "offers for technical assistance or the planning programmes which various International Agencies offer; and yet she herself is not able to provide sufficient personnel" for such purposes. Moshoeshoe II called for "the better and rapid economic development of Basutoland" to support the efforts to bring about better jobs and social services. At the same time, he asked to "restore the Government of Basutoland to the Basotho, under their National Ruler and King, *Motlotlehi* Moshoeshoe II, as in the days of old."[121]

The call from Moshoeshoe II was striking in the way that it presaged the understanding of the rhetorical consensus on development that rural Basotho would largely come to hold by the late 1960s: better jobs, more government services, and increased Basotho popular participation in governance. While Moshoeshoe II was more committed to an executive monarchy than most Basotho and the colonial regime, his argument for a robust conception of development that encompassed more than simply macroeconomic growth helped spread the idea of development more broadly. The message was congruent with the post-1960 BCP grassroots strategy of encouraging district councils to focus on the formation of agricultural and purchasing cooperatives as a way to increase rural incomes and purchasing power.[122] By urging Basotho to think beyond what official development programs like the Taung and Tebetebeng Schemes promised, efforts such as Moshoeshoe's helped set up the conditions for a wide segment of Basotho society to understand and support the rhetorical consensus on development by the time of independence. Moshoeshoe II continued his travels in the mid-1960s, making trips to West Germany in 1962, North America and Israel in 1963, and Sweden and Nigeria in 1964.[123] None of these efforts landed large development projects, but again all of these countries would contribute aid for development to Lesotho in the independence era.

AN EMERGING YOUTH RHETORICAL CONSENSUS

The elite rhetorical consensus on development of the 1950s started reaching a wider audience after the elections of 1960. The first large group that internalized the message was the younger generation, especially those who had access to the rapidly expanding post–primary school system. Tšeliso Ramakhula was in the vanguard of this group as he graduated in 1949 from Morija Training College before going on to earn an agricultural certificate from Fort Cox College in South Africa. After teaching in secondary schools for a few years in the early 1950s, he joined the faculty at the Agricultural College in Maseru in 1955 to train agricultural demonstrators. He had also been an early member of the BCP, though not in a leadership role. He remembered opposition to the idea of independence and to the BCP: "There were some people around who said that Congress wanted to govern ourselves and wanted to drive Europeans away, yet they cannot make even a single pin. Many of the old people were opposed because they were satisfied with the situation and they deemed it actually fit that we should be buying and buying all of the time."[124] Ramakhula positioned himself not just as a supporter of greater political power for Basotho but also as a supporter of the need for development, symbolized by the making of pins. Through this metaphor, he argued that development would allow Lesotho to lessen its economic dependence on South Africa. As he suggests, this was an idea that in the 1950s had not reached too deeply into society, especially among older generations.

As the school expansion continued apace in the 1960s, giving a greater number of young Basotho access to secondary schools and beyond (see table 2.1), more young Basotho began to speak of independence in the language of development. Mohlalefi Moteane was enrolled as a high school student in the early 1960s, and he hoped that independence could bring "a chance for us to make matches. You understand what I mean?

A box of matches."[125] Similarly, Thabelo Kebise, also a student in the mid-1960s, hoped for "new factories in our country and . . . some trains to run through the country, maybe from Butha Buthe to Quthing [from north to south]."[126] Beyond industrialization and railroads, Raphael Leseli hoped that independence would bring infrastructure like "roads and schools . . . [and] hospitals, clinics. Development."[127] Chaka Ntsane explicitly connected independence with increased access to foreign aid, hoping that independence would give Basotho a chance to "not [be] confined to only British circles," meaning that they could approach multiple countries and organizations for development assistance, technical support, and diplomatic relations.[128]

These voices, representing a wide range of political and religious viewpoints, suggest that most young Basotho who were going to school in the 1950s and 1960s came to understand and internalize a connection between independence, increased economic opportunity, and government services. Many of these same individuals also remarked on a generational divide; they said older Basotho were more suspicious of the promises of independence made by politicians and more cynical about the possibility that development would deliver substantive economic change. Ramakhula characterized older Basotho as being "satisfied with the situation [of colonialism and lack of development]," and Michael Mateka was not even sure if his own father participated in the 1965 and 1970 elections because of a deep disdain for politics and the ideas of independence and development.[129] Selborne Mohlalisi recalled older Basotho being wary of independence because of a simple economic calculus: "All they knew was it was the Boer who gives us bread and work."[130]

Even among some younger Basotho, independence was an unknown commodity that worried them. Moeketsi Lesitsi, a teacher, remembered being quite suspicious and fearful of the idea of independence in the 1960s. It was not until sometime in the 1970s that he "came to realize the advantages that could be possible from independence—people could go to other countries for training and learning and we could get money [foreign aid] from other countries."[131] So while the rhetorical consensus on development took root among most young Basotho by the mid-1960s, it was a belief that was full of uncertainty and had not yet become rooted in the rest of society.

The diverse ways Basotho youth expressed their visions for development highlighted that a broad definition of development was necessary.

The diverse meanings attributed to it suggest that rhetorical agreement on development as a category concealed vast differences in how people expected to realize societal changes after independence. There was very little reflection in these accounts as to why older Basotho were more skeptical about the promise of development and independence, with most stating something similar to Mohlalisi, who characterized independence as "a strange subject understood [only] by those that had been to Maseru or read books."[132] In their characterizations of their older compatriots, young Basotho were largely echoing the words of colonial development planners about a resistance to development and lack of knowledge about the concept of independence.

Lesitsi's narration of his gradual conversion to a belief in development hints that experience with projects and political independence could change individuals, but the failure of colonial development projects loomed large for many Basotho. Scott Brumburgh, a Peace Corps volunteer, was stationed in Matelile outside Mafeteng in the late 1960s where he assisted communities in the planning of village water supply projects. He remembered deep resistance to the projects and his personal presence, as the colonial government had earlier allowed South African businessmen to collect money for similar projects. Local memory had these men absconding with the money and constructing nothing.[133] Thus, even after independence when Brumburgh and representatives of the Lesotho government came to villages to pitch the projects, there was deep and understandable skepticism about their desire and ability to complete them. Villagers needed assurances that their investment of time and money would be rewarded with service upgrades. Perhaps, then, the hesitation among the older generations was not skepticism of the idea of independence but a healthy suspicion of promises made by those with power, whether colonial or Basotho, whom they viewed as having disappointed them in the past. The end result, however, was that politicians and younger Basotho saw older community members as being suspicious of development and independence. In order to overcome some of this lingering suspicion, both colonial administrators in the early to mid-1960s and Basotho politicians yearned to deliver "successful" projects with tangible results to entice more people to see development as a path to political independence. Both were hindered, however, by the lack of administrative capacity within the government that marked colonial rule and the post-independence Lesotho government.

FACTORY DEVELOPMENT AND THE WORLD BANK
ROAD PROJECT

External and internal pressures on the late colonial government to facilitate development led to two significant development initiatives in the 1960s: discussions between Moshoeshoe II and the colonial government to open up land in Lesotho for factory development and negotiations between the World Bank and the colonial government concerning a road-paving project. In addition to more pressure from within Lesotho, the colonial government faced a new push in the early 1960s from the Colonial Office in London to prioritize development efforts in the HCT so that the territories did not reflect poorly on Britain in relation to other newly independent African states and the South African Bantustan project.

The issue of development threatened to drive a wedge between the United Kingdom and South Africa, however. The Pretoria regime worried that significant industrial development in the HCT undermined their efforts to encourage South African firms to build factories along the "borders" of the Bantustans, a policy designed to force more Africans to live in "Homelands." During February 1960 meetings in Cape Town, British prime minister Harold Macmillan and South African prime minister Hendrik Verwoerd disagreed on how development in the territories should proceed. Verwoerd, angry at Britain for granting Lesotho the 1959 constitution and holding elections in January 1960, argued that the HCT were "naturally . . . economically interdependent with the Union" and thus the United Kingdom should see South Africa as "economic guardians of the inhabitants" of the HCT.[134] Verwoerd threatened Macmillan that South Africa would take "measures to protect [South African] industries" if Britain "used the Colonial Development Fund to set up European-controlled industries in the Territories." This threat of economic protectionism was accompanied by an offer to the United Kingdom for South Africa to make the HCT "viable economically" by "guid[ing] their economic development and harmonis[ing] it with that of the Union itself," integrating them into South Africa's Bantustan system. For Macmillan, who just days before had staked his international reputation in the "Winds of Change" speech on African nationalists pushing for the end of colonial rule, handing over the HCT to South Africa was not a serious option. Macmillan's rejection of South Africa's offer forced the Colonial Office and local HCT administrators to redouble their development efforts.

In Lesotho, colonial administrators, the monarch, and even many ordinary Basotho equated development with industrialization. In 1960, there were no factories in the territory. One obstacle to establishing factories was the issue of landownership and tenure. Legally, the monarchy held all land in Lesotho in trust and, in conjunction with the local chieftaincy, was tasked with disbursing land and adjudicating land disputes. This meant that non-Basotho individuals could not own land, outside of the small government reserves that functioned as district headquarters. Laws prevented the sale or alienation of land to non-Basotho anywhere in the territory. Support for this state of affairs ran deep as it differentiated Lesotho from Swaziland and the Bechuanaland Protectorate, both of which had some European settlers. Keeping land allocation in the hands of the chieftaincy as a way of precluding outsiders, especially Europeans or South Africans with access to capital, was a defining part of national identity for Basotho of all political persuasions.[135] Factories, however, demanded a capital investment that required security of tenure not available in Lesotho, thus hindering industrialization.

Moshoeshoe II's efforts to solicit development funding made him a natural supporter of industrialization plans. The 1962 scheme, known as the Basutoland Factory Estate Development Scheme (BAFED), set aside twenty-five acres in Maseru near the main border post and railroad station. This acreage was outfitted with water hookups, sewage lines, roads to link with the center of Maseru, and a mile-long railroad siding to allow for direct train connection to the Orange Free State.[136] In addition to being the logical location for a project that was expected to export finished goods to South Africa, the site sidestepped the thorny issue of landownership as it was situated within the Maseru Reserve and required only a sign-off from Moshoeshoe II to come to fruition. It was thus possible to offer owners security of tenure through a fifty-year lease without having to completely rewrite landownership laws throughout the territory or gain the assent of other senior chiefs. The site proved popular, and by the end of the decade, there was a brewery, a large grain milling operation, and a number of smaller enterprises that opened after investment from the post-independence Lesotho National Development Corporation (LNDC).[137]

While Prime Minister Verwoerd and the South African government could not stop these efforts, they successfully hindered further industrial development in Lesotho in the late 1960s and early 1970s. The regime in Pretoria worried that Lesotho's membership in the Southern African Customs Union, which included tariff-free entry for goods into South

Africa, could allow Lesotho-made products to undercut South African manufactured goods due to the cheaper cost of labor in Lesotho.[138] Widespread industrialization in Lesotho was never, however, an imminent threat; South African and multinational corporations were not keen on setting up factories outside of South Africa's major cities. The South African government's unsuccessful 1965–68 efforts to convince Chrysler to locate a new factory in rural South Africa rather than in Pretoria is evidence of this reluctance.[139]

The South African government had additional leverage over companies that considered setting up manufacturing and commercial operations in Lesotho. In 1968, South African pressure scuttled plans for a commercial radio station operating out of Maseru and nixed discussions between Maseru officials and the Honda Motor Company about construction of an engine manufacturing facility.[140] The South African government simply threatened companies with loss of future access to South African markets to gain compliance. Thus Lesotho's industrialization plans in the late colonial period met with only limited success, largely in the realm of import substitution. The reluctance of firms to come to Lesotho, and South African resistance, was compounded by the colonial administration's inability and unwillingness to support industrial development with government funds. So the colonial administration turned to other avenues for development, including multilateral organization funding for infrastructure in the early 1960s.

In 1961, the colonial administration approached the International Development Association, the arm of the World Bank that focused on lending to poorer countries, to seek funds to upgrade Lesotho's road network. Initially they wanted to finance territory-wide expansions and upgrades of the road system to boost export-oriented agricultural production. The lengthy negotiation process, which dragged on from 1961 to 1965, ended up radically changing the scope of the plan. The messy process highlighted the lack of expertise in the Maseru administration in planning and implementing complex projects. Administrators missed deadlines and could not produce technical reports in the timely manner that the World Bank demanded. They also could not agree on whether the project should emphasize macroeconomic growth for the territory or whether it should be run more as a public works program providing employment and skills training.

The initial proposal submitted to IDA in 1961 was a large-scale public works program to increase local employment and upgrade the skills of public employees while also constructing roads. It called for the construction and rebuilding of one thousand miles of rural roads in Lesotho at a cost of £3.88 million ($10.86 million), to be disbursed as a loan. While the proposal mentioned macroeconomic growth potential through the possibility of more wool and mohair exports, it emphasized public works to ensure popular support. Under these initial plans, the Public Works Department (PWD) would run the program as a "field training of artisans, operators and supervisors" who could oversee construction of the entire project.[141] The emphasis on local employment showed the influence of political parties like the BCP, whose agenda after winning the 1960 elections included large-scale public works programs. The plan also reflected the Labour Party orientation of the colonial administration, which was then emphasizing cooperatives and community development.

IDA officials, however, rejected the proposal as written. They sent it back for revisions, noting that it represented more of a "long-term overall road program rather than a specific project" and was not feasible given the lack of trained supervisors in the PWD.[142] The IDA, as an arm of the World Bank, was not interested in giving a loan for a public works program that did not have macroeconomic growth as its primary purpose.

The colonial administration in Maseru was quite slow to meet the demanding bureaucratic requirements of the World Bank. Maseru officials struggled to obtain and compile the surveys and technical reports IDA demanded. IDA officials pressured the colonial administration from the outset of project discussions to bring in South African contractors to complete work rather than attempt to train local people. Thus the project that came to fruition turned into a one-off project that financed a road but did not lead directly to broad-based economic benefits for Basotho. IDA officials made this policy explicit to Maseru administrators as early as 1962, when they noted that the chance of funding would increase if they managed to submit a "self-contained project," meaning not a sprawling public works project. The project needed to include "realistic cost estimates based on field surveys" that were beyond the scope of PWD officials' abilities.[143] The pressure on colonial officials to get any development projects operating in late colonial Lesotho and IDA insistence meant that colonial officials went along with the World Bank's recommendations and cut direct employment and skills training. They acceded to "suggestions" that they utilize outside consultants to prepare reports and have the project work completed by South African construction firms.

Actual construction on the project started in 1965, but the plan to prioritize macroeconomic benefits over direct benefits set the pattern for development that would continue into the independence period. The project also highlighted the tension within the colonial administration: not all department heads were in favor of the original direct employment project. The PWD, a department dominated by South African officials, had never been "particularly enthusiastic" to be in charge of a large public works program and had only grudgingly accepted it "at the suggestion of [other branches of the] Government."[144] The lack of speed with which the PWD responded to IDA requests suggests that they were not competent to run a project of this magnitude, that they were not willing to do so, or both. In May 1963, for example, IDA officials asked for technical reports on road planning within ten weeks. When the reports finally arrived in Washington seven months later (in January 1964), they were so significantly revised that IDA officials had to start over with aspects of the project evaluation.[145] The 1964 proposal eliminated the public works component, replacing it with the contractor-built paved main road stretching from Leribe/Hlotse in the north to the Phutiatsana River in Mazenod just to the south of Maseru. This was the project that received funding and that was completed in 1967.

Despite the elimination of the jobs program from the proposal, the project was the government's first successful application to a multilateral institution. It was one of the first major projects that did not rely mainly on British funding, and for civil servants like Selborne Mohlalisi, this was the embodiment of independence. A junior official, Mohlalisi argued that the civil service was competent and ready to help an elected Basotho government run its own affairs: "We had been trained sufficiently. . . . [T]he expectation was that we would carry on[,] . . . develop the country, be able to manage affairs."[146] Implied in his characterization of readiness was that Basotho civil servants could do a better job than the British had because they were part of local communities and cared more about the national success of projects.

The ability of an independent Lesotho government to solicit and garner post-independence development assistance from a wide variety of sources made Basotho hopeful about the prospects for independence. However, the relatively united front on development put up by Basotho political elites around projects like the IDA road fractured in late 1965 following the BNP victory in the May elections. While all political leaders continued to advocate for development as the route to the realization of independence, their disagreements about particular projects came to the fore as electoral concerns started to dominate political rhetoric and maneuvering. Despite the politicization of development in the years around independence, more Basotho continued to enter conversations linking the necessity of development to the realization of independence.

The road project represented the culmination of the elite rhetorical consensus on development, as politicians of all parties claimed that state-intensive, top-down projects were the embodiment of independence. At the same time, however, the road project's implementation fractured the political consensus as opposition parties vied to undermine the government's implementation of aspects of the project. The government tried to claim the political capital for this showpiece project. At the same time, more Basotho, especially youth, started to act on their own conceptions of development. These performances of development at the grassroots level sometimes aligned with the development initiatives of government, especially in the self-help programs, but at other times these efforts took a wider variety of forms. Young Basotho helped plan, design, acquire funding, and mobilize labor for the implementation of small projects designed to improve the quality of life for people in rural communities.[147] These efforts often included avenues for input designed to bolster participation in governance, locally and nationally, or to assist residents in communities with their basic needs. Small projects, born out of the elite rhetorical consensus on development, helped spread the idea that independence could be a meaningful idea for Basotho in rural and urban communities.

Colonial officials and Basotho officials after independence should have celebrated these efforts as the embodiment of development they had worked so assiduously to cultivate. Instead, the development efforts came to highlight differences between Basotho who saw development as a tool to build participatory structures and political leaders who desired development as a means to centralize government authority.

CHAPTER 3

Working for Development

Centralization, Youth Groups, and the Physical
Infrastructure of Independence, 1960–1968

As the pace of decolonization across Africa picked up through the 1960s,
the 1950s rhetorical consensus on development in Lesotho gradually expanded to a broader segment of society, as aid and development became
more visible and central to the political process. Around independence,
Prime Minister Leabua Jonathan traveled to the United Kingdom, the
United States, the Republic of South Africa, Austria, and West Germany
in a quest to obtain funding for large-scale development. Unfortunately,
despite his 1965 campaign promises to introduce large, centralized projects
like industrialization to Lesotho, the government was forced to rely in the
post-independence era on smaller-scale projects similar to the community
development of the late 1950s. This frustrated top BNP officials and stymied their efforts to utilize showcase projects to build electoral support.
Smaller, locally run projects, however, opened up the kind of opportunities
that younger Basotho hoped to see from independence, like infrastructure
creation and the ability to publicly participate in decision making. Through
these broader based, small-scale initiatives, development became the language and practice of independence in Lesotho.

But the independence era was also marked by increasing politicization
of aid and development because the rhetorical consensus on the importance of development made the delivery of projects central to political

contestation. It also made the projects themselves symbols of political success or failure and thus raised the stakes for participation. The rhetorical consensus led to deep divisions within Basotho society on the merits and politics of particular projects, leading to fierce contestation over project planning and implementation.

The international, or at least Western, consensus on development after World War II revolved around the axiom that economic planning could be "apolitical" because it was a step toward "productive efficiency" that helped "eliminate poverty by enriching everyone."[1] By the 1960s, the Americans, in particular, were explicitly attempting to steer politicians toward elite, centralized planning as a foundation for creating national economies to promote the formation of national identities.[2] Creating a national identity was less a concern in Lesotho, on account of its perceived ethnic homogeneity and the long history of Basotho uniting when they perceived the threat of incorporation into South Africa. The connection between development and nation building was evident in the language of a UNDP consultant in 1965, who called on the Lesotho government to "force the pace of [macro]economic development [to] maintain the unity of the nation."[3] The BNP government gave lip service to the idea of national unity in the early independence period, but it was focused primarily on promoting development for partisan political gain. Relatively inexpensive community-based projects were the norm through the late 1960s because funding for larger projects was not available.

In March 1966, Setho Letsie, minister of works, posts, and telegraphs and communications, announced the start of a self-help program designed to encourage development projects such as constructing new gravel roads and bridle paths, planting trees, providing piped water to villages, and building new classrooms. This program attempted to draw on Sesotho culture, making reference to "communal practices like the *matsema* [community work parties initiated by chiefs]" in order to "stimulate the interest and participation of the people with the efforts of the Government in economic and social development."[4] In addition to being a new development program, self-help projects explicitly made a break with the colonial regime, which in 1950 had outlawed *matsema*. Thus, in bringing forward the self-help program, the BNP stirred up nationalist sentiments by referencing a banned colonial-era cultural practice. In the new self-help program, laborers were paid only in food aid donated by the U.S. government in partnership with the World Food Programme (WFP). The goal of self-help was to "transform" food aid into a "capital asset" to allow for cheap infrastructure creation and improved agricultural productivity while also meeting the basic needs of the population.[5]

The rhetoric used by the self-help planners, however, fell back on the colonial assumption that Basotho were apathetic to the idea of development, as well as tacitly accepting the new polarized partisan environment that kept people from participating. The language the minister used made it clear that he viewed Basotho as needing a push from government to see how they might personally benefit from participation. Self-help, Letsie claimed, allowed people to "feel that the projects are theirs and not the government's. In this way they will be ready to maintain works initiated by themselves" as a way of helping bring about "full independence and growth to nationhood."[6] Letsie's view here elided the growing politicization and polarization around development, failing to acknowledge that participation in projects was, by 1966, an indication of political allegiance rather than a statement of either support for or rejection of development. This was true for many young Basotho, who eagerly embraced the self-help model of community development but did so through youth organizations. They were not rejecting the ideas of development or self-help but rather the cynical politicization of certain projects by the government and the opposition.

The increasingly vitriolic tenor of political discourse and the relative dearth of projects magnified the importance attached to every development effort, no matter how small. The increased politicization led to more national attention on development programs. Many Basotho bemoaned this politicization, but, ironically, the spotlight it trained on even the smallest projects meant that the elite rhetorical consensus on development morphed into a society-wide consensus that made independence synonymous with development for the entire population by about 1970. While government and international agencies provided important support for projects, the widespread adoption of self-help development projects was possible only because of the initiative taken by young Basotho to implement projects in places underserved by government. A continued rise in school enrollments contributed to a concomitant increase in the number of youth organizations, which played a key role in organizing projects through which young Basotho could implement or "perform" their visions of independence through development. It was through their participation in these organizations and projects that Basotho youth constructed their visions for the nation. For the most part, such visions, rooted in grassroots and participatory-democratic forms, came into conflict with the desire of the BNP government to centralize its authority over development in order to win more electoral support and to gain increased funding from international organizations. But even when the trend in Lesotho's development projects was toward centralization and conflict, the ability of youth to continue to work for their own visions helped them keep faith in the eventual ability of development to bring about a desired independence.

ATTEMPTS TO CENTRALIZE DEVELOPMENT IN THE 1960s

Among the political elite, support for development remained as strong in the 1960s as it had been in the 1950s. With politics intensifying in the decade, leaders were less inclined to agree on how particular projects should come to fruition, but they all shared a vision of centralized, planned development that could be harnessed for nation building. The 1959 constitution had pushed political leaders in the 1960 elections to embrace decentralized community development by vesting development control in district councils and village committees. The community development projects of the early 1960s thus gave local people in many places their first taste of control of land and development issues. The committees that controlled projects after 1960 enabled "active participation by large groups of people" and allowed nonchief actors to be responsible for "social services, economic development and land questions."[7] At the same time, however, these structures posed a considerable threat to chiefs' already diminished ability to control land allocation, and they also threatened government technical departments, which previously enjoyed a free hand to run rural projects.[8] Council- and committee-led development projects also increased politicization of projects by giving elected bodies control, which meant that some Basotho rejected these decentralized efforts because of their partisan implications. On the whole, however, the desire of local communities to obtain development projects led Basotho politicians to call for more projects and more local control in 1960 due to the political advantages on offer for being seen as competent leaders. This changed dramatically by the end of the 1960s as politicians shifted to more centralized development plans.

The high point for decentralized development came during and in the immediate aftermath of the 1960 elections in which all parties supported the idea in their respective platforms. The Marematlou Party called for the "national attainment of self-rule through local initiative in different fields of development" to allow individuals to "assume increasing responsibility in promoting national well-being." The party also expected cooperation between chiefs and commoners to increase "agriculture, health and educational services."[9] The Basotho National Party similarly called for government to be "in Basotho hands," so that administrators could "press for the utmost development of . . . local industries for the local needs of the population (carpentry, shoemaking, wool spinning, fruit canning, etc.)."[10] Finally, the Basutoland Congress Party demanded "self-government in Basutoland by the Basotho NOW"; party leaders wanted immediate legislative powers to be better able to regulate "administration, education, commerce, industry, state finances, and land tenure."[11] This unanimity on development was a product of the 1950s rhetorical consensus, but that consensus was not predicated on a particular form of development. Thus the emphasis on decentralized community development was not a deep-seated commitment but resulted from the terms of the 1959 constitution that placed most power in the hands of district councils.

Shortly after the 1960 elections, the leadership of all parties started to push for more centralized development projects as a way of encouraging the colonial administration to devolve more powers to Basotho. This would allow leaders to pursue the political changes they hoped to see while also consolidating political power in their own hands (or so they hoped) after independence. Basotho political leaders were also responding to internal and external pressures for more centralized development. A few dedicated members founded the Communist Party of Lesotho in 1961, and their founding manifesto decried the lack of development in Lesotho by asserting, "[The] land and natural resources are hardly developed at all. There is no industry."[12] Externally, the focus of key funding agencies like the U.S. government was centralized, planned development. Therefore, leaders such as Moshoeshoe II and members of the Executive Council adopted this stance to garner more funding.[13]

As the political contention of the 1960s increased, the rhetorical consensus on development began to fracture into disagreements, not on whether the government should pursue development, but in which form the eventual projects should arrive. Political leaders of all parties increasingly argued for centralized, planned, state-run enterprise, while younger Basotho, who were not necessarily opposed to larger projects, wanted to retain some aspects of popular participation and control over projects at the grassroots. As Marc Epprecht and Andrea Nattrass note, this was not really a binary choice but rather one in which the diversity of opinions expressed by Basotho who were not part of the political elite did not fit neatly into simple characterizations.[14] In addition, the issue of top-down versus decentralized control was further complicated by the intense politicization of aid and development. This politicization led to more local resistance in the 1960s as the legitimacy of individual politicians and the parties themselves became tied to project success or failure.

With the 1964 constitution promising the next electoral winners the opportunity to lead Lesotho to independence, political concerns among Basotho politicians came to dominate debates about development and the forms that projects took. Peter Khamane, a leading figure in the BNP and post-independence government, thought that with development the country could be "very rich," because it possessed water resources, had the potential to produce diversified foods for export, and likely held valuable minerals. "We were hoping," he said, "for the minerals that are now showing up in the mountains where the diamonds are."[15] Khamane, who got his start as a Catholic Church Boy Scout organizer, was a close adviser of BNP leader Leabua Jonathan, and he knew that the riches and jobs that projects generated needed local staff. Hence, when Gabriel Tlaba reported that many of his peers in Catholic school Boy Scout troops ended up in the security forces, he confirmed that Khamane's and the BNP's plan for development included a healthy dose of patronage since the party relied heavily on the Catholic Church and its schools for educated supporters in the independence period.[16] These new patronage opportunities encouraged political leaders to secure as much development funding as possible and to centralize plans in order to maintain control of direct employment opportunities. Khamane's memories of the government's hopes for large-scale, centralized projects is emblematic of the transition in the 1960s in the attitude of political leaders to the idea of development as a strategy for consolidating political power at the center.

Despite this change in attitude by political leaders, the lack of funding for development and resistance to colonial agricultural schemes in the late colonial period meant the intensification of development efforts consisted primarily of some small-scale projects and continued expansion of the education system. The government sponsored and carried out some of the projects, but private groups like churches also continued to operate projects. The Catholic Church still encouraged *kopanos*, and the PEMS church maintained many chapters of the Homemakers' Associations, while other church-affiliated groups carried out small community projects as well.[17] The planned secondary school expansion funded by the Colonial Development and Welfare Act continued apace, too. Through the 1960s, the number of secondary and high schools expanded and the number of students enrolled rose almost twelvefold between the early 1950s and early 1970s.

While most of the schools maintained an academic focus, the colonial regime and missions continued to push for vocational and technical education in their efforts to create a tiered educational system. However, students continued to scorn such education as inferior and second-rate. This was especially true in the context of the rhetorical consensus on development. There was a school strike in 1960 that engulfed both Basutoland High School and Lerotholi Technical School (known colloquially to this day as Fokothi). These two schools were situated down the street from each other in Maseru. The colonial report in the aftermath of this disturbance seemed to hint that the Fokothi students saw their education as inferior in light of the rhetorical consensus on development. The report pinned the blame for the strike on the fact that Fokothi graduates were "not regarded by employers as trained artisans, but as rather superior labourers; and the boys themselves, who had hoped to find positions of responsibility, discover that their four years of training are of little value to them."[18] There was plenty of work in the territory for carpenters and bricklayers, two of the main categories of labor that Fokothi taught, but this was not regarded as remunerative enough and could not lead to "positions of responsibility" that young, educated Basotho desired. Of course, vocational and technical education had long been relatively unpopular with Basotho youth because they did not see it as a pathway to white-collar employment, or as a way to avoid the pathway of labor migration to South Africa.[19] This played out at Leloaleng Technical School in the rural Quthing District as well, where the principal noted in 1958 that less than a third of the school's forty-eight students were from Lesotho. He dolefully noted that he had difficulty "persuading [students from Lesotho] to apply."[20] Fokothi and Leloaleng were the two oldest and best vocational and technical schools in Lesotho. So if Basotho students at both institutions came only grudgingly and rarely had their expectations met, it stands to reason that the rejection of vocational and technical education was widespread. Further contributing to the low status of this type of education was the sense that the gains of independence would accrue primarily to those with an academic rather than a technical education.

This made scholarships to study abroad particularly important to both Basotho politicians, who could use them as patronage opportunities, and Basotho students, who could access opportunities not available locally. With strong Pan-Africanist connections, Ntsu Mokhehle and the BCP obtained some scholarships from Ghana and the Eastern Bloc. The Ghanaian connection was especially important because the Ghanaian government issued valid travel documents for Basotho students, which were essential if they wanted to take up scholarships from the Eastern Bloc. With its Cold War orientation, the colonial government did not easily give permission to study in communist countries.[21] Colonial officials recognized, however, that the scholarships represented opportunities for individual students that were not available from other sources. Resident Commissioner Chaplin wrote in 1961 about Basotho students attempting to get to Czechoslovakia: "How can [Basotho] restrain their children from such temptations when the opportunities to study in Great Britain or the USA are so pitifully small, and their own facilities in Basutoland so inadequate?"[22] The colonial regime feared, though, that many Basotho students who took up scholarships were not legitimate students. They worried that "scholarships" were merely a cover for BCP members wishing to get "trained in subversion" so they could destabilize the region on their return.[23] This was not just a British concern, as South African government officials worried about this as well. Likewise, after independence, the anticommunist BNP was almost as suspicious of the intentions of Basotho students as its colonial predecessors had been, and the BNP worked closely with South African authorities to monitor Basotho students leaving for or returning from study abroad.

Basotho students, for their part, were genuinely curious about the global ideologies they encountered through education, even if government officials and politicians saw education and scholarships primarily through the lens of the Cold War and the struggle against apartheid. Mohlalefi Moteane remembered being fascinated by world events at school: "We started reading about what was happening in the rest of Africa, in Ghana. . . . We would read about the Kennedys."[24] Similarly, Simon Phafane knew where to find communist literature in Maseru and often purchased some, despite being a committed royalist: "I knew where [Motloheloa, leader of the Lesotho Communist Party] operated from, I passed through Maseru I would go out there and pick up some. And many of us had access to this and again it was a militant kind of language which young people, many of them, enjoy."[25] These recollections suggest that while some younger Basotho may have been invested in Cold War ideologies, many more were genuinely curious and sought to utilize scholarships and education more generally to learn about how the world worked and to further their own dreams.

Cold War politics, and the fact that colonial Basutoland was still under British rule, dictated where most Basotho went with formal requests for development aid in the late colonial period. Moshoeshoe II traveled in 1962 to Washington, DC, accompanied by Executive Council members Charles (C. D.) Molapo of the BNP and S. S. Matete of the MFP. While British administrators facilitated the visits and arranged for particular meetings, the Basotho leaders, in particular, Moshoeshoe II, set the agenda. The Basotho leaders were cognizant of what other emerging African states and leaders garnered in terms of funding at independence. Tom Mboya's lobbying efforts, which resulted in hundreds of scholarships for Kenyan students (including a young Barack Obama Sr.) from the United States, were especially appealing. Scholarships held the promise of more trained Basotho civil servants, as well as a cadre of younger Basotho loyal to particular parties because they owed their training and positions to the patronage that top political leaders had dispensed. While Moshoeshoe and the Executive Council leaders did not return from Washington with such an offer in hand, the Basotho envoys requested the colonial administration in Maseru to get in touch with British authorities in Nairobi as soon as possible to ascertain how Mboya managed to obtain this aid.[26]

The Basotho leaders met with a variety of agencies in Washington and Ottawa, and the range of projects for which they requested aid suggested the shifts in strategy already under way in the early 1960s—from decentralized community development toward larger, more centralized development projects. The Basotho leaders did explore the possibility of American funding for "the provision of village water supplies, on a community aid basis," which was in keeping with the smaller scale of development projects then under way.[27] The main thrust of their mission, however, was requests for larger-scale aid programs to assist with further education expansion, the transfer of the university from the Catholic Church to government control, and an expansion of the health care system.[28] Further, the British High Commissioner in Pretoria, Sir John Maud, encouraged officials in Maseru to have the delegation seek funding for projects like "roads, power supplies, [and] dams."[29]

The transition of the political leadership from community development to centralized development was facilitated by the fact that the administration in Maseru, despite the Colonial Office push of the 1950s, never really bought into the idea of community-led development. Resident Commissioner Chaplin wrote to the Commonwealth Relations Office in May 1960 to ask its officials to halt discussions with the UN Special Fund and CDW officials because "it is now not justifiable to give a costly community development scheme priority at the expense of the Agricultural, Educational and Medical development schemes."[30] The colonial push for more centralized development projects allowed for a smoother transition to Basotho politicians who also embraced centralized, Basotho-led development. The colonial resistance to community development also came from the same technical departments, where administrators never embraced the idea of losing their authority to district councils after 1960. Wallman reported Agricultural Department officials feeling that "responsibility had been given to the Basuto [sic] Councils prematurely."[31] While the technical departments offered the most entrenched resistance, the central administration was also wary of too much decentralized control, as a report on the manner in which district officers could assist with agricultural development projects being run from Maseru noted. The soil conservation officer commented that Basotho "will have to make sacrifices. Only after they have been strictly controlled and disciplined to the requirements of conservation will they ever be able to develop along the lines of a progressive community."[32] This conception of the Basotho population needing "control" and "discipline" was certainly not decentralized, and its authoritarian tone bemoaned the unwillingness of rural communities to submit to centralized guidance when they were used to more laissez-faire policies.

The views of the colonial administration in Maseru, however, were not monolithic. Some officials pushed for stronger community-based projects. In the same report where the soil conservation officer berated the Basotho populace for being unwilling to sacrifice, another, unnamed colonial official pinned the blame for failed development projects on a wider variety of actors. Most of the blame in this analysis fell to "the lack of trained personnel and quite often an ill-conceived and wrong approach on the part of Government" that was "unilateral."[33] Still, despite the occasional voice of dissent, the majority opinion within the colonial regime was that Basotho were the primary cause of development failure and thus that decentralized development could not be the solution. With more Basotho making their way into the upper echelons of the civil service during the 1960s, authoritarian modes of thinking about development were becoming the norm for Basotho civil servants as well. They received reinforcement for these views from the language of development planners like the UNDP expert Kaul, who wrote in 1965 about the "pathetic contentment" of Basotho regarding development.[34] The colonial inheritance, thus, included the view that Basotho outside government were fundamentally opposed to and unprepared for active participation in development projects.

Multilateral institutions like the International Development Association also encouraged Basotho politicians to abandon decentralized development in favor of centralized, state-driven projects. An example of the IDA's attitude is provided by the exchanges between the IDA and colonial and Basotho officials regarding the construction of the road between Leribe and Maseru (see ch. 2). The IDA forced the Maseru administration to change a system of public works into a centralized, contractor-built project. Since it was the IDA that had the money and controlled whether the project came to fruition, colonial and Basotho officials had to acquiesce to the changes in order to move the project forward.[35] While Basotho politicians like Jonathan were happy to claim credit for the IDA road in 1967, when project work finished, British colonial officials largely oversaw the early stages of the negotiations.

Although it took nearly four years of negotiations, the IDA road project was but one of many notable successes officials had attracting development funding in the mid-1960s. These successes, even prior to the arrival of formal independence, helped convince Basotho politicians that large-scale aid from non-British sources could be a fruitful post-independence development strategy. The Ford Foundation and USAID in 1964 funded the transfer of Pius XII University College in Roma to the colonial administration, under the name the University of Basutoland, Bechuanaland Protectorate, and Swaziland.[36] The World Food Programme funded a school meals scheme that provided lunches to hundreds of thousands of primary school students across the country, contracted with Catholic Relief Services in 1965 to provide emergency food supplies to alleviate drought, and provided assistance in the self-help Food-for-Work scheme that built roads, village water supplies, and improved sanitation facilities. In the first three years of these programs, funding from the WFP, the U.S. government under Title II of Public Law 480 (Food for Peace), and the Lesotho government totaled around $3.4 million, with Lesotho responsible for only 13 percent of total program costs.[37] UNICEF was active in Lesotho starting in 1959. The organization worked mainly to improve maternal health and child nutrition by partnering with clinics and schools. These increases in aid primarily from multilateral institutions in the years prior to independence, combined with aid packages that other African countries received at independence, gave Basotho leaders hope for significant aid increases after the formal transfer of power.

For several reasons, including rudimentary communication networks in the country and the small scale of many of the projects, ordinary Basotho were largely unaware of development efforts under way in the territory. Some programs, however, began to break through and come to the attention of larger numbers of people. One project in particular, the school meals scheme, probably had the widest reach of any project in the territory. This program, alongside a variety of district council–sponsored programs, provided most Basotho with their first experience of development in rural Lesotho during the period from 1960 to 1968. These programs were quite diverse, including road and bridle path maintenance, the stocking of local fisheries, the building and maintenance of local health clinics, and the construction of village water and sanitation projects (fig. 3.1).[38] The wide range and scope of these projects ensured that, by the late 1960s, most Basotho were familiar with at least one project.

While development projects were unevenly distributed in the country, by the late 1960s few Basotho were unaware of development initiatives, even if all they knew was that such projects tended to be heavily politicized. District council efforts, in particular, faced political polarization, despite Ström's claim that there was widespread acclaim for their work.[39] Wallman's assertion that people's perceptions of council-run projects tended to correlate with political affiliation was supported by Basotho such as Michael Matekas, who noted that the polarization of projects led to rifts in communities and even within families.[40] Peter Millin, a government agricultural department worker in the 1950s and 1960s, confirmed that small-scale projects had penetrated the majority of rural settlements by mid-decade and that opposition largely ran along partisan lines. Even a cooperative Wool Growers' Association program that allowed Basotho sheep owners to bypass European traders (who dominated all commerce through the colonial period) and ship their wool directly to buyers faced some resistance. This program enabled wool from Lesotho to be la-

Figure 3.1 "Matheson, Alastair. Men harvest fully-growth [*sic*] carp from a fish pond near Roma. Fish, together with eggs and vegetables, are providing a valuable supply of much-needed protein in Lesotho." Africa America Institute Records (MS 849). Special Collections and University Archives, University of Massachusetts Amherst Libraries.

beled and "classed by trained Basotho wool classers" and shipped to East London in South Africa, with a check for the wool then being sent back to Lesotho. However, the agricultural department still had to "battle," in the words of Peter Millin, for this program because of a general suspicion of the colonial government.[41] These cooperatives, however, were more popular than council-run schemes because they increased rural household incomes directly and because they allowed farmers wide latitude to participate or not on their own terms.

The 1960s can thus be characterized as a period of transition for development in Lesotho. Not only the political leaders but also young Basotho and others not at the top echelons of political power increasingly supported development, as the rhetorical consensus on development started to penetrate Basotho society more widely. But the broadening of the consensus—agreement that "development" was necessary for and a marker of independence—actually led to less agreement on the form that projects should take. Political leaders, by and large, moved toward a model of development that focused on centralized projects leading to consolidation of political control at the center. Ordinary Basotho were not opposed to such centralized projects. After all, these were major infrastructure improvements. However, they were also strongly in favor of development projects that featured avenues for popular participation. There was certainly no widespread resistance to the idea *or* the practice of development generally speaking, but individuals and communities hesitated to support particular projects because of the political implications of such support.

For many, ideas of development and independence remained a bit nebulous as the 1965 elections and the 1966 transfer of power approached. Philosophical agreement between political leaders did not translate into national unity, as the 1965 electoral campaign saw every candidate promise to deliver more aid for development and called such foreign assistance a symbol of national independence. Despite efforts by individual Basotho to retain control over participatory projects, it was the top-down intensification of political rhetoric and contestation by the mid-1960s that was driving the process of state formation. Lesotho was "an entity coming into being," similar to how Mann described Mali at independence, and politicians contested the control and terms of this birth through the language and practice of development.[42]

THE POLITICAL STAKES OF AID AND DEVELOPMENT AT INDEPENDENCE

The growing intensity of the Cold War and the increased reliance of the governments of Basutoland and Lesotho on both Western donors and South Africa made the intensification of political contention in Lesotho a matter of international diplomatic concern. Donor priorities in many cases drove and shaped the form that development projects took in Lesotho's late colonial and early independence periods. The British government in London and the colonial administration in Maseru both utilized aid to entice Basotho leaders to make choices to put the territory and future country on a firmer financial footing. This was also of interest to leaders in South Africa, who worried about political instability in Lesotho and, in the midst of their fight against the opponents of apartheid, feared the prospect of a hostile, independent government within their borders. Basotho, meanwhile, continued to grapple with their own uncertainties regarding the desired results of development and the national and local politicization that accompanied development. Thus, as Lesotho continued to move toward independence, the politicized nature of development was obvious and evident to all, and conversations about aid at the governmental and village level rapidly slid into discussions about what independence meant for Lesotho and what forms institutions should take after formal decolonization.

All the potential Western funders of development in Lesotho encouraged Basotho politicians to focus on projects that made macroeconomic development the first priority. A 1960 memo from the British chancellor of the Exchequer spelled out the calculus of aid donations to places like Lesotho, noting that poor countries needed "higher rates of investment and of increase in the stock of capital per head" to grow their economies, but if this money had to come from domestic sources it had to be "extracted . . . only by a rigorous totalitarian regime—hence the need for financial help from outside."[43] The British government, therefore, in addition to feeling a lingering colonial obligation to continue funding development in Lesotho, saw its development assistance through the lens of staving off the potential advent of totalitarianism and communism.

Planners in Great Britain were rather late in coming to grips with the concepts of either macroeconomic growth or political independence in Lesotho. As late as 1959, the British Colonial Office did not foresee starting discussions on Lesotho's independence for at least another decade, so British officials had to scramble to formulate plans during the early 1960s.[44] Even with the implementation of the 1959 constitution, some British officials did not fully support moves toward full independence. In 1961, Britain abolished the position of High Commissioner, placing the British ambassador to South Africa in charge of the HCT. Thus, when in 1963 outgoing Ambassador Maud noted, "By the standards of even 10 years ago none of the [High Commission] Territories is yet ready for self-governance, let alone independence. But such standards have changed abruptly," he was speaking of the unease about independence that remained among some in the Colonial Office. He noted that these officials would not stand in the way of self-rule but rather had to work with local politicians to ensure that the territories could "stand on their own feet when the time comes" through "increased financial aid" for development.[45] In the case of Lesotho, this was a radical change; colonial policy since the Pim Report held that Lesotho had no potential for growth and should function as an agrarian labor reserve for South Africa.

Once the colonial administration regarded an accelerated schedule for independence as a fait accompli, it focused on devising ways to reduce the potential future drain on the British Treasury that the prospect of an undeveloped, independent Lesotho presented. On the eve of negotiations over the 1964 constitution, the British ambassador to South Africa, Hugh Stevenson, wrote to the Colonial Office assessing Lesotho's viability for independence, politically and economically. He called the medium-term macroeconomic outlook for Lesotho "gloomy" because the budgetary gap the territory faced was "substantial" over the next few years. He struck a less pessimistic tone regarding big development projects in Lesotho for the long term, noting that "there is a lot which can and indeed must be done to improve the economy of Basutoland," including dam projects, agricultural improvements, and the start of industry. The goal of investing in Lesotho's infrastructure, Stevenson noted, was to "increase the national income even if [the projects] did not increase per capita [income]."[46] So the financial position of Lesotho on the eve of the 1964 constitutional negotiations portended a short- and medium-term need for British financial assistance to balance the budget for the independence government. There was, however, hope among British officials that before too many years of independence, a steely dedication to macroeconomic development projects on the part of the Lesotho government could bring about enough GDP growth to eliminate the need for recurring budgetary assistance and aid for development.

With the 1964 constitution thus pointing the way toward independence, political leaders and parties contested the April 1965 elections with renewed vigor and an emphasis on centralized macroeconomic development that was quite different from the 1960 campaign. In 1965, all parties utilized foreign funds to finance campaign operations and put forth a vision of independence that saw Lesotho as a significant player in the international arena, able both to solicit development funds and to play a key role in regional and global political contests. The main role of outside money was to fund the electoral campaign. The BCP had the largest domestic funding base because of its strong support from Basotho who had formal employment, including migrant miners and civil servants, but even the BCP had to rely on foreign funders. The funding for the parties mapped fairly neatly onto Cold War lines, with the BCP getting money from China, the BNP getting money from South Africa and West Germany, and the MFP receiving funds from the USSR. The BCP received over £20,000 ($56,000) from China through its Pan-Africanist connections, which China maintained in its quest to become more influential globally in a two-superpower world.[47] The BNP funds came from countries, individuals, and institutions like the Catholic Church that broadly supported the party's anticommunist stand. This included, most controversially, the apartheid regime, which gave use of a helicopter, among other assistance.[48] The MFP's funding from the USSR was less ideologically coherent, since it was an amalgam of Royalists, senior chiefs, and discontented former BCP members. Party leader B. M. Khaketla wrote to U.S. State Department officials in 1962 accusing Mokhehle and the BCP of a double standard, claiming they "hobnob with communists" but now want "western countries . . . to think that he is their friend." So Khaketla positioned himself and the party as a moderate nationalist alternative in the hope of securing support. But he undercut his own position by admitting that he did "not wish it known that our Party is receiving assistance from America."[49] This desire for secrecy came about because Khaketla represented only one wing of the party. Without funds, Khaketla's faction lost out in internal struggles to South African refugee Joe Matthews's faction. Matthews was a major fund-raiser for the ANC and the SACP and was able to also raise funds for the MFP from the Soviet Union.[50]

Funding from abroad became a key campaign issue as all parties attacked the source of their rivals' funds. The BNP best managed to make the case that its successful solicitation of funds from abroad—including the universally reviled apartheid regime—was a useful skill that held the promise of more development funding after independence. This was partly a reflection of the more defensive stances that the BCP and MFP had to adopt on account of their support from communist governments in a region where the anticommunist side of the Cold War had the upper hand. The remaining settler colonies in the region like South Africa, Rhodesia, Angola, and Mozambique were all virulently anticommunist, and the BNP held out its anticommunist position as evidence that it could garner more support from the United States. But the BNP's most impressive political trick was to turn South African assistance from a liability into an asset in a country where resistance to South Africa shaped national identity.

Party leaders like C. D. Molapo and Leabua Jonathan argued that the assistance represented the future ability of a BNP-led Lesotho government to negotiate with South Africa on an equal footing and was the precursor of more "access to non-communist sources of foreign aid for development projects."[51] This argument helped the BNP to a narrow majority in Parliament, but with only 40 percent of the vote, it was a precarious victory and one predicated on a popular mandate to deliver a significant uptick in the number of development projects to the populace at large.

Even with a popular mandate on development, the BNP government at independence faced real political risk by attempting to rely on South African funds for development. First, as explored later, there were plenty of cabinet ministers in the South African government opposed to spending money to assist Lesotho. Second, many Basotho, even BNP supporters, worried about creating even more dependence on South Africa. And third, the vitriol engendered by soliciting and accepting such money drove some people away from participation in the political process and threatened to undermine support for independence. Moeketsi Lesitsi came to the conclusion that national politics were too unsavory for his tastes, so, as a Catholic schoolteacher, he shied away from political activity.[52] Similarly, Armelina Tsiki "had a very negative attitude toward the parties . . . [and] really didn't like this idea of politics and independence" because of the climate that political contestation created.[53] But there were also specific concerns about South African involvement. Mohlalefi Moteane remembered "the support that was given by the South Africans to the BNP . . . [but also the questions about] those things [politicians] say they will be able to do once independence comes."[54] Further, concerns about South African involvement and the idea of political contestation were so worrisome to some Basotho that, as Michael Mateka recounted for some older community members in his home village, they wanted politics to "disappear so that maybe we can begin to work."[55] This wide range of reactions to party politics underscored the degree to which Basotho understood how politics and development were linked and how the rhetorical consensus on development had spread broadly into Basotho society.

For those who did not understand the connection between aid, development, and independence, however, the need for BNP leader Jonathan to contest a by-election in order to get into Parliament in 1965 brought these issues to the fore. Jonathan lost a contest for the constituency near his home in the rural Leribe District in the April 1965 general elections. To get Jonathan into Parliament so that he could take over as prime minister, the BNP MP from the safe constituency of Mpharane in the Mohale's Hoek District resigned.[56] It was in this by-election that the importance of aid as a proxy for development and independence came into clearest focus. The BCP and MFP united to run only one candidate in the hope of keeping Jonathan out of Parliament and forcing new elections as the BNP had a parliamentary majority of only one. The South African government, which had given the BNP over R15,000 ($21,000), announced a "personal" grain gift from Prime Minister Verwoerd to Jonathan on the eve of the by-elections.[57] Jonathan had not asked for the gift, despite South African claims to the contrary, and his first reaction to the announcement of the gift was "surprise" that caused him to "nearly fall out of his chair laughing." By the very next day, however, Jonathan embraced the gift as evidence of his ability to get even the hated apartheid regime to supply Lesotho with development assistance. He profusely thanked Verwoerd and publicly made the by-election a referendum on his ability to garner foreign aid.[58]

Jonathan personally oversaw the delivery of the grain gift as a way of angling for electoral support but also for the public relations boost it imparted. For the Mpharane constituency, where most of the grain went, it was distributed through the network of Catholic missions and expatriate traders that had helped deliver the BNP electoral victory.[59] Opposition leaders protested the gift on the grounds that it was an illegal campaign contribution under electoral law, but the colonial administration was unwilling to disallow it.[60] Long after the election, Jonathan continued to refer to the gift as a way of demonstrating his personal competency, since it was gifted to him in the "capacity as Leader of the National Party" and because of his role as overseer of importation and delivery.[61] The grain delivery forced Jonathan and BNP officials to coordinate the distribution of grain among the chamber of commerce, Catholic missions, Save the Children, district commissioners, and employees of the agricultural department.[62] This large-scale coordination was an important test for BNP officials, who faced questions from colonial officials about their competency to run the government given how few had experience. Jonathan's victory in Mpharane allowed him to take up the post of prime minister, but it also ratcheted up the pressure on the BNP government to deliver visible development results. At the same time, Jonathan's victory heightened the resolve of opposition parties to deny the BNP credit for development initiatives as a way of undermining the government's political legitimacy with the electorate, furthering the politicization of aid and development.

BNP leaders undertook an intensive, multiyear promotional effort to publicize any and all development projects that the government sponsored. In August 1966 Jonathan opened a new bridge at Hlotse in the Leribe District, praising the project for being "built almost entirely by Basotho" and arguing that the cooperative spirit of the project "symbolizes our determination to let no obstacle stand in our way to achieve a prosperous and go-ahead Lesotho."[63] Similarly, the pro-government newspaper, *Lesotho News*, printed descriptions of every completed small project. On the front page on April 25, 1967, headlines proclaimed, "Six-Month Self Help Campaign" and "Second Self Help Programme for Lesotho," and on June 27 a long article was headlined "Girls' Hostel Opened at Butha Buthe Secondary School."[64] As the headlines suggest, these were not massive development projects but smaller, less capital-intensive projects that the government hoped would carry more political significance than the rather small total expenditures might otherwise suggest.

At the same time that the BNP government attempted to gain political capital by publicizing small development projects, the opposition increasingly attacked it for not providing enough development opportunities. BCP members of Parliament pressed the government hard to provide more services for rural areas (especially in locations where the BCP represented constituencies) and also attempted to highlight the gap between the BNP's campaign promises and popular expectations. In October 1965, to take a representative month, BCP MPs posed parliamentary questions about the lack of good roads leading to the diamond diggings at Let'seng-la-Terae and the seeming inability of the Public Works Department to construct new roads in rural areas across the country. The MPs further complained about the lack of postal agencies, health clinics, and school expansion in specific rural communities. In response to all of these concerns, the BNP ministers responded in ways similar to that of the minister of works, Setho Letsie, who noted that "Lesotho urgently needs an efficient, good and well planned roads network" but that funds were short and the needs long, so the government could build roads or other services only "where the need has been proved."[65]

Basotho found attempts by both parties to politicize development too simplistic, but a variety of protests against specific development projects in the early independence era showed the degree of political division within society, between parties but also within them. In terms of development, most Basotho agreed with Raphael Leseli that independence was supposed to bring about physical infrastructure that facilitated the delivery of government services.[66] Politically, then, the BCP critique of the BNP and its protests against the lack of infrastructure creation were tapping into a fertile vein of discontent in Basotho society, especially because it was infrastructure connected to everyday services like clinics and postal agencies. The BCP went beyond just parliamentary speeches; March 1966 protests over new grazing rules erupted in violence in the Leribe District near Ficksburg and in Butha Buthe. These incidents, according to British intelligence officials, represented mainly protests "against the suspension of District Councils," or, in other words, protests against the BNP's attempt to legislate the centralization of development.[67] But the protests also represented conflict within the BCP between local and national interests. The national BCP leadership was in that same month courting the senior chieftaincy, who dominated the upper house in Parliament, in the hope of getting their support for a resolution to postpone independence until new elections could be held.[68] The senior leadership was unsuccessful, and local protests against the "chieftaincy on fronts of grazing, tree planting, [and] land allocation" continued into April.[69]

The conflict between local and national political interests within the BCP ranks mirrored tensions between competing visions of development in the independence era. The national BCP organized resistance to National Tree Planting Day in 1968 in response to the government's attempts to make the event an appeal for national unity. Prime Minister Jonathan and Moshoeshoe II appeared together at Khubetsoana outside Maseru, assisted by local youth club members. Events all over the country aimed to plant over 200,000 trees. The government mouthpiece, *Lesotho News*, reported that BNP leaders hoped to "arouse great interest among the general public and it is hoped that it would be a truly national affair this year."[70] Of course, in the intensely politicized environment of early independence Lesotho, the day was not one of national celebration but rather of conflict. The BCP had its supporters "uproot [the trees] or sent animals to break them" in an effort to physically demonstrate that the government did not enjoy the support of local communities and that the BNP was not bringing the national unity as claimed.[71]

Basotho desire for more development projects increased steadily in the late 1960s. As they encountered more projects, Basotho became increasingly savvy about how the politicization of aid and development affected them personally. The BNP government was therefore under more pressure to continue to deliver on its promise of more projects, but it experienced difficulty soliciting large projects in the late 1960s. Part of the problem was Prime Minister Jonathan's diplomatic inexperience. In an April 1967 visit to Austria, he spent most of the trip asking for technical advisers and Haflinger studs for Lesotho, while Austrian officials, confused about a general lack of solicitation for more substantive aid, called his trip the "most unpolitical [visit] they have ever experienced from a politician."[72] But the blame for this state of affairs did not rest entirely on Jonathan's shoulders; the lack of administrative capacity in Lesotho to initiate and administer projects and the inability of major funders like USAID in Washington to start new bilateral aid relations in the 1960s also contributed.[73]

Jonathan's quest for foreign aid for development took him across the globe from the United States to Western Europe and even to Taiwan. He desperately hoped for significant U.S. aid but actively entreated the apartheid South African regime too. As Jonathan was one of only a handful of African leaders willing to even talk with apartheid officials, he hoped to receive some development assistance as a reward. His requests were met with some encouraging signs, including the only personal meeting that Prime Minister Verwoerd had with the leader of an independent African country prior to his assassination and one-on-one meetings with Prime Minister Vorster later in the 1960s. In the main, however, the South Africans were unwilling to provide capital for development programs in Lesotho. Most of their aid took the form of food donations, private medical charity efforts, and technical advisers seconded to the government.[74] While the BNP welcomed all of this assistance, it did not amount to the large-scale funding to create showpiece infrastructure or widespread employment that Jonathan needed to bolster his political standing at home. This was especially disappointing because of the amount of political capital Jonathan had expended reaching out to the apartheid state. He faced heavy criticism not just from the domestic political opposition in Lesotho but also from other African states in the Organization of African Unity in Addis Ababa. Still, for Jonathan and for Basotho more generally, the early independence period was marked by the start of a number of smaller development efforts, even if these were heavily politicized.

GRASSROOTS REACTIONS AND RESPONSES TO
DEVELOPMENT EFFORTS

The politicization of development that started in the late colonial period continued into the independence era. The variety of projects that began during this time reflected the changes taking place in government centralization efforts but also the manner in which Basotho at the grassroots made connections between development and independence. Decisions about whether and how to participate in projects remained highly dependent on the political orientation of individuals and communities. The projects detailed below show the myriad ways in which the politicization of projects played out and the ways in which people in communities across Lesotho had the ability to help shape development efforts put forth by the state in the first years of independence.

The most important large-scale project from the perspective of the Lesotho government was the water scheme because of its potential to generate significant new revenues for the Lesotho government. The British started preliminary studies for this project in the 1950s, and discussions between British officials and the South African government about diverting the Caledon River, the border between Lesotho and the Orange Free State, dated back to the 1930s. By the early 1960s, however, the South African government refused to negotiate further with the colonial administration, as the South Africans feared that a disruptive change at independence might scuttle the project no matter what agreements they managed to make with colonial officials. South African water planners projected that some transfer from Lesotho would become necessary in the decades after the 1960s in order for the mining and industrial sectors to continue expanding in Johannesburg and the Witwatersrand. The connection between increased water supply and economic growth encouraged the South African cabinet to open discussions with Jonathan's government just months after independence in December 1966. While the water was obviously the most important aspect of the deal, the project also held out the chance for the beleaguered apartheid regime to have an independent African state as a diplomatic ally. South African foreign policy in the late 1960s attempted to engage friendly African states to prove it could be a good neighbor, as part of efforts to push back against its increasing isolation on a continent now largely free from colonial rule.[75]

In Lesotho, a project of this magnitude attracted political contestation at the national level, and that happened shortly after the commencement of discussions. Jonathan was quick to highlight the possibilities of his gamble on the apartheid regime, as he did in a triumphant parliamentary speech in which he belittled the BCP for arguing against the opening of talks on May 11, 1967.[76] The discussions for the project, however, were wide ranging and slow moving because of their political and technical complexity. The talks churned through several rounds in the intervening years, but no formal agreements or infrastructure construction had started by 1969. The BCP made sure to point out the lack of tangible results in its political attacks from 1966 to 1969. They called Jonathan's engagement attempts with South Africa a failure and argued that this policy led to no development projects of note *and* close ties with the despised apartheid regime. Jonathan and the BNP were nervous because there was nothing tangible to show the electorate on the water project. Heading into the 1970s elections, this issue promised to dominate much of the conversation. Lord Fraser, owner of one of the largest trading companies in Lesotho and a firm BNP supporter, made this clear in a 1969 letter to Prime Minister Vorster. He asked Vorster to speed up negotiations in the hope of being able to deliver on a deal prior to elections. Even if that was not possible, Fraser asked Vorster to arrange for a photo-op of "Chief Jonathan digging the first spade full of earth" at the site of the dam project. This would "impress the electorate" by showing the "first sign of work . . . to the people," even if the "real work were much delayed."[77] While this did not come to pass, the letter suggests the degree to which the optics and politics of development mattered in post-independence Lesotho.

Electoral pressures on the BNP government were, of course, not new in 1969. After winning only 40 percent of the vote, the BNP leadership knew the government needed to deliver development projects to win over more of the electorate. In 1965, the colonial government and the BNP had plans in place with the WFP to forestall a potentially calamitous famine, as the spring rains necessary for planting were late. When the rains finally came in January 1966, obviating the need for direct famine relief, Jonathan and the cabinet pressed for aid deliveries anyway as symbolic proof of their ability to provide tangible services to Basotho. British officials reported that the cabinet was "embarrassed by what they have said to people about outside aid and are reluctant to reduce demands on account of the improved situation."[78] Similarly, immediately after independence in early

1967 Jonathan asked the United Kingdom to frontload its development funding package because, in the estimation of British officials, "his government must show as early as possible (and definitely before the next election in 1970) that they are bringing some advantageous results to the people of Lesotho following independence."[79] Thus, from the moment the BNP government took power in 1965, the perception of competence that resulted from aid and development was of utmost importance to Jonathan and the BNP leadership.

In response, the BCP actively worked to oppose development projects as part of a broad campaign to deny legitimacy to the BNP government and set the stage for its own increased electoral support. Motsapi Moorosi, a casual BCP supporter but not a party member, remembered that the BNP government had to "battle, really battle . . . [to build up] infrastructure, the roads, farming, agriculture, you name it," in the late 1960s. He reflected that the BNP "did well to my surprise, honestly," given the political struggles of the time.[80] These battles, as Moorosi called them, happened because the BCP fought tooth and nail against BNP projects as a way of denying the party legitimacy. There was more than a little schadenfreude in these actions as they undermined the success of efforts similar to the ones started by the BCP and run through the district councils, like cooperatives earlier in the 1960s. However, the BCP reaction was pure politics, as well as a response to BNP efforts at the grassroots to derail earlier projects for partisan gain. As an example of the rhetorical vitriol, Shakhane Mokhehle, a BCP leader and the brother of party leader Ntsu, took a swipe at BNP development when, in a 1967 speech in Parliament, he sarcastically asked if a newly announced industrialization program was going to employ people on an "in-kind basis" as self-help programs from the time did.[81] While voters ended up punishing the BNP in 1970 for the lack of progress on development, Moorosi's comments suggest that Basotho who were not strong partisan supporters saw the politicization of development as detrimental to the realization of projects in the form and variety they desired.

One of the best illustrations of the political interplay regarding development programs and the ability of Basotho at the grassroots to influence the positions taken by national leaders was the reaction of both major parties to the arrival of U.S. Peace Corps volunteers in late 1967. Prime Minister Jonathan was deeply invested in this program since he personally negotiated it with the Americans. The first group of volunteers landed at the Maseru airport to great fanfare in late December, and the individuals took up positions primarily in education and cooperatives.[82] The Catholic newspaper *Moeletsi oa Basotho*, a strong backer of Jonathan and the BNP, published a front-page article with two black-and-white photographs of the arrival.[83] This was news reporting, but it was also a response to BCP attacks on the program that dated back to at least October 1967. Ntsu Mokhehle made one of his more vitriolic attacks in Parliament on November 2, calling the volunteers "unwanted guests" and "foreign spies," using language similar to his earlier denunciations of civil servants seconded from the South African government.[84] The Peace Corps was but one target in this speech, however, as he lumped together all of the major governmental development efforts, including a 1967 diamond mining agreement with Rio Tinto, the presence of large numbers of South African civil servants, and the Vorster grain gift. Mokhehle termed these various initiatives a conspiracy by the BNP government to "sabotage . . . the sovereignty of the country" by giving away control to foreign governments and companies.[85] Later in 1968, he insinuated the volunteers might really be CIA spies and concluded that the volunteer presence in rural Lesotho "undermine[d] the UN resolutions on non-interference . . . in the affairs of other states."[86] The strident nature of anti–Peace Corps rhetoric from BCP leaders encouraged BCP supporters to harass the volunteers. Dennis Caspe, living in Mafeteng with his wife, Sheryl, in 1967 and working as an adviser to a tractor cooperative, remembered that BCP supporters "just hated us and were abusive, openly hostile."[87]

The BCP attacks were not only about internal politics in Lesotho. Pan-Africanists across Africa had long attacked the Peace Corps because it was a U.S. government program on a continent where many were skeptical of American intentions. From its inception in 1961, when the first program opened in Ghana, until 1980, African governments either temporarily or permanently evicted nine of the twenty-four Peace Corps programs across the continent, with many African leaders accusing volunteers of being CIA spies.[88] Mokhehle and the BCP tapped into these currents, but they did not simply import ideas from other African states. They localized the rhetoric. The BCP referred to the volunteers through the Sesotho translation of Peace Corps as the "Army of Peace," and the image of young, mainly white, "soldiers" residing in rural Lesotho was a concern to many Basotho given the tumultuous history of land dispossession by Afrikaners from the Free State and British officials in the nineteenth century.[89] With permanent European settlement forbidden in Lesotho during the colonial period, the volunteers' presence in villages and towns, living among the population, was a new and potentially threatening phenomenon. Peace Corps volunteers (PCVs) were not the only outsiders; the British Voluntary Service sent about twenty-five volunteers to the country, and the American organization Crossroads Africa periodically sent groups of North American students, but the alignment of Cold War politics with the BNP/BCP political divide in Lesotho made the Peace Corps the target of highest visibility.[90]

The vitriolic level of the attacks on volunteers working closely with local communities, however, did not resonate for many Basotho, especially those who came into contact with them. One staunch BCP supporter, Mohlalefi Moteane, was confused by the attacks at the time and was still unclear as to what their purpose had been over forty years later, calling the rhetoric from party leaders "misplaced criticism."[91] Zakes Mda, another BCP supporter who participated in the verbal harassment of PCVs in 1967, noted that they "disarmed us with their friendliness," and the campaign quickly fizzled.[92] The campaign also lost momentum because local people who had contact with volunteers quickly came to realize that the "sympathies" of most volunteers, in the words of Dennis Caspe, "lay with the people [the BCP] who were nominally harassing us."[93] At some level, too, BCP criticism of the Peace Corps was simply political theatrics. U.S. diplomats in Maseru noted that BCP leaders do not "attack the Peace Corps privately as rigorously as [they do] in public."[94] The lack of grassroots support for the campaign against the Peace Corps and the fact that the leadership did not wholeheartedly believe in their own criticisms meant that the attacks quietly faded away by mid-1968.

Just as grassroots unease with the attacks on the Peace Corps played a role in putting an end to the BCP's campaign against it, so too did local sentiment play a key role in the success or failure of many of the tractor cooperatives and cooperative industries. Some of these schemes received assistance from PCVs who were assigned to local branches of the Lesotho Credit Union Scheme for Agriculture (LECUSA) to assist in the financial operations of the groups. District councils had started pilot programs for similar initiatives prior to independence, but the central government investment in LECUSA and international volunteer assistance helped broaden their scope throughout the country. These schemes proved more popular and durable than colonial agricultural schemes because they offered avenues for popular input and were typically autonomous at the local level, but they also ran into trouble on issues of funding and financing. They also, in some places, fell victim to the national polarization of development, demonstrating again how political positioning often determined the success or failure of particular development projects.

The tractor scheme in the Mafeteng District, originally called FARMECH, started in 1961 when the newly elected district council decided (against the wishes of the agricultural department) to take out a £45,000 ($126,000) loan to start a tractor-hire program. The goal was to improve wheat production in the lowland portion of the district and raise individual income for Basotho farmers by increasing tractor plowing and fertilizer inputs. The council was responsible for getting the scheme to generate sufficient income to pay down the debt, but this proved difficult. The council also struggled to communicate with project villages because of the poor road system, and it faced declining interest in the project area because the cost of hiring tractors rose substantially between planning and implementation. Finally, the program faced resistance from the agricultural department in Maseru from the beginning since agricultural officials saw the district council as encroaching on their jurisdiction. The biggest source of friction, however, was politically based resistance from Basotho who regarded the scheme as an attempt to build legitimacy for the BCP-run council and, thus, the BCP in general.[95]

The calculations about whether to continue supporting the project or letting it fade away were complicated when project managers applied for a financial bailout loan from the central administration in Maseru in 1964. The Mafeteng district commissioner, ever concerned about social stability, worried that rejecting the loan and attempting to repossess the tractors could "cause a political furor" or lead to the tractors being burned rather than local people allowing repossession.[96] Moreover, local chiefs and BNP supporters strongly opposed the project, with chiefs fearing the project would undercut their already precarious hold on land allocation and rank-and-file BNP members aware that "every achievement of the Scheme thus reflects back on the Congress Party [BCP] and every setback detracts from its political reputation."[97] Thus Basotho public opinion in the project area was deeply divided on the potential benefits *and* the politics of the project.

There was some merit to the claims of project politicization, as BCP project managers attempted to hire only party supporters. This was done out of a desire to dispense patronage in an area where local jobs were scarce, but it was also designed to keep BNP supporters from sabotaging the project from within. In this acrimonious context, then, the assessment by the permanent secretary for local government in Maseru that FARMECH was a "welfare scheme" rather than a development project, because it was not being "run strictly on business lines," is a drastic oversimplification of the political complexity on the ground and the political maturity with which local Basotho read the implications of the project.[98] Certainly the troubled finances of the scheme called into question its ability to increase rural household income, but its inability to muster widespread support throughout the project area could not simply be boiled down to one tidy explanation.

The FARMECH scheme was the first tractor cooperative. Although it had financial difficulties, the proliferation of LECUSA branches around the country after independence attests to the commitment by the government and overseas donors to the model of rural agricultural cooperatives. These schemes were popular with Basotho politicians because shiny new tractors plowing fields were a tangible sign of rural development and suggested the competency of the individual leaders who managed to garner funds from Maseru or sources abroad to purchase the machines. Support for tractor plowing ran high in areas of less political contestation. Clark Tibbits remembered the tractor scheme he assisted in the Roma Valley being "very successful," with "stands of corn done with tractors, and hybrid seeds ... [producing] huge ears on stalks," when he lived there in 1967–69.[99] Dennis Caspe remembered the scheme was also popular in the Mafeteng District; there were "fights about when [people] could use the tractors" after the first rains of planting season. Despite their popularity, the cooperatives found it almost impossible to make a profit. Caspe noted that the financial accounting was "just all smoke and mirrors" in the cooperative he advised, and Tibbits noted that the programs "gradually declined as there were not enough resources to sustain it—the high cost of inputs."[100] By 1970, twenty tractor cooperatives operated across the country in every district except for Mokhotlong. As a whole, they lost over R7300 ($10,220) in 1970, and the government expected a slightly larger loss, R9500 ($13,300), in 1971.[101] With its focus on soliciting larger projects, in the 1970s the BNP government was less inclined to support programs that were losing money at significant rates. In the late 1960s, however, the government funded the tractor programs even when they were losing money because they were a rare operational development program.

Village cooperative industries (also called *kopanos*) were similarly de-signed to help communities start income-generating activities in rural areas, and because of their roots in earlier Catholic and colonial government projects, they were also operating in the late 1960s. Cooperative industries typically set up weaving ventures or other forms of small-scale craft production, aimed at attracting a burgeoning tourist market (fig. 3.2). Like the tractor schemes, though, many of the cooperative industries projects became enmeshed in the politicization of development in the independence era. This result was not guaranteed, as a *kopano* that suc-ceeded for a time at Ha Paki showed. Ha Paki was a village at Mazenod, the site of a large Catholic mission outside Maseru that included the headquarters of *Moeletsi oa Basotho* and the Catholic printing press. The cooperative was originally set up by the French Canadian Catholic pastor at the Mazenod church. The *kopano* carried out weaving and spinning op-erations, with many of the local villagers supplying wool for the project or working as spinners and carders. Ted Hochstadt, a PCV who arrived in late 1967, reported that the *kopano* operated on nonpartisan lines, with BCP and BNP members working well together. This was surprising, as Mazenod was certainly not immune to the BCP/BNP contestation. In fact, Hochstadt also reported that in 1968 "the BCP uprooted all the trees that I and other Ha Paki villagers planted on National Tree Planting Day."[102]

But the Ha Paki *kopano* enjoyed the support of those in key posi-tions. The BNP-leaning headman served as the president of the organi-zation, while the weaving managers, who were crucial to its economic profitability, were BCP supporters. The managers "hire[d] spinners and weavers without regard to their political affiliation," to ensure that the jobs were spread among the various local villages in the project area.[103] The Ha Paki *kopano* suggests that political differences were not insurmountable in early independence Lesotho. However, it was clear that for a successful outcome those in charge had to make sincere and conscious efforts to avoid politicization. It also helped that the organization had acquired the weaving equipment from abroad through its Catholic Church connections and therefore was not dependent on government inputs to fund and run its operation. The *kopano* at Ha Paki ran into difficulty by the early 1970s when accusations of nepotism undermined trust in the organization and "skilled weavers and spinners [were replaced] with unskilled ones."[104] While administrators certainly faced pressure to hire family and friends,

Figure 3.2 "British Information Services. Miss Eliza Letsoela
teaches local villagers in the handicrafts center of Roma University
College, July 1963." Africa America Institute Records (MS 849).
Special Collections and University Archives, University of
Massachusetts Amherst Libraries.

there was also an organizational goal to rotate people through jobs "periodically to allow other [community] members to benefit financially from
the weaving operation."[105] In other words, similar to the tractor schemes
that were generally losing money, Basotho were making conscious choices
to run the cooperative programs in ways that prioritized perceived community fairness over economics. The Basotho administrators were creating
projects designed primarily to help a larger number of people. These were
deliberate moves made in consultation with community members—from

the least skilled wool cleaner to the village headman and the technical staff hired to run the business operations—that, at least for a time in the late 1960s, allowed people to make the *kopano* the instrument for realizing the better life promised at independence. This was not "freedom from" colonialism or apartheid-induced regional economic imbalances but rather a local community utilizing donated materials, their own skills, and administrative structures to remake their community along lines they desired: in short, independence.

The different ways in which Basotho were mobilizing and organizing around development projects represent deep engagement that cut across most sectors of society by independence, or at least shortly thereafter. This represented, on the one hand, the triumph of the rhetorical consensus on development. On the other hand, the continued fierce conflicts over implemented projects, ranging from nonparticipation in tractor cooperatives to fiery speeches in Parliament and the uprooting of newly planted trees, also suggests that whatever agreement was present among Basotho was, in many places, counterbalanced by disagreements over how development should proceed. Despite these conflicts, development remained the rhetoric and ideology that drove the thinking and actions of many Basotho because of the malleability of its definition and because Basotho acting in youth and community organizations could organize and carry out projects on their own with minimal assistance.

ALTERNATIVE PATHS TO DEVELOPMENT: YOUTH ORGANIZATIONS

Young Basotho, in particular, were early and eager adopters of the language and practice of development-as-marker-for-independence, and they wanted development not just for themselves, but to improve the communities in which they lived. Generally speaking, young Basotho were not opposed to growth in the GDP, more government revenues, and the increased tax base that were the key indicators of development success for the BNP government and international funders. They were, however, more focused on the increased economic opportunities, expanded services, and participatory avenues that defined development for them. Young Basotho, by dint of their early adoption of the language of development, played a key role in introducing many Basotho to this idea through their work on projects. Utilizing youth organizations, younger Basotho helped to construct projects in their communities that embodied their visions for independence through development. These efforts were a type of performative nationalism, as Basotho youth were physically building the communities in which they wanted to live. As earlier discussions of the wide political divide among Basotho should make clear, this performative nationalism through development was not monolithic in terms of conceptions of nationalism, independence, or the forms development should take. The diversity of youth organizations, in fact, allowed the message and practice of development to spread throughout the country; a monolithic "youth" pushing for one particular form would have met with political resistance in many places. Working through groups like the Boy Scouts, Girl Guides, Lesotho Workcamps Association, Junior Red Cross, Homemakers Associations, and student Christian groups, young Basotho worked for the development and independence they wanted to see in Lesotho.

Youth organizations have a long history in Lesotho, especially at the oldest elite secondary and teacher-training colleges. The colonial government was slow to organize and support other youth organizations financially. It was not until 1961 that the colonial government hired Lena Mphuthi, a South African–born Mosotho, as the first youth organizer. Her remit was to start youth clubs that focused on sport, handicrafts, and other recreational activities. The first of these was based at Fraser's Memorial Hall near the airport in Maseru. The initiation of this position was a direct result of the formation of political youth wings in the previous years and their perceived radicalism.[106] The government worried most about the BCP Youth Wing, but the strength of youth organizations in the Catholic Church, and the institutional support it provided to the BNP, brought about the darkest fears of politicized Basotho youth fighting pitched battles in the streets with "Congress on the one hand and the Catholics on the other."[107] Thus the government hoped to channel youthful energy into seemingly innocuous activities, and the youth club model quickly expanded beyond Maseru to include other major towns like Leribe/Hlotse and Mafeteng. The government had long provided nominal support for school-based youth groups, and the school expansion that started in the 1950s precipitated a rapid increase in the number of youth who had access to formal organizations. Over ten thousand Basotho youths affiliated with a wide variety of clubs, for example, attended the first National Youth Day rally in April 1967.[108]

The 1960s were a golden age for youth organizations in Lesotho. Because there was a shortage of trained and qualified adults to mentor and lead the various chapters, in many cases, older Basotho youth had effective control, which allowed a cadre of young Basotho who came of age in the era of independence to initiate, organize, and shape the policies and actions of the groups. This was even true for one of the oldest youth organizations in the British Empire, the Boy Scouts. The first Scout chapter in Lesotho was founded on January 2, 1914, and Scouting along with Girl Guides enjoyed a constant if limited amount of financial support from the colonial government.[109] In the 1960s, however, the Boy Scouts nearly doubled their number of active members, from about 1,100 young men in 1951 to over 2,000 in 1964. Girl Guides membership rose in a similar fashion, though it started from a higher base of about 1,600 in 1951.[110] The churches that sponsored most schools in Lesotho were eager supporters of clubs like this because they were a way to connect with Basotho youth, thereby cultivating them for later full church membership. This goal was important enough that the Catholic Church, the largest sponsor of troops in Lesotho, moved Peter Khamane from the primary school classroom to a full-time position as organizer for Scouting and Guiding in Catholic schools in 1957.[111]

The relative autonomy of Scout and Guide troops gave their members and the young teachers in charge of them space to develop important leadership skills that they utilized through the independence period. Gabriel Tlaba described Boy Scouts at St. Theresa's Minor Seminary in Roma, the heart of the Catholic educational establishment in Lesotho, as "self-supporting." The older members served as troop and pack leaders, and they had a free hand to organize activities like camping trips that entailed planning all logistics and negotiating the donation of supplies from individuals and local shops. For Tlaba, these skills directly translated into his later leadership of groups like the University Christian Movement and his career as a teacher and administrator at the Lesotho College of Education.[112] Likewise, a young female teacher in the rural Mafeteng District struggled to find others at her primary school willing to help with youth organizations. She was personally overseeing both the Girl Guides and Junior Red Cross. "*No one*" helped her, she exclaimed, because they were "not interested" in youth organizations. She even looked for help at the nearby high school, but the staff was unwilling, and she had to "pull up by [herself]," which meant that some groups went without leadership.[113] This leadership void meant that Basotho students and young teachers had lots of autonomy within the structure of their groups.

Some organizations had competent leadership, and this helped them produce a generation of young Basotho attuned to needs within their communities and willing to work to bring about change. Alexander Sekoli, who earlier had been scoutmaster of Peter Khamane's troop, was the scoutmaster at St. David's (Catholic) Primary School in the Berea District. Sekoli mobilized his boys to volunteer on community projects, including the government's self-help water supply programs. Sekoli's troop helped transport pipes from the district offices to villages and contributed the volunteer labor necessary for project completion in the early independence period.[114] Through this work, the youth in Sekoli's troop, who were assisted by their sister troop of Girl Guides, ensured the success of the water supply projects by taking charge of the logistical issues that often threatened to sabotage small-scale development projects like this. Not surprisingly, Sekoli reported that his Scouts were liked "very much" by the local communities for providing this type of assistance free of charge.

In a similar vein, Armelina Tsiki joined the Girl Guides at St. Rodrigue Secondary School in 1965, a troop under the supervision of a young Mosotho nun teaching at the school. For Tsiki, a big attraction of the organization was the opportunity to learn and practice personal "leadership skills," but it was also a group populated by "girls who had responsibility and at the same time who were always the first to give the helping hand whenever there was need."[115] Her group focused on practical handicrafts like basket making, sewing, and knitting. While Tsiki remembered selling a few items for personal profit over the years, most of the items the group made were given away through the school as gifts to visitors or donated to older Basotho in surrounding communities. Helping older residents "in their fields on Saturdays" to ensure a suitable planting season and harvest and donating their handmade hats and gloves to the elderly in winter were some examples of how Tsiki and her peers were working to bring about the changes they wanted to see in their own communities. This work was surely religiously motivated, but it was also fundamentally political. Tsiki rejected the form of community building promoted by the political parties. She had a "very negative view of the political parties," because they spoke ill of the churches and fostered a spirit of disunity in the country. This drove her to conclude that she "really didn't like this issue of politics and independence." The actions of Tsiki and her Girl Guide peers suggest, however, that these young Basotho women had a fundamentally different understanding of politics, independence, and community building that was informed by their own religious visions for how independent communities should operate.

While the Catholic Church sponsored the majority of Scout and Guide troops, the other major churches also supported a variety of youth organizations that were especially active from the 1950s. In 1955 the Paris Evangelical Mission Society appointed the Swiss missionary J. Zimmerman as its youth organizer with a remit to expand church youth organizations beyond the schools. This was due in part to Zimmerman's and the PEMS's suspicion of groups that took government funds, like Scouts and Guides. They worried that these groups had an undue focus on "mould[ing] the citizens [the government] needs" rather than independent-minded believers.[116] This led Zimmerman and the PEMS to focus their energies on projects outside of government efforts, and they built the Mophato oa Morija, an ecumenical youth center at the main PEMS mission station at Morija.

The Mophato, Sesotho for "Initiation School," became an important site for Basotho youth to assemble and discuss religious ideas, but it was also a popular meeting place for a wide variety of groups with interests other than spirituality. The Mophato opened its doors in 1956 to "offer training that empowers Basotho youth based on their culture." It hosted many PEMS church events but also many groups that had only a loose connection to the church.[117] An Easter 1964 meeting at the Mophato, for example, drew seventy young Basotho Christian leaders of all denominations for a weekend retreat. Against the backdrop of the 1964 pre-independence constitution, the participants discussed the intersection of "independence and politics" in the context of a simultaneous desire for "a deeper understanding of their Christian faith."[118] These types of discussions were important for Basotho interested in bridging the political divides in Lesotho, which closely corresponded with religious affiliation, but the Mophato played an important role beyond Lesotho as well.

Two of the more popular youth groups among educated Basotho were the University Christian Movement (UCM) and the Student Christian Movement (SCM), which had chapters in schools in Lesotho and South Africa. Daniel R. Magaziner's work on the UCM in South Africa found the organization to be one that allowed young South Africans to envision a new future through a Christian framework, despite bleak times in the present.[119] Though the situation of Basotho youth in the 1960s was not as dire as that of South African youth due to the repression and lack of opportunity under apartheid, Basotho youth utilized the UCM and SCM as forums to discuss contentious issues and use faith to try to bridge political and religious divides. Merely participating in groups that operated across the denominational divide in Lesotho was a fundamentally political act, especially for young Catholics. Gabriel Tlaba matriculated at the University of Botswana, Lesotho and Swaziland in 1967 as part of his training to be a priest. Simultaneous with the commencement of his studies he wanted to broaden his experiences, and he joined the UCM, intrigued by its goal to have conversations across denominational lines on a wide variety of topics.[120] Like many Basotho he was also attracted to the UCM because it had branches across South Africa and was a vehicle for meeting similarly curious young South Africans. Tlaba, like most Basotho students, abhorred apartheid and wanted to have some connection to the campaign against it but also saw that the problems of Lesotho could never be fully resolved as long as apartheid existed. The goal of UCM participants was, in Tlaba's estimation, to "live our Christian life amongst the political situation and struggles that we were in at the time," referring to struggles in both Lesotho and South Africa. Chapter meetings centered on how individuals could stay true to scripture while working for economic justice and political change. These conversations seemed more meaningful because of the presence of Basotho of all religious denominations and because of the regular contact with UCM chapters in South Africa. The cross-border and interdenominational conversations attracted Tlaba, but it was the egalitarian nature of the group, where members participated as "equals" in the conversation, that most appealed to him.

The emphasis on egalitarian relations in some student-run and youth-led organizations marked the early independence years and was attractive to many Basotho students. Another group where this was true was the Lesotho Workcamps Association (LWA), a university-based group that organized service-oriented trips over school holidays. Chaka Ntsane, an LWA member from his early days on campus in 1966, remembered that the group was very popular because it was inclusive: "Students from different walks of life, from different schools, from different political parties, different religions. It was never anything that was along any of either political, religious or sectarian lines, and I think this is why quite a few students were interested."[121] The LWA projects included constructing infrastructure like health clinics, school classrooms, and windmills in communities around the country, and the group partnered at times with Crossroads Africa, the U.S.-based group that brought students from the United States and Canada to participate in projects and foster individual ties across national and cultural lines.[122]

For Ntsane and his peers, however, the aspirational rhetoric of independence mixed with the language of development in groups like the LWA to produce projects in which young Basotho literally built the types of communities they wanted to see. Ntsane and his peers were frequently "talking about development [and] taking responsibility" for ameliorating conditions of poverty in Lesotho. They wanted to "contribute to the situation in our own land [because] if we didn't start when we were young, we would have to do things in our middle age that we should have done in our youth."[123] Ntsane's view likely reflects, to some extent, a narrative he developed through his long career as an agronomist in the governments of Lesotho and South Africa, but still, the work of the LWA was tangible. Young Basotho were building the health care and community infrastructure that, in due time, led to the provision of more social services, an important aspect of the independence expectations of many Basotho. The LWA projects were an example of young Basotho physically constructing their visions for an independent Lesotho. Of course, the LWA was not immune to the intense partisanship of the time, with some leaders like Ntsane also being members of the BNP Youth League. However, the group understood the potential for its work to be undermined if it was seen as partisan, and it worked to combat this. In 1968, for example, its major project was the construction of a school in Morija, a hotbed of support for the BCP and home of the original PEMS mission station.[124]

Lest we think that a belief in independence through development was held only by elite Basotho who had access to secondary or tertiary education, community-based groups like the Homemakers Association were working for similar ends. Maleseko Kena lived in Tsoelike Auplas, a rural village in the far southern Qacha's Nek District, where she was active for a time in politics through the Women's League of the BCP. She quit this group, feeling disillusioned because they "were not doing anything for the nation."[125] Her eyes lit up, though, when talking about the Homemakers because the organization "had power." This power was gained through effective organizing, especially around household subsistence, a key development concern for rural women across Lesotho. The group hosted events in which members taught each other how to "cook, prepare foods, sew, can fruits and all sorts of things. . . . [They] knew how to get things done." In Auplas, as in communities across rural Lesotho, economic livelihoods were shaped by the patterns of labor migration to the mines and by the vagaries of climate. Therefore, helping more people stretch limited household budgets was an important development project. Kena, for instance, was then able to utilize more of her limited household income for school fees, as she educated all seven of her children. The Homemakers Association was not new—Epprecht noted that it was central to rural development strategies as early as the 1930s, and there were over 160 chapters operating in the territory by the early 1950s—but in the 1960s chapters like the one in Auplas provided a space for women to work collectively for the types of communities they wanted to see at independence.[126] The women of Auplas did not all agree politically, as Kena found when in the 1960s and 1970s she worked with apartheid refugees and was confronted with disapproval from many in the community. The Homemakers Association, however, provided a space where they could all work to creatively surmount some of the structural economic obstacles that life in the shadow of apartheid and in post-independence Lesotho presented.[127]

Almost none of the young Basotho saw and characterized their work in youth and community organizations as political, despite the fact that they were engaged in helping make and shape communities and policies. In large part, they contrasted their efforts in these organizations with the explicitly political work of the Youth Wings of the political parties, entities that earned a bad reputation in the 1960s and 1970s for their central role in endemic political violence. Basotho youth, however, were keen participants in efforts that Gilbert Ramatlapeng characterized as the "politics of mealie pap," which he defined as a better life whereby people in Lesotho could find work, eat better, have basic services, and live a life free from "rule by other people," whether colonial rulers or autocratic Basotho.[128] Clara Rapholo, a teacher and Girl Guide leader, captured this dynamic well. She, like many, disavowed any political motivation for her work training students and helping them build community, but she "wanted to pass [the values she had learned] along to her students" and wanted them to have the "same experiences" she had with groups like the Girl Guides to give them the foundation for building careers and communities.[129] The youth and community groups that young Basotho utilized to bring to fruition aspects of their visions for independence were resilient ones that allowed these individuals to remain optimistic for the future, even if the political changes and development efforts of the government were not meeting their expectations. The ability of group members to organize and physically construct the artifices of independence through their own efforts helped keep hope alive despite the stark polarization and politicization of development in the immediate post-independence period from 1965 to 1970. The elite rhetorical consensus on development of the 1950s had laid the foundation for the community-building projects of the 1960s to be symbolically meaningful beyond just the local communities in which they were operating.

CONVERGENCE OF CENTRALIZATION AND POLITICIZATION: THE ABOLITION OF DISTRICT COUNCILS

The BNP government was willing to support local projects carried out by youth organizations, provided they fit within its framework for acceptable projects. However, in the long-term, the BNP leadership saw centralized development as the key to political legitimacy at home and increased funding for development from abroad. Thus they saw decentralized development schemes like FARMECH in the Mafeteng District or even the Home Industries project in Mazenod as threatening. If such programs that were initiated and run by local or district level officials succeeded, they undermined the claims of the BNP government to have brought development to communities, threatening their electoral support. The BNP government was driven by an increasingly urgent need to consolidate and claim more support as the 1970 elections approached, and development projects were the vehicle through which this could happen. Thus a key goal of the BNP government from the time it took power in 1965 was to neutralize the district councils by removing their mandate to control local development efforts. In August 1965, the BNP government first proposed a system of indirectly elected ward and village councils reporting to local chiefs, a key constituency that largely supported the BNP.[130] While this proposal fell by the wayside as independence preparations took precedence over local government reform, the desire to centralize development and eliminate the opposition-supporting councils remained after independence.

In addition to the BNP leadership's desire to centralize development planning and implementation for domestic political purposes, they also faced pressures from international agencies mandating centralized planning as a prerequisite for getting funding. The World Bank/IDA road project managers frequently lamented the lack of a planning department in the Maseru government in the early 1960s. Similarly, in 1965, a British Overseas Development Ministry official wanted a "well-conceived" and planned development program in place for Lesotho in order to raise the "productive power of the economy [and] . . . increase its taxable capacity."[131] The colonial government never implemented the recommendation to have a planning office because of the cost, and the BNP government was reluctant to start such an office after independence because it suspected the political loyalties of most of the trained civil servants who could have staffed it. Jonathan's suspicions of the civil service caused him to blame them for sabotaging development projects, and he dismissively referred to them as "low caliber."[132] Expatriates in Jonathan's government had a similarly dismal view of the Basotho civil service. The Dutch chief economist J. W. Biemanns criticized it for not being "development oriented," though he presented no evidence for this charge.[133] Jonathan used such characterizations to his advantage and applied for British government funding for an all-new planning department that he could then stock with his personal appointees, outside the strictures of the civil service commission. In this way, he could get politically loyal Basotho into positions of power and authority while keeping the office firmly under his own control. In later years, a planning official noted that aid for development "was the most urgent and primary concern of the Government in establishing a central planning agency."[134] The desire to have a powerful central planning department under the personal authority of the prime minister foreshadowed Jonathan's use of development as the primary strategy for increasing government centralization in the 1970s, and it is clear that this was the objective from the earliest days of BNP governance.

The BNP efforts at centralization culminated in the April 1968 abolition of district councils. The move effectively neutralized the BCP's advantage in grassroots organizing. It also curbed the power of the constitutional monarch by abolishing the Department of Finance operating from the royal village of Matsieng, moving its authority to the newly consolidated Ministry of Finance in Maseru.[135] These changes were obvious attempts to ensure that the benefits from politicized development projects accrued to the BNP government rather than to other political actors, and they mark one of the first salvos of the 1970 election campaign. With development firmly entrenched as the language of independence, these moves made clear how important it was for BNP electoral prospects to be able to claim successful development initiatives. That the idea of development and project implementation could play such a central role in Lesotho politics during the independence era was possible only because the 1950s elite rhetorical consensus on development had now reached most segments of Basotho society. This had happened through the ability of the government to attract some international funding for development initiatives and the publicity that surrounded such projects but was in larger part due to grassroots efforts by young Basotho actively participating in small-scale development initiatives through school and community groups. Their efforts to remake communities in their image of independence were important not only to those who now had access to new and improved infrastructure but were also symbolically significant as actions that allowed more people to grapple with what independence could or should mean. This increased national consciousness of development and independence shaped how many Basotho understood the 1970 elections and the subsequent coup and period of authoritarian rule. Many Basotho, having seen the possible fruits of independence through grassroots activism and development, were able to retain faith in the idea that development would someday bring about positive change despite a bleak near-term political situation.

CHAPTER 4

The Internationalization
of Lesotho's Development

The 1970 Coup

In July 1965, recently installed Prime Minister Leabua Jonathan wrote in a note to British Government Representative Sir Alexander Giles that he was "most anxious to initiate discussion of the Oxbow [water] project with South Africa." He asked if Giles could "arrange for confidential enquiries to be made on behalf of the Basutoland Government" to start exploratory talks.[1] After many twists, turns, and occasions on which both sides walked away from the table, the project came to fruition as the Lesotho Highlands Water Project in the 1980s. In the 1960s, the Colonial Office generally supported the water project, as it had been funding preliminary studies since the 1950s. Its officials counseled caution since they anticipated South Africa would be eager to enter into discussions to alleviate water shortages in the ever-growing Witwatersrand area. The Colonial Office wanted the Basutoland government to "avoid any appearance of undue eagerness to bargain."[2]

The South Africans, for their part, were not willing to discuss the water project until Lesotho was independent because the Pretoria regime worried about negotiating with an unfriendly government. Prime Minister Jonathan, however, was anxious to start discussions. He wrote with increasing urgency in April 1966 to the Colonial Office requesting R100,000 ($140,000) to fund more preliminary studies, noting he could not "overstate the importance to the whole of Basutoland's economy of getting Oxbow started.... [M]y government is becoming increasingly distressed by the protracted delay in the release of funds for this essential work."[3] The urgency Jonathan showed to jumpstart development initiatives became a regular feature of the early post-independence period because the Lesotho government had pinned its political future on the provision of development projects.

The water project, however, moved slowly. The South African cabinet felt no great urgency to move on it. Jonathan and the BNP government held only the slimmest parliamentary majority, so the South Africans worried the government might fall, to be replaced with a less friendly regime. The South Africans, far from feeling weak, thought they had the upper hand in negotiations because they were the "only potential recipient of the water and power" from the scheme. In addition, some apartheid cabinet ministers had serious reservations about putting control of vital resources in the hands of an independent African government. They also correctly anticipated that in the short term the Lesotho government needed the project more than any other interested party.[4] Still, the looming long-term need for water, a late 1960s push for diplomatic allies among newly independent African states, and the presence of an administration in Maseru open to the possibility of cooperation with the apartheid state meant that preliminary talks started on the project shortly after Lesotho's 1966 independence. The initial talks proceeded slowly, but they led to an announcement on February 23, 1968, that the two countries would commence formal talks on the project.[5] Formal talks represented the high-water mark for Jonathan's engagement policy with South Africa in the early independence period, and with that came a rising level of confidence within the government that it just might be able to deliver significant new development projects. The 1968 announcement seemed ideally timed for the party to potentially reap a development windfall in the upcoming 1970 elections.

For all the optimism the talks engendered among BNP leaders, however, the populace was largely unaware of them since they produced no visible jobs or new infrastructure. It was hard for Jonathan to point to tangible proof that engagement was benefiting Basotho, and this led to frustration among citizens. Many found the lack of visible progress on the water and hydroelectric scheme emblematic of a general inability of the

Lesotho government to deliver on large-scale development projects in the immediate post-independence period. The time government leaders spent on this project also kept them from overseeing or finding funding for more of the smaller projects that brought the development results that most Basotho desired. Few Basotho objected to the water project, but on account of its projected decades-long duration, it would certainly not deliver quick, visible results.

In the January 1970 elections, voters punished the BNP for not delivering on their promise of development, allowing the BCP to win convincingly. In the wake of the elections, however, the BNP annulled the results, mounted a coup by suspending the constitution, and declared a state of emergency. This forestalled a transfer of power and ended representative political governance in Lesotho until 1993.

The shock of the BNP coup effectively marked the end of postindependence euphoria, especially the hope for rapid development. The crackdown that put opposition politicians in jail or caused them to flee into exile publicly silenced critical opinions about government development initiatives. The postcoup period also forced a reevaluation of employment goals for many Basotho, as jobs in the civil service became dependent on membership in the ruling BNP. In addition, the government intensified the politicization of development project delivery, with projects coming only to villages that supported the BNP. Despite these setbacks, however, many Basotho still maintained hope in the promise that development and independence would eventually result in a better life in Lesotho. They sustained this faith in part because even in authoritarian Lesotho, the stark contrast between conditions at home and those in apartheid South Africa were noticeable. There was also an increase in international development assistance to Lesotho that started in the early 1970s and helped keep hope alive.

After the coup, the Lesotho government needed to reestablish legitimacy at home and abroad. Again, it turned to development to secure these aims. Soliciting international funding for government operations and development projects remained the top priority. In the wake of the coup, however, the Lesotho government faced a new financial crisis: its two biggest funders, the United Kingdom and the United States, cut off budgetary and development aid. This situation threatened the ability of the government to maintain power, despite South Africa repeatedly propping up the regime with money for the security forces. Political concerns

at home in the United Kingdom caused the British government to reinstate aid in June 1970 just when the situation was getting dire for the Lesotho government.

In an ironic twist, the postcoup Lesotho government was better able
to solicit development funding from international donors. The authoritarian crackdown meant that the government could control popular protest and dissent. Hand-picked communities received government largesse
in the form of development projects, which then allowed the government
to tout its legitimacy to other funding agencies, thereby claiming a broad
popular mandate to govern. The undemocratic consolidation of power by
the BNP government allowed it to garner more foreign funding for development, but it also made its grasp on power even more dependent on this
international funding. This dependence pushed the government to implement policies that increased bureaucratic control of projects at the expense
of local input in order to continue to attract future funding.

POLITICIZATION OF AID AND DEVELOPMENT COMPLETED:
LATE 1960s

By 1968, Jonathan, buoyed by the start of formal talks on the water project
with South Africa, was feeling more confident in his ability to deliver on
development promises. Thus the tone of his budget and development
speech on March 20, 1968, in Parliament was quite upbeat. He noted that
the Lesotho government had attracted very little development assistance
in the past three years, but he quickly tried to spin this into a political
victory by arguing that the paucity of funding had forced the country to
decolonize more rapidly by focusing on "self-reliance." He contended that
Lesotho was therefore less dependent on U.K. aid, with "greater independence in running our state affairs."[6] This was simply not true, as the precarious financial situation of the Lesotho government during the U.K. aid
suspension after the 1970 coup highlighted.

Jonathan also claimed that the goal of self-reliance would lead to
more development funding from sources other than the United Kingdom.
He wanted people to believe that the effect of Basotho working together
for small-scale development projects would convince "foreign governments and international funding institutions" of the "future viability of our
country's economy," and they would then want to give more money for
development.[7] Jonathan needed self-help programs to run efficiently and

effectively because politically the government had backed itself into a corner rhetorically by promising to bring the results they were producing in rural areas. He could also tout the national unity they supposedly demonstrated. Self-help would bring together "the whole Nation" since "hardly any foreign aid will be forthcoming if our people ... do not apply themselves with all their power to increasing their productivity."[8]

Jonathan and the BNP leadership surely believed in the importance of development efforts in Lesotho, but they were also using development projects in an attempt to build support for the party. Jonathan used the language of national unity in his speech, but a mere two months later, he announced that the IDA-funded road would be named after him. Similarly, in December 1968, he named the recently renovated airport in Maseru after himself, to remind people that he was the driving force behind these public projects.[9] He consistently took the opposition to task for their resistance to BNP development efforts, calling those who interfered with anti–soil erosion programs and tree-planting efforts "traitors" for "deliberately ruin[ing] our soils" and saying he would "have no mercy for the sabotaging elements of our society, for those who maliciously throw away the source of our children's bread [the land]."[10]

All of this made clear how Jonathan viewed development by 1968. He wanted his government to be firmly in control of projects, running them from Maseru. These centralized projects, then, would legitimize the ruling party, though they did not lend themselves to having meaningful community participation or dissenting voices. This vision was certainly not unique in post-independence Africa, but prior to 1970 it was hotly contested by the opposition.[11] The particular ferocity of early post-independence politics in Lesotho made debates about development central to political contestation.

The BNP's self-help programs, the primary way in which it delivered development from 1965 to 1970, made the task of consolidating political authority tricky. In many ways, these programs were successors to the community development initiatives of the 1950s. They were designed to run with popular input and initiative, but this was clearly untenable under the BNP vision. Jonathan's South African special economic advisers, Professors D. V. Cowen and Owen Horwood, laid bare their strategy for self-help in 1967. The projects "should not be haphazard ... [and they] should be coordinated into a proper plan, District by District," so that the "electorate can see something actually happening on the development front and be given faith in their own country and its Government, which is the foundation of political stability, on which economic stability so much depends."[12] Allowing significant popular participation in project planning and implementation was not conducive to "proper planning" and was therefore politically risky. This is why self-help was not the preferred vehicle for high modernist development programs that did centralize state power and cement political authority, like Ujamaa in Tanzania and the Akosombo Dam in Ghana. The Lesotho government, however, could afford only self-help so that was what it used.

The BNP development initiatives were facing an intransigent political opposition, some elements of which were willing to sabotage development efforts for political gain. They felt justified in this open opposition because of the naked politicization of all development projects by the government. Catholic schools, for instance, in contrast to Protestant ones, received more resources for new classrooms, supplies, and supplementary features like libraries and laboratories because of the strong Catholic support of the BNP.[13] Refusing to participate in development projects or destroying already completed projects was an opportunity to protest the government and call its legitimacy into question. Given Lesotho's high poverty levels, however, the number of Basotho who could reject development efforts outright in their own communities on grounds of political principle was quite small. The provision of public services like water projects and school buildings was attractive.

The intensified politicization of development, however, made obtaining formal employment in Lesotho and even in South Africa more fraught. Prior to 1970, the BNP had little control over labor recruitment. The official labor-recruiting network for employment in South Africa consisted of 144 agents working for eight agencies out of twenty-eight offices throughout Lesotho. In 1967, the recruiters, according to South African authorities, were "overwhelmingly BCP supporters," and they "not only [gave] preference to BCP supporters when recruiting, but actually turn[ed] away BNP members and discriminate[d] against them." Prime Minister Jonathan complained to the South African authorities that he was concerned about this state of affairs. He wanted to "deal with the matter as soon as possible."[14] Having BCP recruiters controlling, to some extent, the flow of migrant laborers into South Africa hurt the BNP, and the party faced more limited prospects for fund-raising at home. Replacing the recruiters was attractive because it would allow the government to reward its most loyal party members with important jobs in

Lesotho, move more BNP supporters into positions of formal employment in South Africa, and control an important patronage network.

Opportunities to reward their own supporters with civil service jobs were not as readily available as Jonathan and BNP leaders would have liked because the Public Service Commission (PSC) played an important role in protecting civil servants from arbitrary firings and politicization. Despite the fact that the PSC was supposed to act as a check on politically motivated purges of the civil service, the BNP leadership managed to create an environment in which opposition-supporting civil servants worried about their jobs and faced limited prospects for moving up within the bureaucracies. Even in the pre-1970 period, the PSC could not protect the most outspoken civil servants from losing their jobs. Tšeliso Ramakhula, for example, was a staunch BCP supporter who lost his teaching position at the Agricultural College in Maseru after the 1965 elections.[15] Often, merely the suspicion of opposition sympathies was enough to keep people from promotions. Selborne Mohlalisi was never a party member, but his membership in the Lesotho Evangelical Church (the successor to the PEMS church) meant that others maneuvered to shunt him aside from a role he felt he deserved in the prime minister's office. He ended up taking a less prestigious position in the Department of Education instead.[16] The Peace Corps made note of the deleterious effects of the general attitude of suspicion among civil servants. A late 1960s memo commented that "political affiliations [are given priority] over skill in the civil service," and this was hindering the ability of government to carry out development projects.[17]

The 1970 coup and concomitant suspension of the constitution allowed the BNP to make these purges more widespread. Without a constitution, the BNP eliminated the PSC and instituted a party membership requirement for civil service employment (Liphephechana). With this new requirement and no constitutional protections, over six hundred civil servants lost their jobs in the immediate aftermath of the coup.[18]

It was not just the civil service that felt the effects of the coup directly. Youth organizations found their funding and degree of support politicized in new ways. The BNP government, like the colonial government before it, saw an opportunity to build long-term support by reaching young Basotho during their formative years. The prime minister sent Peter Khamane, the former Boy Scout leader and one of Jonathan's most trusted political operatives, to Israel, Taiwan, and Malawi in an effort to bring

Young Pioneers–style organizations to Lesotho.[19] On his return, he established the Lesotho Youth Service, an organization dedicated to cultivating a "broad programme of skills training, agriculture, and development projects" for Basotho youth.[20] The ambition of Jonathan and Khamane, however, was to build a cadre of youth willing and ready to serve as the government's political shock troops, as organizations like this did in Malawi and Ghana.[21] The residential camp model utilized by Hastings Banda in Malawi, for example, never materialized in Lesotho, but Khamane's promotion to the prime minister's office after the coup highlights the importance the BNP placed on youth mobilization. The BNP Youth League also functioned as an extrajudicial enforcement arm of the BNP government from the 1970 coup until the BNP lost power in 1986.[22]

The postcoup government was not just satisfied to substantially increase its support for explicitly political groups. It also drew from existing youth groups, like Boy Scouts and Girl Guides at Catholic schools. In Gabriel Tlaba's account, these organizations became sites for the grooming of future BNP leaders. Student leaders in the Scouts and Guides often moved straight into party leadership, and the upper ranks of the police and security forces drew heavily from Catholic school Scout groups.[23]

Youth groups presented a potential threat to the government as well as an opportunity, especially groups at the university. At the Roma campus, students came from Lesotho, Botswana, and Swaziland and other countries in the region. The government assumed that most students there—domestic and foreign—supported the opposition because the stronger anti-apartheid and Pan-Africanist views of the BCP resonated with the relatively cosmopolitan mix of students. BNP officials were fearful that student organizing would derail the government's efforts to build closer ties with South Africa. The Lesotho government actively monitored groups like the UCM because its members regularly crossed the border for meetings and maintained connections with individuals and groups banned by the South African government.[24]

The BNP government also worried about university students emulating South African protests and the global student protests of the late 1960s. Following three disruptive months of protests in 1968 at Fort Hare University, Minister of Education Anthony Clovis Manyeli went to the Roma campus to warn students not to engage in similar efforts. His December 1968 message to the students was to focus on their studies and stay out of politics.[25] Manyeli made a thinly veiled threat that students who were too active in politics could lose their scholarships/bursaries if they were "found guilty of embarrassing the government." He tried to be even-handed by calling on students to remain "legitimate critics" of policy without "assum[ing] the role of enemies."[26] He also challenged them to tie their studies into national and regional economic needs. He hinted that future bursaries might be contingent on individuals taking up fields of study linked to development needs: "Teaching, agriculture, engineering, and medicine."[27]

THE ROLE OF DEVELOPMENT IN THE ELECTION CAMPAIGN OF 1970

The rhetoric of development played an even larger role in the 1970 election campaign than it had in 1965, as politicians and the electorate saw the elections as a referendum on the BNP development efforts over its five years in power. The triumph of the rhetorical consensus on development meant that most Basotho understood and spoke of independence in the language of development, so every completed project or failure to bring about significant change in communities loomed large.

The BCP platform was far different from the overconfident version that had been put forward in 1965. The 1965 plan had simply called for "strong cooperation between a new Lesotho and the foreign countries." The 1970 election manifesto, in contrast, called for sixteen specific projects ranging from "developing mohair-weaving, fruit-preservation, tinning of beef, butter-making, [and] leather tanning" to "dams for irrigation and electricity" and a "living wage for workers."[28] The big-ticket water project was included, but most of the projects listed were smaller-scale, community-level development projects such as cooperatives, self-help projects like village water supply, and pottery production. This was consistent with the BCP's charge that BNP development efforts were too centralized and not reaching enough communities. Through this emphasis on smaller, community projects BCP leaders were also demonstrating a new commitment to listen and respond to the concerns of the grassroots membership.

The BCP's campaign, thus, focused not only on mobilizing its own supporters with the promise of such projects but also on winning over disaffected BNP and MFP supporters who had not seen development projects in the number or the type that they desired in the post-independence era.[29] Whether a victorious BCP would have abandoned their mid-1960s focus on centralized, politicized development in favor of a more decentralized program is, of course, unknowable. The BCP would have faced similar pressures from funding agencies to emphasize project "planning." It is likely, too, that they would have also faced significant structural obstacles to consolidating political control through grassroots development initiatives. The party's campaign rhetoric, however, showed a marked shift back toward the more decentralized model of development favored by a large number of its supporters, in particular, Basotho youth.

The BNP, on the other hand, continued to call for and focus on centralized development. Development plans occupied the first paragraph of the election manifesto. While the idea of citizen participation was not entirely absent, it was clear the government did not intend to markedly change its program. Public participation was encouraged only through a top-down system that reserved planning for central administrators. The BNP government hoped to introduce a new "National Planning Consultative Council representing national groups or associations directly involved in the economic and social spheres in their respective districts." The council would not shape overall development strategy or specific project implementation but was to be "consulted and informed of planned development programmes and [issued] progress reports." In other words, the council was primarily designed to help the central government disseminate information to organizations and communities from which the government expected cooperation. In addition, the BNP called for continuing the self-help program, increasing local employment, and expanding services in education and health care as "poverty, ignorance and disease stand out as the greatest enemies of our people."[30]

At every stop on the campaign trail, the BNP and its standard-bearer, Jonathan, beat the drum of successful development delivery. As the 1970 elections approached, Jonathan and other BNP ministers increased the frequency with which they appeared at the opening of new self-help projects like school libraries and village water supply projects.[31] The ministers had prioritized development delivery their entire time in office, but ensuring ministerial presence at the opening of self-help projects encouraged friendly newspapers like the Catholic Church's *Moeletsi oa Basotho* and the government-run *Lesotho News* to devote even more coverage to development efforts. BNP leaders hoped this coverage would feed a countrywide narrative of progress since independence, especially among their base of rural Catholics. The reality, however, was that the BNP government had failed to secure a single new large development project from its preferred funders—South Africa, the United States, and multilateral institutions like the World Bank.

Some BNP ministers had discovered their talent for turning any development opportunity, no matter how small, into one or more completed projects. The American chargé d'affaires in Maseru had a small amount of money from USAID with which he could support ongoing projects. USAID's development priority for 1969 was agricultural projects. The Ministry of Agriculture, however, seemed incapable of identifying projects that could benefit from this scheme. The Lesotho government seemed likely to miss out on this opportunity, as the funds would no longer be available as of the start of the new fiscal year. At the deadline, Sekhonyana 'Maseribane, minister of the interior, suggested that the money be repurposed to support existing self-help efforts like village water supply and school classroom construction projects. The Americans noted that these projects were "well-geared," and they were "able, and more than ready, to supply the Mission with viable self-help schemes."[32] Not coincidentally, 'Maseribane, as deputy prime minister as well as minister of the interior, was a key figure in formulating the BNP electoral strategy. Thus the infusion of American money into existing projects kept self-help at the forefront of government initiatives aimed at demonstrating its ability to deliver on promises. The influence of 'Maseribane, however, meant that self-help was even more politicized since communities most sympathetic to the BNP government received the lion's share of funds.

Besides the small amounts of U.S. support for self-help, the Lesotho government received assistance from South Africa. This assistance, however, primarily took the form of technical advisers seconded for a limited time from the South African civil service to Lesotho, along with funding for security force upgrades. These efforts generated enough goodwill that the Lesotho government refused to condemn South Africa or its apartheid system at the OAU and UN in the late 1960s.[33]

South African aid was quite controversial in Lesotho. In Maseru the presence of many South African refugees made Jonathan's policy of keeping a number of seconded South Africans as his close advisers especially unpopular. In the rural areas, the close cooperation between the South African police and the newly formed Stock Theft Unit in the Lesotho police force became a significant electoral liability for Jonathan. The collaboration allowed uniformed South African officers to operate jointly with the Lesotho police in the mountains where theft was common, but this was highly unpopular in districts the BNP won handily in 1965.[34] Thus the political rhetoric about South Africa during the 1970 campaign focused on how the relationship between the Lesotho government and South Africa might change. With Basotho from all over the country intimately aware of the indignity and inhumanity of the apartheid system from their experiences with border posts, migrant labor contracts, and family stories, it was clear to all that a BNP victory portended little change.

In addition to highlighting the development projects completed under their watch, the BNP leaders threatened on the campaign trail to withhold development assistance from communities that did not support the government at the ballot box. The Kolonyama constituency in Leribe was one Jonathan particularly wanted to win. It contained the village where he grew up, and he had been handed a humiliating electoral loss there during the 1965 general election. The constituency also contained the only factory in the country located outside Maseru, a candle-making venture established by the government in Kolonyama in the late 1960s. Jonathan gave a bombastic speech there in October 1969 in which he warned residents that if they did not vote BNP, "development priority [would be] given to those constituencies that do."[35] At other campaign stops, he was less bombastic but delivered the same general message: support the BNP or lose access to self-help development projects. In the Berea District village of Sebitia in early December, Jonathan "pointed at several completed village water schemes at Peete's and Ntsoso's and mentioned those under construction at Mokabo's and Nkutu's" and noted that the government planned to "bring further development to the constituencies which would vote it back into power" at the elections.[36]

These threats reflected the political reality that most BNP development projects had been completed in communities that clustered around the lowland road system—communities that had largely supported the BCP or MFP in the 1965 elections. The most visible project was the new IDA-funded tar road that ran through Maseru to the northern town of Hlotse/Leribe. The only industrial development the government had managed to start was concentrated in Maseru and along the road.[37] The clearest expression of how much development meant to Jonathan, and how he expected to win an election that was a referendum on BNP development efforts, came in a speech he gave in December 1969 in the BCP stronghold of Mafeteng:

If you think that the roads we have constructed are a good thing, return us to power. If you think the electricity we have brought to Lesotho is a good thing, return us to power. If you think the air services and airstrips we have established and improved are a good thing. If you think the industries we have brought to Lesotho are a good thing, return us to power. If you think the food aid we have brought to this country is a good thing, return us to power. If you reject the Basotho National Party, then you reject the developments we have achieved.[38]

Unfortunately for Jonathan, Basotho voters were only too willing to judge the BNP government on these grounds, and they did so in the January 27, 1970, elections. Voters resoundingly rejected the BNP, returning its candidates in only twenty-three of the sixty parliamentary constituencies. While the MFP managed to carry one constituency, the BCP was the overwhelming victor with thirty-six seats.[39]

THE CHANGING POLITICS OF AMERICAN AND SOUTH AFRICAN ASSISTANCE

The two most promising non-British sources of aid for the Lesotho government in the early independence period were the United States and South Africa, both of which were controversial. South Africa already wielded outsized influence over Lesotho on account of its economic power, and U.S. assistance was tied into Cold War aims that did not always resonate with popular sentiment in Lesotho. Jonathan eagerly and actively pursued both in the early independence period because they offered the best chance to reduce his government's extreme dependence on the United Kingdom for budgetary and development assistance. The opposition BCP worked to limit the amount of aid that either country could offer, and they proffered stiff political opposition to projects like the Peace Corps program, as well as any and all South African assistance. The BCP saw in such opposition many political advantages. Not only would they hinder the success of BNP government initiatives, but at the same time the BCP could demonstrate ideological opposition to the apartheid regime and skepticism regarding the motives for American interest in Lesotho. The positions each party took on foreign aid from these two countries are representative of leaders' attempts to merge political ideology with electoral strategy in the early independence period.

In Lesotho, as in many other places in Africa, accepting aid from the United States during the 1960s came with political baggage because of the intensity of the global Cold War. These concerns came out in discussions about the Peace Corps program that Jonathan personally negotiated for Lesotho and that started operations in late 1967. As early as 1962 Moshoeshoe II had made inquiries about the Peace Corps when he was in Washington, DC. By the late 1960s, the Peace Corps was, by cost, the largest non-food-aid development program in operation in Lesotho. It had a budget of around $1.1 million and thus was a signature program for Jonathan and for his boast that the BNP government could attract significant foreign assistance for development.[40] When the first volunteers arrived in December 1967, Jonathan personally greeted them at the airport and used every possible opportunity to spread the news of their arrival as evidence of government competency.

The opposition, as noted in the last chapter, used the Peace Corps program to attack Jonathan, U.S. assistance in general, and the volunteers themselves. This ranged from Frank Phillips, who recalled being "often yelled at in the townships around Maseru," to Tom Carroll, who remembered his first months in Mafeteng as being "pretty tense for a while" because people would "yell" and threaten him in the streets, and Bill Reed, who connected the opposition to the Peace Corps to the U.S. government's "policies toward apartheid."[41]

The comment by Reed was especially prescient because the Peace Corps program was not just controversial among local political activists in Lesotho. It also threatened to derail the relationship Prime Minister Jonathan was trying to build with the South African government. Top officials in Pretoria resented the presence of a group of young, mainly white, volunteers living in rural African communities. Their relatively successful imbrication in rural villages and towns threatened apartheid ideologies about the incompatibility of the cultures of different racial groups. South African authorities went out of their way to make it harder for the program to operate. The first two groups of volunteers, who served from 1967 to 1971, could not get South African visas, and the South African government put tremendous pressure on Jonathan to have less contact with the Americans. The U.S. chargé d'affaires initially had "difficulties in getting to see [Jonathan] after he became Prime Minister" because of "South African pressure."[42]

Jonathan had to stand firm against the South Africans to keep the Peace Corps program but also to keep other advisers that the Lesotho government received from multilateral agencies. The South African government wished to isolate Jonathan so that he had only South African assistance and seconded South African advisers. Therefore they also made life difficult for World Bank and UN personnel. The South African secretary for foreign affairs, Hilgard Muller, wrote to Jonathan in 1967, telling him that *"carte blanche"* visas for UN personnel in Lesotho would not be forthcoming because "the Republic was skeptical about the activities of UN officials."[43] The South African authorities did this, in part, as a response to the increasingly hostile reception that South Africa's apartheid policies received in the 1960s at the United Nations and from the World Bank. Thus Jonathan faced domestic political opposition to the Peace Corps program as well as pressure from South Africa at the same time that he desperately needed large prestige programs like Peace Corps and the water project to bear fruit through development successes.

The continuation of relations with South Africa and the decision to seek South African aid was, therefore, a high risk–high reward proposition for the BNP government. If it could get substantial development funding from Pretoria, it could conceivably convince enough Basotho that it was not selling out Lesotho's sovereignty to the hated apartheid regime. If the BNP failed to bring home projects or if the projects came with too many strings attached, however, the party left itself open to easy political attack for being too cozy with the apartheid government. As it played out, the BCP's claims that South Africa would not provide the amount or the forms of assistance that the BNP desired largely proved prescient. Pretoria's aid was generally confined to seconded officials and technical advisers rather than funding for programs and projects, and this left the BNP open to the charge that it was not truly independent because it had to rely on apartheid officials in sensitive positions like chief electoral officer and Chief Justice of the High Court.[44] Seconded South Africans also served in developmentally sensitive fields like forestry, agriculture, health, and small-scale mineral exploration. Tellingly, however, though Lesotho asked for experts to assist in mining and industry, South Africa was not willing to comply since this might threaten South African economic hegemony in the region.[45]

The South African government also played a two-faced game on economic policy, as it thwarted many efforts by the Lesotho government to industrialize. The Pretoria regime was never particularly interested in giving "donations to Lesotho or any other country," and it only grudgingly gave seconded advisers as aid-in-kind, claiming to be focusing on the development of the Bantustans.[46] The government in Pretoria also worried that giving direct financial assistance to Lesotho opened South Africa up to diplomatic embarrassment if it then turned down further requests from other poor neighbors.[47] The assistance on offer from South Africa was designed primarily to boost the regime's claim that South Africa was a good regional neighbor and was part of a late 1960s push by South Africa to gain diplomatic allies.[48]

The South African regime could not, however, constrain the efforts of its own private citizens like the cigarette and manufacturing magnate Anton Rupert. When Pretoria turned down Lesotho's request in 1967 to provide R1 million ($1.4 million) to jump-start the work of the new Lesotho National Development Corporation (LNDC), Rupert became the LNDC's patron, personally funding the salary of its South African director and serving on its advisory board.[49] The South African cabinet had no interest in contributing to this parastatal organization, calling it a threat to its Border Industries and Bantustan policies.[50] In July 1967 Jonathan finally convinced the British government to provide start-up money for the LNDC and to finance a few projects, which were in operation prior to the elections of 1970. The British minister of overseas development agreed to this on the condition that the board was constructed to be "as far as possible independent of government."[51] This came about because the prevailing view of the High Commissioner in Maseru was that the Jonathan government was "incompetent" in the realm of planning and implementing development projects.[52]

Thus the political situation concerning aid for development remained quite dynamic in Lesotho in the early independence period. The British, whom Jonathan reviled at times in speeches, rescued his pet industrialization project in 1967–68. The American presence in development was relatively new, but the Peace Corps played a significant role in domestic politics, and the Jonathan regime hoped to obtain more and bigger projects from the Americans in the near future. The South Africans remained the most difficult in terms of donor calculus because of the history of contestation over land and because of the unpopularity of apartheid. Jonathan's optimism that he could wrangle significant development assistance from South Africa did not die completely in the late 1960s, but the lack of movement on projects of any scale other than water project negotiations certainly tempered his enthusiasm. Notably, he did not make much of his South African connections in the campaign for the January 1970 general election. Therefore, when South African Prime Minister Vorster declared in 1971 that he did not "believe in hand-outs, but rather in offering help in such a way that developing countries can with self-respect help themselves," it was the final straw.[53] It was then that the Jonathan government started to contemplate a more complete diplomatic break (see ch. 5). This rupture pushed Jonathan and the BNP toward engagement with an even wider world in hopes of securing development funding.

THE 1970 COUP AND THE SUSPENSION OF WESTERN AID

The Jonathan regime's annulment of the results of the 1970 election was possible only because of its support from the South African government, in particular, its direct financial support of Lesotho's elite security forces. The Jonathan regime was hurt most in the months after the coup by its lack of an aid package from the United Kingdom. The government in Maseru had been negotiating a new deal with the British government during the last months of 1969 but had failed to sign the official paperwork to finalize a new three-year deal before the elections. This mistake stalked the government's efforts to deal with the domestic and international fallout from the coup, especially because other Western countries, including the United States, also cut ties after Britain's decision. While the Jonathan regime attempted to muddle through with stopgap funding, it was facing difficult choices by the middle of 1970 because the government was running out of money.

When British and U.S. aid resumed in June 1970, it came at a pivotal moment. Instead of having to make hard choices about political concessions and about which programs to cut, the Jonathan regime halted negotiations with the opposition, resumed solicitation of aid from abroad, and consolidated domestic power in an autocratic fashion. Development assistance was, thus, an instrument that directly supported unrepresentative government in 1970s Lesotho. Moreover, the BNP's use of development assistance enabled it to sideline domestic politics and make opposition to particular development projects illegitimate. In October 1970, Jonathan declared a five-year "holiday" from politics, and thus outlawed criticism of development by deeming it politically motivated. This was a key step along the path to making development an "anti-politics machine" by 1975.

The voting results from the January 1970 election trickled in over a period of days because the terrain in many places was so rugged, especially in the far-flung mountain constituencies where election officials sometimes had to transport ballot boxes using donkey trains. The campaign had been nasty, especially with regard to development, with the BCP attacking "the lack of development in the vast bulk of the country, most notably in the Maluti," and the BNP attacking the BCP for its "nihilistic opposition to . . . useful development [e.g., self-help], even amounting to sabotage."[54] The South African press reported that the race was close but, as it does to this day, reported mainly from Maseru and filed mostly personality-driven stories detailing differences between leaders.[55] Election day was peaceful, with the police, newspapers, and even government-run Radio Lesotho reporting no serious incidents—a stark contrast to what Jonathan and elements of the South African press claimed in the subsequent days.[56]

Voters judged the BNP government harshly, primarily on its development record, and the BCP claimed an outright parliamentary majority. Early returns showed the BNP picking up a couple of seats in the Leribe District along the newly constructed IDA-funded road. This included Jonathan's home constituency of Kolonyama. However, the BCP made major gains in the foothill and mountain constituencies that had solidly supported the BNP in 1965. It was in these areas that "no economic development of any note had taken place" and "highly unpopular" moves like the expulsion of individual Basotho diamond diggers from Let'seng-la-Terae and joint Lesotho–South African Stock Theft Unit patrols caused voters to switch their support to the BCP.[57] The stage seemed set for a transition of power in Lesotho.

From all accounts, the prime minister was prepared to hand over power peacefully, but hardliners in the cabinet convinced him otherwise. Deputy Prime Minister Sekhonyana 'Maseribane, Matete Majara, and Peete Peete secured a pledge of support from South African authorities and convinced him to hold onto power instead.[58] So on Friday, January 30, 1970, Prime Minister Leabua Jonathan took to the airwaves of Radio Lesotho and announced a state of emergency and the suspension of Lesotho's constitution. Basotho greeted the announcement with a mixture of shock and disbelief. Simon Phafane, working as a low-level adviser in the office of King Moshoeshoe II, went to the bar at Lancer's Hotel to check on the mood for the king and found BCP supporters loudly proclaiming that there was no way Jonathan could get away with it.[59]

South African support for the coup was crucial to its success and was driven largely by worries about how the BCP might support groups like the PAC and the ANC. While South Africa had been largely unwilling to directly fund development efforts in Lesotho, it had paid to upgrade Lesotho's security forces in 1967. The funds paid for two new companies of the elite Police Mobile Unit (PMU).[60] Along with the funds came increased coordination of the PMU, in particular, with the Special Branch of the South African Police. In 1969, South Africa provided more security assistance in the form of an interest-free loan to finance the construction of a new police training college in Maseru. It also gave almost R400,000 ($560,000) per year to finance a further doubling of the PMU from four to eight regiments.[61] This was all done out of the fear of the BCP coming to power and allowing Lesotho to be used as a frontline base by anti-apartheid organizations. By December 1970, the South African government funded a full third of Lesotho's security budget, a percentage that only increased through 1972.[62]

While there was no violence in the days immediately after the election, the state of emergency declaration and the arrest of opposition leaders led to sporadic violence in the subsequent weeks. Much of the violence in Maseru happened at the hands of the BNP Youth League. Some of this violence was directed at opposition supporters in general, but there was a concerted effort by top BNP leaders, in particular, Deputy Prime Minister 'Maseribane, to get staff at the government printing works to admit to electoral fraud. A British memo dated February 3 stated:

> Assaults were not confined to Maseru or Maseribane's house and were carried out by certain Basotho police officers, members of either BNP Youth League or Young Pioneers and BNP supporters of both sexes. Questioning related both to alleged misuse of ballot papers and concealment of arms. . . . In some cases witnesses said they had given false statements at gunpoint to satisfy their interrogators.[63]

The report went on to describe how the expatriate British man in charge of the printing works, while not having been assaulted, was pressured to "admit that ballot paper could have been stolen in transit from South African printers, or from government press security store, and that false ballot paper could have been printed on government press machines. He denied that any of these suggestions were possible."[64]

In addition to the targeted political violence in Maseru and other towns, several larger gun battles between state security elements and opposition forces occurred over the next few months. The biggest battle involved a group led by a former deputy commander of the police, Clement Leepa, near Ha Tšiu, about twenty miles from Maseru. The fight with the PMU occurred in early February, but the government did not manage to kill Leepa and disarm his group until March 3.[65] A second major conflict took place between a group of individual Basotho miners, known as Liphokojoe (jackals), and the PMU near the Kao Mine in the mountains of the Leribe District in early April.[66] Most of the violence, however, took place in the periurban neighborhoods outside Maseru and in villages across the country as the BNP Youth League clashed with the most outspoken opposition supporters.

The British Labour Government under Harold Wilson suspended aid for budgetary support and development assistance in the immediate aftermath of the coup. This was relatively easy to do because Jonathan and the BNP government had failed to finalize a new aid agreement with the British government prior to the elections. The initial independence aid agreement that went into effect in 1967, delivering £3.1 million ($8.65 million) in assistance, was set to expire on March 31, 1970.[67] During late 1969, the two governments had multiple rounds of talks to negotiate a new aid package. The final meetings took place in early December in London, and the two sides agreed on £2.625 million ($6.3 million) in budgetary aid and £4.5 million ($10.8 million) for development assistance over a three-year period starting April 1, 1970, and ending in 1973. The aid in this package skewed more heavily toward development funding because the administrative capacity in Maseru had improved since independence but also because Lesotho was set to receive more government revenue to support recurring budgetary items from a renegotiated Southern African Customs Union.

The goal of the development aid was to help Lesotho wean itself from reliance on the British government. The overarching goal of British planners was to help the Lesotho government "diversify their sources of development aid" by earmarking much of the aid for the Lesotho government's upcoming required contribution to big development projects already in the planning stages with the UNDP and the Swedish International Development Cooperation Agency (SIDA).[68] Jonathan delayed signing the final aid offer in early January 1970 because he wanted the "formal decision . . . [to] be taken by [the] Cabinet . . . [and] there [was] no prospect of [the] Cabinet's meeting until after elections on 27 January."[69] This turned out to be a grave tactical error, as it was far easier for the British government to rescind an unsigned agreement than to abrogate one that had been signed. Without this British aid, the Lesotho government was in a precarious financial position, and the lack of British funding support vexed Jonathan's government in the months following the coup.

The withdrawal of the aid offer was formalized on February 7, 1970, and other Western governments quickly implemented sanctions as well. Harold Wilson's government claimed it was "impossible . . . to regard our relations with Chief Jonathan and his Government as unchanged" since the regime had "seized power unconstitutionally."[70] The United States and Sweden cut assistance for Lesotho and pledged not to start any new programs, though the United States continued to fund the Peace Corps program and did not withdraw the volunteers.

The cuts in foreign assistance, particularly British budgetary support, necessitated immediate planning by the Lesotho government for a new and significantly diminished financial future. Lesotho had a small financial cushion because of the manner in which revenues were received from the Customs Union. This meant it would be late 1970 before the cash on hand ran out. Still, proposed government cutbacks would by midyear amount to a "national disaster," slowing development progress and likely causing "insupportable damage to the government in power," according to a March 1970 British assessment.[71] This financial pressure pushed Jonathan to release opposition leaders from prison and start talks about a unity government or a negotiated political settlement.

Convincing Britain to release its promised aid was surely the most expedient short-term financial solution for the Lesotho government. However, it was not certain that Britain could be convinced to relent. Jonathan's government therefore redoubled its efforts to diversify sources of funding. An obvious source, especially for increased defense funding, was South Africa. As key supporters of Jonathan and the coup, the apartheid regime did fund three more platoons of the Police Mobile Unit in late February, the third expansion of the force in three years.[72] Within the Lesotho cabinet there was debate about the potential for further South African funding for non-security-related items. Hardliners, led by Deputy Prime Minister 'Maseribane, wanted the government to push for even closer relations with South Africa in hopes of bringing the water project and other major development initiatives to fruition. Moderates, meanwhile, backed Jonathan, who advocated for diversifying the sources of development funding.

The effort to diversify development almost ran afoul of internal BNP cabinet politics and South African influence. This was most evident in a March 1970 effort to evict the Peace Corps from Lesotho. On March 25, Jonathan's primary secretary for foreign affairs, Joseph Kotsokoane, met the U.S. chargé d'affaires, Stephen Gebelt, to ask for a "temporary withdrawal" of the Peace Corps program and the repatriation of its outspoken country director, Dave Sherwood. Kotsokoane noted that Jonathan was under "more pressures than you may know" from the South African government and hardliners in his own cabinet led by 'Maseribane.[73] Gebelt pointed out that a "mass exodus would have a strange effect outside Lesotho" since Jonathan claimed to have the country under his control when pleading with British officials for an aid resumption. Further, the withdrawal of the Peace Corps would signal to other potential donors that South Africa was not only propping up Jonathan's security but was able to veto or evict any development program with which it disagreed.

The next day, Jonathan, in a personal meeting with Gebelt, made it clear that he no longer wanted the entire program to leave. He did, however, demand the expulsion of a small number of volunteers who, he claimed, had "involved themselves in internal politics" that directly contributed to violence around Mafeteng.[74] One of the evicted volunteers worked only with South African and Dutch engineers at the Department of Public Works in Maseru and had no regular contact with Basotho, especially those in politics.[75] The other volunteers accused of being politically active had arrived only in early 1970 and had very little understanding of internal politics in Lesotho. There had been no Peace Corps involvement in violent acts, but volunteers from this period who personally knew some of the other evicted volunteers noted that they worked closely with BCP-supporting civil servants and had access to government transport as part of their jobs.[76] The eviction of a few volunteers was a workaround measure that allowed Jonathan to save face with South Africa as well as members of his cabinet while not compromising his own longer-term hope of garnering new aid from U.S. and other non-British sources.

Jonathan not only liked the work the Peace Corps did, but he was betting the political future of his administration on the arrival of significant U.S. aid to solve his development dilemma. The United States had, however, joined British efforts to cut aid to Jonathan, and the American diplomats in Maseru loudly supported British efforts to withhold any new aid from the regime in the hope of bringing about a democratic solution to the political crisis.[77] The U.S. State Department even dictated on February 9 that there were to be "no new self-help projects for now," taking away the small amount of aid ($25,000) U.S. diplomats had used to support community projects.[78]

Despite this, and despite the U.S. Congress's ban on creating new stand-alone USAID programs, Jonathan still held out faith that there would be new projects. In this, individual AID administrators in Washington and in the regional planning office in Zambia assisted Jonathan, because they were keen to start new programs in Lesotho. Some of these officials continued to plan for projects in Lesotho for which discussions were already under way by the time the aid ban took effect. Four days after the ban, a USAID memo noted that American efforts to get more development funding into Lesotho would encourage "other countries . . . to join as donors." The memo continued, "We have in mind, for example, West Germany, South Korea, [and] the Scandinavian countries."[79] The USAID author was either unaware or unconcerned about the American aid suspension, as well as the fact that Sweden and other Scandinavian countries had suspended aid too.

The bureaucratic agenda of USAID—to start and complete projects— worked to the advantage of Jonathan and the BNP in the postcoup period. Administrators at the regional USAID office in Zambia, for instance, wrote to the top U.S. diplomat in Maseru in late February 1970. They were trying to create a framework for future USAID agricultural projects to "contribute to economic and political stability" while also "provid[ing] real benefits for individuals." These efforts included USAID officials making a formal visit to Lesotho in May 1970, again despite the aid ban still being in place.[80] The result was that Lesotho was well positioned to forge ahead with larger projects funded by the United States immediately after the aid suspension was lifted.

The mixed signals that the United States, in particular, was sending allowed Jonathan greater leeway to consolidate political power and avoid making concessions to the opposition after the coup. The BNP government started talks with opposition leaders in March to explore the possibility of a power-sharing, national unity government. These meetings continued through April and May and seemed to make some progress, but despite some initial optimism no such agreement ever materialized.[81] The talks were important, however, as a symbolic gesture of reconciliation in the government's effort to get British funding restored.[82] The Lesotho government could let the talks flounder, though, because of ongoing USAID efforts to make plans for a large agricultural development scheme designed to reduce Lesotho's "heavy dependence on [food] imports." USAID bureaucrats wanted to coordinate the project with "the British, nationalist China, and other donors."[83] Jonathan's knowledge of such discussions, and of the formal visit of USAID personnel in May, rendered the British and American aid suspensions less effective in wringing political concessions from the BNP government.

Within the British government, there was worry too about the possible consequences for Britain's influence in Lesotho and southern Africa of withholding aid. The Commonwealth Office, for instance, worried about accusations that it was treating the African-run Lesotho more harshly than it had treated white settler–ruled Southern Rhodesia over the 1965 Unilateral Declaration of Independence.[84] Further, the British government worried that if Jonathan's attempts to solicit funding from other sources were successful, it would diminish British influence in Lesotho and therefore contribute to a regional decline in British influence. In March, Jonathan had tried to accept the withdrawn British aid package. His "acceptance" letter included a threat to "look elsewhere for assistance" if the British did not reinstate the offer.[85] This led the British High Commissioner in Maseru to argue for a resumption of aid not only as a way of maintaining British influence but also as a way of avoiding a potentially worse fate. Jonathan was, in his estimation, "from among the Basotho National Party, the best we have," and resuming aid might "strengthen [Jonathan's] hand . . . over the more irresponsible ministers" and calm the volatile domestic political situation.[86]

The British continued their suspension of aid through April and May because of financial reports in April that the Lesotho government was able to function without it. The key British ally in the region, Botswana's Seretse Khama, also supported keeping the suspension in effect. While officials in London worried about reports like the one from the Maseru High Commissioner in March, their fears were assuaged to some extent by an April report from Mr. Glaze, who had served as deputy financial secretary in the Lesotho Ministry of Finance. Back in London at a meeting with officials at the Foreign and Commonwealth Relations Office, he concluded that "no great damage had yet been done by the suspension of British aid. . . . Lesotho's administrative capacity could rapidly be restored to normal provided that there was not a long delay in resuming flow of aid."[87] Khama's opposition to the resumption of aid to Lesotho also loomed large. He thought that the British aid suspension was the only hope for forcing Jonathan into a democratic solution to the coup, writing in early June, "Resumption of aid, if not resumption of relations, would fairly obviously be [a] triumph for Jonathan and would confirm him in his purposes and harden his attitude to the need for any accommodation with his political opponents. It could well provide the factor which finally ruled out the possibility of a multi-party political solution."[88]

Despite Mr. Glaze's report, however, from the perspective of the Lesotho government, the aid suspension was beginning to cut deep by April and May, particularly in the realm of the development projects the Jonathan regime so desperately needed. The first program to face the new financial reality was a planned FAO-UNDP area-based agricultural pilot project designed to improve rural agriculture and increase household income in the Leribe District. The Lesotho government found it necessary to postpone the launch of the project because the money to fund the government contribution was part of the canceled British aid package of 1970–73. Even if the government had the money, the UNDP representative worried, "cooperation of local people on which success depends, cannot . . . be assured in present conditions [rural unrest]."[89]

Delays in long-planned projects like the Leribe FAO-UNDP project helped convince Michael Stewart, British secretary of state for foreign and Commonwealth affairs, in late April that the British government needed to work for normalized relations and an end to the aid suspension.[90] The entire British cabinet, however, did not yet support this plan, so the aid suspension remained in effect. Ministers still hoped that continued diplomatic pressure could lead to some sort of negotiated political settlement between the BNP and opposition leaders.

For his part, Jonathan sent mixed messages on compromise. He continued talks with opposition leaders into May, but his government had also forced Moshoeshoe II into exile in the Netherlands in April, accusing him of encouraging illegal political rallies.[91] The fissures in British-U.S. solidarity concerning the suspension of aid became larger in May with

U.S. officials holding informal conversations with Timothy Thahane, the highest-ranking Basotho member of the Planning Unit, about the provision of more aid from the United States to replace British aid.[92] The lack of violence after the pitched battle in April at the Kao mine also augured well for Jonathan's ability to gain renewed recognition from Western powers, which might enable aid to be restarted. He therefore allowed the talks with the opposition to languish.

Still, the time from April to early June was a nervous one for the Lesotho government as no announcements of renewed recognition from the United Kingdom or new aid from the United States were forthcoming. The April battle at the Kao mine proved to be the last large flare of violence in the immediate postcoup period, which allowed the U.K. government to certify by June that the BNP had "effective control" of the territory, and thus it could restore diplomatic recognition, paving the way for renewing British financial assistance. The British cabinet in mid-April allowed Michael Stewart to recognize the Jonathan government when he saw fit, but it encouraged him to do so slowly and deliberately. Stewart's argument that carried the day in London was that Britain propped up plenty of leaders who had "sinned against the canons of democracy far more flagrantly than has Chief Jonathan."[93]

The final concern for the cabinet was getting the blessing of President Khama of Botswana. Through April and May he rebuffed British efforts to recognize the Jonathan regime, arguing that the aid suspension was the only thing keeping Jonathan at the table with the opposition. By early June, however, he reluctantly changed his position to support renewed British recognition on the grounds that the suspension was hurting ordinary Basotho for the political sins of their leaders. In doing so, he worried, presciently as it turned out, that resuming aid "finally ruled out the possibility of a multi-party political solution."[94]

The British government leaned so hard on Khama for support on the Lesotho issue because the Labour government faced its own political pressures ahead of a general election scheduled for mid-June. Labour leaders worried that Lesotho might be an issue for Tory attack, as they had suspended all aid to one of their poorest former colonies. This was not just a hypothetical worry either, as Conservative MP John Biffen had raised this issue in Parliament back in March, asking whether the British aid suspension "imperils the whole economy of Lesotho."[95] So on June 12, 1970, just days ahead of the general election in Britain, the British government restored diplomatic ties with Lesotho.[96]

The renewed recognition of the Jonathan government allowed Great Britain to gradually restore aid. In August, the two countries formalized an aid agreement along the lines originally agreed to in December 1969. The United States quickly followed Britain's lead and restored full ties diplomatically and resumed development assistance. Since U.S. planners had continued to work on Lesotho development schemes, they picked up their work with only minimal disruption. Thus, by early August, officials from USAID, the Lesotho government, and the IDA started formal talks on the area-based agricultural project that came to fruition in 1972–73 as the Thaba Bosiu Project (see ch. 5).

The resumption of relations between the United Kingdom and Lesotho did not lead to the complete normalization of Lesotho's foreign relations or domestic politics. Sweden, for instance, continued to withhold previously promised funds from the authoritarian government. The Jonathan government used the resumption of aid from the United Kingdom and the United States to end talks with the opposition. In a quest to legitimize its extralegal rule, the BNP implemented a plan to outlaw political activity. First floated in March during talks with the opposition, the plan initially proposed to outlaw parties because they had "succeeded only in dividing people." Further, this would allow Basotho to come together for "national unity" in order to "put more emphasis on their social and economic development."[97] In October 1970, Jonathan put this into practice, declaring a nationwide five-year "holiday" from politics, effectively banning political parties other than the BNP, which could cloak its work in the guise of government business.[98] Jonathan and the BNP were able to remove development from the realm of political contestation only after they consolidated an authoritarian regime. Thus the resumption of aid that normalized autocratic rule played an important role in limiting the ability of ordinary Basotho to influence and have a voice in development projects.

BASOTHO REACTIONS TO THE COUP

For most Basotho, the coup and the security crackdown that followed did not make sense. There had been little violence in late colonial Lesotho and certainly no widespread uprising against the colonial regime or chiefly authority. The combination of development and independence had, until 1970, held out the promise of a better life for all. The violence and loss of representative government structures were shocking to many and disrupted some of the promises of independence. Governmental development efforts, however, did not falter, and in many places the number and scope of development projects increased after the coup. The first Five-Year Plan put forth by the Lesotho government was published in 1971. In the introduction, Jonathan called for more development to assist Lesotho's drive for an "actual independence" by "rous[ing] the dormant national dynamism and channel[ing] it towards the solution of the problem of the country's economic emancipation."[99] This type of rhetoric opened spaces for young Basotho to continue to work for their visions of development and to have hope in independence, even as the government lurched into more authoritarian tendencies.

At independence, Alexander Sekoli was forty-two years old. He taught and led the Boy Scout troop at St. David's Primary School near Mamathe's in the rural Berea District. He had followed politics since the founding of the BCP in the early 1950s and, like many Catholic schoolteachers, supported the BNP at elections. His primary focus, though, was on the Scout troop. He led his Scouts in development projects that ranged from planting trees to helping older community members in the fields and assisting with government-run self-help village water supply projects. In the late 1960s Sekoli had his Scouts assist with the transport of needed supplies, like pipes for the water projects, from district headquarters at Teyateyaneng (a distance of about 15 kilometers). These projects, as Sekoli related, were not merely service opportunities for his Scouts; they were also a way for him to raise awareness of the meaning of independence in local villages. He "personally went around telling people" about the projects, and he relished his role as an intermediary between local communities and government administrators at the district headquarters. The volunteer labor of his Scouts was required to bring the water projects to fruition.[100]

Sekoli's Scouts were venturing into the heart of politicized development in the late 1960s, however. Sekoli, as a Catholic schoolteacher who supported the BNP and who could acquire the materials for scarce water supply projects, clearly had good connections with government officials. In his recounting, however, he deliberately and consciously did not officially join the BNP. He recognized the politicization of development work. He commented, "I was so active that [BNP leaders] had asked me to join the party, but I was afraid because I was loved by all the parties, BCP and

BNP." He did not want to upset the delicate balance he had worked out in the communities surrounding St. David's.[101] Sekoli was making an important political point by attempting to keep his Scouts as free from the politics of development as possible. In his own words, he wanted independence to include "a widening of opportunities" in education and in services that rural Basotho could access, like the piped water. The newly built water taps improved lives by reducing the number of hours women in the villages spent hauling water and keeping the water supply safer from livestock contamination. As Sekoli understood, water projects provided not just water but also hope for the residents of the communities that independence and development went hand in hand.

Sekoli's desire to keep politics out of development work and to engage Basotho of all ages in the projects was shared by many rural residents during the independence period. The provision of services through small-scale projects, despite their sporadic, haphazard, and politicized placement, helped build and maintain hope among a larger number of Basotho that development could bring about the benefits they envisioned from independence. The crackdowns that followed the coup dampened some Basotho hopes and dreams for independence, but for many the hope in the possibilities of independence survived even the new, more repressive environment. The growing strength and reach of the global anti-apartheid movement and the significant increase in project funding from a variety of international sources during the 1970s helped nurture and keep alive a long-term hope that development and independence could transcend the short-term political setback and usher in a better Lesotho.

The political violence of the coup and its aftermath indelibly marked the period in the minds of most Basotho. They started using the Sesotho term *Qomatsi* when referring to the period of unrest. Its literal translation was "State of Emergency," but most people used it more broadly to denote the early years of the 1970s when the threat of political violence was pervasive. This popular linguistic conflation of the state of emergency with social and political unrest makes it clear that few could ignore politics completely.[102]

Some older Basotho, however, were not surprised by the violence of 1970. Gabriel Tlaba remembered many older Basotho taking a "we told you so" attitude toward disillusioned younger Basotho.[103] Tšeliso Ramakhula similarly implied that many older Basotho saw the path to independence as one leading to impetuous leadership and violence. He characterized older Basotho as being disdainful of independence as they sarcastically asked, "If we govern ourselves, whose son is to govern us?"[104]

For most Basotho, however, Qomatsi and its attendant disillusionment still elicited strong responses in the twenty-first century. In 2008, Thabelo Kebise shouted angrily, "[It was] unforgettable to people who have seen it." Selborne Mohlalisi noted that Qomatsi still "had a pervasive influence on the politics of this country." "We still discuss it with our children and relatives," he said. "We still recount the brutalities and everything because people have got it into their head that they must still remember the atrocities."[105] Both Kebise and Mohlalisi were personally affected by threats of violence, which certainly had an effect on the degree to which they continued to feel strongly about it. Still, the political violence of Qomatsi casts a long shadow for many in Lesotho.

In addition to violence, the coup allowed for the full-scale politicization of the civil service. The BNP government, after suspending the constitution and abolishing the Public Service Commission, instituted the Liphephechana system, whereby a BNP membership card became a prerequisite for a government job.[106] This new requirement meant that for many young Basotho the dream of securing a job in the civil service in Lesotho vanished. Mamapele Chakela came from an active BCP family. Her uncle Charles was party treasurer in the 1960s and cousins Lebenya and Koenyama were also in party leadership. She trained as a secretary, obtaining a colonial government bursary to study in Nigeria in 1964. Chakela held a series of jobs in the government after independence, but she was quickly moved on from department to department. BNP officials worried about her passing government secrets to politically active family members. With trained secretaries in short supply, though, Chakela was never without work prior to 1970. In April 1970, however, she lost her post in the Economic Planning Unit. She was then blacklisted and threatened by the BNP Youth League, which caused her to flee to Botswana, where she lived from July 1971 until 1973.[107]

The effects of Qomatsi and Liphephechana were not confined to those with elite political connections either. Raphael Leseli came from the small village of Makhalaneng ha Lekota in the foothills of the Maseru District. His parents were active in the local chapter of the BCP and encouraged him to join the Youth League, which he did in 1965 while still enrolled in school. He completed his Junior Certificate (secondary school) at Maseru Community School in 1969. Leseli's independence vision included not having to go to South Africa for work because he regretted that his father was always away in Bloemfontein "working at the railway" and was thus gone most of the year.[108] Growing up without his father at home had a profound impact on Leseli, and he wanted to get a job in Lesotho after completing his education.

Unfortunately Leseli's timing was terrible; he finished school on the eve of the 1970 elections. Therefore, when he went to look for work he knew it was fruitless: "If you are supporting the wrong party, they will throw out [the application]."[109] He knew this from direct family experience, as his older brother lost his job with the Post Office in the wake of the coup on account of his long BCP affiliation. Raphael, who wanted to join the police force, instead reluctantly went to the offices of The Employment Bureau of Africa (TEBA), the hiring consortium of the South African gold mines, and he signed on to be a clerk at the President Steyn Mine in Welkom, South Africa. He worked there from 1971 to 1998. Still, Leseli said, "I was disappointed because I didn't want to go to the mines." The promises of education and independence were that he could "stay in Lesotho and work in Lesotho," but the new reality was that his political affiliations denied him that chance.

Despite this disappointment, Leseli managed to create a bit of his independence dream for his family. First, he was able to come home every month because of changing labor conditions in the mines and his position as an aboveground clerk. Second, he was able to move his family from remote Ha Lekota to Roma by the late 1970s. Ha Lekota, he said, "was too far, [had] poor transport, [the] schools are not there, [neither were] clinics or hospitals, so I came nearer to those things."[110] The presence of this infrastructure was, for Leseli, one of the main attractions of independence. When asked, he simply stated that he hoped to see development after independence. So, despite his disappointment at being unable to fulfill the domestic employment part of his independence vision, the incremental progress in infrastructure creation allowed him to maintain faith in the idea of Lesotho and to keep his family there while he was away working at the mines.

Having access to new and improved infrastructure helped many Basotho maintain hope in the eventual efficacy of independence, despite the disruption of Qomatsi. This was true for a teacher in the Mafeteng District, a card-carrying BCP member who wished to remain anonymous. In the late 1960s and early 1970s, she hid her political affiliation for fear of being fired from the Anglican school where she worked. The threat of physical violence with the specter of the state behind it made the postcoup

period significantly worse. She remembered the police as being "very trou-
blesome" and also recalled that many people dissembled, "pretend[ing] it
[the BNP] was their [party of choice]."[111] Despite this climate of fear, she
supported her husband's continued education, and he ended up with a
teaching certificate from the Teacher Training College (TTC) on the out-
skirts of Maseru. This was made possible in part because her home was on
the road system, allowing for easier travel. Similarly, the school expansion
of the 1960s included improvements to TTC, with some funding from
international donors. The roads and schools enabled the teacher and her
husband to maintain their rural home and enabled her to keep her job in
spite of the postcoup conditions.

It was not just Protestants and opposition supporters who fretted
about the unrest of Qomatsi and its potentially deleterious effects on their
visions for the nation and independence. Gabriel Tlaba, jointly enrolled in
the Catholic seminary and the university in Roma, remembered shortly
after the coup that "it became *very clear* that things were not rosy. People
were just looking for their own, you know, good and not the common
good."[112] In particular, he mentioned the threat of physical violence that
was poisoning interpersonal relations and disrupting the relationship
between people and the government. Brother Michael Mateka, another
Catholic school teacher, lamented the lingering effect of violence on the
hopes and dreams of Basotho, explicitly linking the threat of violence to
development: "You can't develop a country when you are at each other's
throats."[113] Catholic voices speaking out against politicized development,
the job reservation system, and the violence of Qomatsi are significant because Catholic Basotho youth stood to benefit the most from post-1970
changes. They suggest that there was a large segment of the population
that even after the coup continued to envision a common national identity
unencumbered by political or religious litmus tests.

The disappointment people across the political spectrum felt as a
result of the coup was still palpable in early twenty-first century interviews, though it was sometimes hard to untangle the disappointments
precipitated directly by 1970 from other bouts of violence that have periodically engulfed Lesotho in the intervening years. The latter include attacks by South African security forces in the 1980s and the 1998 invasion
by forces from Botswana and the postapartheid South African government. There were also episodic assassinations during the period of BNP
rule, from 1970 to 1986, violence during the army's 1986–93 rule, and

spates of political violence after Lesotho's return to multiparty parliamentary democracy in 1993. The Qomatsi violence, however, was singular for many Basotho because it came first. In some ways it conditioned Basotho to see violence as a relatively normal feature of political life. Many Basotho after Qomatsi took a rather more cynical view of political elites, seeing them as willing to resort to violence in order to solve problems that could and should have had an amicable solution.[114] Selborne Mohlalisi noted that Qomatsi still pervaded the consciousness of many Basotho and had helped regularize political violence in Lesotho, comparing 1970 to the 2008 ZANU-PF crackdown on supporters of the Movement for Democratic Change in Zimbabwe.[115]

For all the fear and disillusionment that Qomatsi engendered, small-scale development efforts through governmental programs and the grass-roots efforts of Basotho in youth organizations continued. These allowed many Basotho to maintain hope that development did not necessarily have to be a casualty of the political dysfunction that characterized the post-1970 period. And despite becoming more politicized, youth organizations remained popular and continued to increase in number and size as primary and secondary school enrollments continued to climb.

While Basotho from Lesotho constituted the majority of new enrollees, the number of South African students in Lesotho also rose through the 1970s, peaking after the Soweto uprisings of 1976. The South African students served as tangible reminders for Basotho youth that conditions in Lesotho, however bad, paled in comparison to the bleak future young South Africans faced under apartheid. Moeletsi and Jama Mbeki, the two youngest sons of the imprisoned ANC leader Govan Mbeki, attended schools in Lesotho. Chaka Ntsane, whose family helped host Moeletsi, remembered that one of Moeletsi's most prized possessions was a letter from his father, sent from Robben Island.[116] Similarly, Mohlalefi Moteane, a classmate of Jama's at Peka High School, reported that all the students knew who Jama's father was. They also understood that "most South African families who wanted their children not to go over to Bantu Education sent them" to Lesotho.[117]

The contacts that Basotho had with South Africans also showed them that there were plenty of people in South Africa who looked to Lesotho and other independent African states as examples. Gabriel Tlaba noted that many of the South African students he met through the University Christian Movement looked at Lesotho's independence "with envy."[118] Raphael Leseli recalled that his South African colleagues in the Welkom mine "wanted [South Africa] to be like Lesotho," that is, politically independent.[119] These experiences with South Africans, on both sides of the border, who saw Lesotho as a model for their own liberation helped temper, to some extent, the disillusionment that young Basotho were feeling in the postcoup period.

Of course, the fact that conditions were worse in South Africa did not assuage all the concerns young Basotho had about the direction of Lesotho after the coup. Tlaba was disappointed that independence had not delivered "better economic structures" in the country, but his exposure to outsider perspectives on Lesotho's independence allowed him to appreciate the changes that had taken place.[120] Being surrounded by the apartheid state did not directly aid Basotho in their quest for an independent state that fulfilled their desires for improved economic and political conditions, but in this particular instance, the contrast between the situations in Lesotho and South Africa provided perspective for continued struggle and hope.

Another mitigating factor in stemming a descent into complete disillusionment was, ironically, the increasing ability of the Lesotho government to attract more development assistance from abroad. Despite evidence that the resumption of British aid functioned primarily to prop up the authoritarian Jonathan regime, some Basotho still hoped that foreign aid and development assistance could help solve the political impasse within Lesotho. They also had to hope that stipulations regarding technocratic competency imposed by funding agencies might force the hand of the Lesotho government. They had to believe that international actors could force their way through local political impasses. Michael Mateka noted the need for an outside push for Basotho to surmount internal political divisions:

> The bulk of the development on that side [South Africa] is on the shoulders of the Basotho, all the farms, all the [mines] you find the managers are all Basotho. Why can't they do it in the country? Here we have inherited that envy, that jealousy, and if I see you succeed I think you are trying to show you are better, so I destroy what you have achieved, or worse I bring you down.[121]

While few held out hope, as Mateka did, that foreign development assistance would solve seemingly intractable domestic political problems, many still saw foreign funding as a marker of independence. The particular meanings and implications of foreign assistance, however, tended to be mediated through a partisan lens, as well as personal ambition. BNP supporter Chaka Ntsane remembered 1968 for the arrival of Taiwanese agricultural advisers, and he recalled feeling a surge of pride because Lesotho was finally free to "associate with any country that [it] wanted and be guided by what these countries had to offer."[122] Studying agriculture and having strong family connections with the ruling party, Ntsane stood to benefit personally from programs like this. Similarly, BCP supporter Mohlalefi Moteane specifically noted that independence for him included the ability of Lesotho to "decide to belong to the UN institutions."[123] For someone whose ambition was to go abroad to study and then return to Lesotho for a professional career, more UN and multilateral agency connections also held the potential for future personal gains.

The relations the Lesotho government was building scared some Basotho. Motsapi Moorosi worried about the Lesotho government making policies that might damage relations with South Africa. Since he was attending high school in Lesotho while his parents lived in South Africa, Moorosi feared being stranded on one side of a border he needed to cross. He also worried that Lesotho's political stances would have an impact on his burgeoning athletic career, for which he received sponsorship from the President Brand Mine in Welkom.[124] Basotho were discerningly evaluating the development connections that arrived during the late 1960s and early 1970s. While there were some like Moorosi who worried about the implications of particular programs and connections, in general the increased connections bolstered the sense among Basotho that independence was meaningful because it was offering more opportunities.

The early post-independence period, 1966 to 1970, saw very few high-profile development projects funded by the Lesotho government or foreign entities. This started to change in the 1970s after the coup and the resumption of aid from the United Kingdom and the United States. Lesotho officials had set the stage for more successful development solicitation through their efforts in the late 1960s, but until the postcoup period these did not bear fruit with organizations like the World Bank, FAO, WFP, or UNDP.

For many Basotho, in another ironic twist, independence was not a concept that was clear in their minds until after multiparty democracy gave way to authoritarian rule. The lack of visibility that development projects had in the pre-coup period made it hard for the populace to make tangible connections between the abstract ideas of development and independence. Catholic high school teacher Moeketsi Lesitsi articulated how this lack of visibility contributed to a sense in the minds of many Basotho that the meaning of independence took time to realize. For Lesitsi, it was only in the 1970s that independence came into focus. This was a bit surprising because he was teaching at a Catholic school at independence, he had worked as part of the 1965 census, and he had been a poll worker during the 1965 elections. He had also received free transport to attend the Maseru independence celebrations of October 1966, yet during the 1960s he "didn't even know what independence meant." After the coup, however, he finally "realized the advantages that could be possible from independence. People could go to other countries for training and learning and we could get money [foreign aid] from other countries."[125] All the outward markers of political participation and symbolic nation building could not make real, even for a schoolteacher and Sesotho-language poet, the abstract ideal of independence.

The final irony of postcoup development funding paving the way for more Basotho to understand and internalize what independence meant was that international funding constrained the ability of the Lesotho government to control and independently operate development programs. Dependence limited the ability of the government to exercise hard-won sovereignty. In addition, the authoritarian turn in government after 1970 limited the ability of ordinary Basotho to have meaningful input in project planning and implementation. So while more people had dreams of independence, especially as they revolved around hopes for development, they were less able to act on these dreams. By bringing in more externally funded projects, the Lesotho government was taking deliberate strides toward the "anti-politics machine" of depoliticized project delivery that hindered the ability of anyone locally to control development.

POSTCOUP CONSOLIDATION AND THE NEED FOR DEVELOPMENT FUNDING

After the 1970 coup, the Lesotho government needed development aid even more than it had in the early independence period. The BNP badly needed to win back its supporters and convince opposition supporters it could be a legitimate government. In order to do this, the government turned yet again to development.

The aftermath of the violence, implementation of a political test for civil service jobs, and suspension of political parties caused a rapid change in expectations for many Basotho. Most saw the repressive, nonrepresentative government as a step in the wrong direction for Lesotho. The Anglican bishop of Maseru, J. A. Maund, reported in February 1970 that "ordinary people, of whom [the] great majority are opposed to Jonathan's actions, are bewildered and hoping for some kind of intervention."[126] Maund was talking about some sort of economic or political intervention to relieve the people of the burdens posed by the threat of government violence, but he could have been talking about development interventions as well. The hope for development that nurtured Basotho through the political reforms of the colonial era also helped sustain them through the period of disillusionment that followed the coup. The majority of Basotho had come to believe, rather strongly, by 1970 that development just made sense, and there was no other way forward.

This hope, however, was a double-edged sword that was not clear to most at the time. While development held out the promise of a better material life, its implementation entrenched an autocratic, nondemocratic government in Lesotho by lending it legitimacy at home and abroad. The BNP government made the case that it could best procure the funding for development projects so in demand from the population. Thus the suspension of basic political rights, fought for and a crucial part of the independence vision for so many, helped the government garner more foreign development assistance. The five-year "holiday" from politics that Jonathan declared further alienated Basotho from their own government and development projects by removing what little public input had been present previously. This was especially problematic because the "holiday" coincided with a rapid increase in the number and scope of projects after 1970. The increased funding for development in the mid-1970s allowed the BNP to "rebuild a public service decimated by the purge of opposition elements" and take control of the rhetoric and process of development.[127]

The contrast with the relatively open political environment of the early independence period was a particularly cruel blow to younger Basotho. The inability of people to have a say in political or development processes led to alienation from the government and started to foster among Basotho an even more negative view of politics and politicians. Moeketsi Lesitsi, despite being a staunch government supporter, characterized politics and the government in the post-1970 period as being "very dirty" and "ungodly."[128] Lesitsi was the same man who noted that it was only after 1970 that he came to understand independence. Thus he embodies the double-edged effects of development in the postcoup period. At the same time that development was opening eyes to the potential benefits of independence, the government was deploying it actively to build barriers to meaningful popular participation in government projects. The government's primary aim was to project state power into the rural areas.

The postcoup government was, through deliberate and inadvertent actions, setting the stage for the "anti-politics" machine era of development projects that was in full effect by the mid- to late 1970s. For Basotho, perhaps the ultimate irony of development efforts was the way that larger development projects focusing on agriculture forced local people and the government to relinquish control of decisions about land allocation and use. The issue of sovereignty over the land had been central to Basotho national imaginings since the era of Moshoeshoe. Losing control of these processes of land allocation, to be clear, while written into the contracts of formal development projects, was not simply the result of international funding agencies foisting agenda-driven projects onto poor, powerless Lesotho. It was also the logical result of a series of administrative and political decisions, in large part driven by public pressure, stretching from the late colonial period into the independence era that positioned the idea of development as the single most important national priority throughout Lesotho.

James Ferguson's inability to find the Lesotho government's explicit intention to build bureaucratic state power through development in the post-1975 period is not surprising, as its roots lay much earlier.[129] By the time Ferguson encountered the Thaba Tseka project, questions about whether development should be encouraged at all cost had already been settled in Lesotho's politics for at least half a decade. The "anti-politics machine" emerged in its fully fleshed form starting in 1975, but it was constructed out of the 1950s and 1960s rhetorical consensus on development, the efforts of colonial and independence-era governments to control, centralize, and utilize development to promote their own political agendas in the 1960s, and the authoritarian turn of the Lesotho government during the early years of the 1970s.

CHAPTER 5

Authoritarianism, Aid, and the Anti-Politics Machine, 1970–1975

After the coup, Lesotho's foreign relations played an increasingly important role in determining how much development aid the country received. The Jonathan government was increasingly able to solicit and receive aid for large development projects. This was, in part, due to shifting aid policies at the international level that favored the world's poorest countries, a category for which Lesotho qualified. The increase in aid funds, though, was also a result of Lesotho's 1972 shift away from the apartheid regime and the changes the BNP government implemented in terms of bolstering the government's internal planning capacity. The authoritarian turn allowed the government to consolidate political control and run development projects as a means of entrenching the scope and reach of its power in the country.[1]

The early 1970s were a time of great transition in Lesotho: from democracy to authoritarianism and from small development projects to large ones. Even with development increasingly serving as the backbone of state control over rural areas, the increase in the number and scope of development efforts in Lesotho heartened many Basotho. Those who did not agree with the scale or scope of particular projects, however, had few opportunities to meaningfully express their views. Development projects in

Lesotho did not provide better economic opportunities, more government services, or increased public input into governance for many Basotho, and disillusionment increased. The development projects and political spaces that opened in the 1970s, though, offered the chance for Basotho to help bring about part, if not all, of their visions for a better life.

Meanwhile, the arrival of the first large-scale projects, with the earliest and most significant being the IDA- and USAID-funded Thaba Bosiu Rural Development Scheme, helped entrench the powers of the government. This newfound power and increased reliance on foreign funding sources rather than a popular mandate to govern made projects less amenable to input from local people at the same time that development efforts continued to bolster Basotho hopes in the ability of future development to improve their condition. The irony of these simultaneous processes is that neither was dependent on the projects meeting their stated objectives and goals, which meant that projects continued to "fail" to meet their stated objectives with regularity.

While support for the BNP government in the postcoup period was relatively weak, the development projects that it brought to the country contributed to a sense that progress was being made toward a desired vision for independence. The continued presence of the apartheid regime next door and the ability of development projects to fulfill some of the expectations of independence helped individuals keep a Havelian hope alive. Many Basotho had to compromise and change the goals they initially had for independence, but in finding their dreams and aspirations partially fulfilled, Basotho continued to strive for the full attainment of their goals despite bleak political conditions in Lesotho and South Africa.

SHIFTING SOUTH AFRICAN POLICY AND THE NEW DEVELOPMENT REGIME IN LESOTHO

Jonathan's move away from South Africa in the early 1970s was a calculated risk. Some of the danger was mitigated in the postcoup period by the rapidity with which negotiations with the United States, in particular, on the Thaba Bosiu Scheme progressed. Increased connections between the Lesotho government and international organizations like the World Bank and agencies of the United Nations also played important roles in giving Jonathan confidence that enough financial assistance was on its way to Lesotho for him to be able to cut ties with the apartheid regime.

As events showed, Jonathan's turn toward sources of development funding other than South Africa paid off. Throughout the 1970s, funds for development poured in as never before. Yet the risk in turning away from South Africa was quite real at the time Jonathan had to make it, as his speech on the occasion of the sixth anniversary of independence in October 1972 noted: "It is difficult to tolerate being discriminated against when you yourself discriminate against nobody. Peaceful coexistence is a two-way traffic and the key to cooperation and good neighborliness. If it is one-sided, it is no longer coexistence."[2] This bold change in foreign policy made it even more crucial for the BNP government to identify, solicit, and obtain new and continuing sources of aid for development since the diplomatic rupture scuttled talks on what was supposed to be the government's showpiece development scheme: the water project.

In the early 1970s, Jonathan and the BNP government continued to deploy the rhetoric of development much as they had in the pre-coup era. Without formal political opposition the rhetoric was aimed at building national unity and a common national purpose, especially among young Basotho. In December 1971, at the opening of a new Mathematics and Science Center in Maseru, Jonathan personally challenged Basotho students to "spearhead developmental regiments in all spheres of growth from road construction to tree planting. I want every school to implement at least one development project within their village as a contribution to nation-building."[3] Even with many young Basotho skeptical of the BNP regime, or cynical about its motivations, the continued use of such rhetoric helped maintain the power of the rhetorical consensus on development.

The Lesotho government's shift in policy on South Africa in 1971–72 was abrupt and surprising to most Basotho since engagement with South Africa had played a pivotal role in the BNP's 1965 and 1970 electoral campaigns. Many BNP supporters were undoubtedly surprised because of the party's long-held promise that South Africa would come through with significant development assistance for the government. It was also surprising because of the degree to which South African funding undergirded Lesotho's security forces and, thus, the BNP's hold on power.

During 1970 and the first half of 1971, relations between Lesotho and South Africa showed few signs of change. As late as July 9, 1971, a high-level meeting between cabinet members from both countries discussed whether Lesotho should open its anticipated consular office in Johannesburg or Pretoria, and South African officials wanted to know if "it would embarrass the Lesotho authorities if South Africa were now to purchase land in Maseru for a consular residence and whether building was better than buying." Lesotho officials assured the South Africans that while there was a shortage of suitable property available in the central city, they "would of course be happy to help in the matter" of finding and arranging for the purchase of land.[4]

Thus it was surprising when, in his October 1971 Independence Day speech in Maseru, Jonathan abruptly shifted the position of the Lesotho government by calling on South Africa to engage with other African states and South African liberation groups through a framework called the Lusaka Manifesto.[5] The manifesto was written by the Conference of East and Central African States in 1969 and adopted by the OAU, an organization with which Jonathan had a rocky relationship because of his policy of engagement with South Africa. The Lusaka Manifesto called for African governments to engage in dialogue with the apartheid regime as long as South Africa recognized the liberation groups as legitimate political opposition and committed to protecting human rights.[6] Jonathan's stance advocating for the terms of the Lusaka Manifesto was significant because it signaled his desire to engage more with the other independent states of Africa while also suggesting that he was moving away from Lesotho's prior, unconditional close ties to the regime.

Jonathan shifted the Lesotho government's South African policy for a number of reasons, but it was not a coincidence that the changes occurred in concert with what looked to be significant increases in the ability of the government to garner development funding from other foreign sources. It was in August 1971 that the prospects for significant new funding and new programs from the UNDP, the International Labour Organization (ILO), the International Bank for Reconstruction and Development (IBRD, an arm of the World Bank), and USAID came into focus.

It was the cumulative effect of promises made by all these organizations that gave Jonathan confidence. In October 1970, the United States told Jonathan it was planning to double aid to Lesotho, from $115,000 to $230,000, in the 1971 fiscal year because Lesotho represented a place to "display our oft-expressed interest in the viability of a Black African nonracial country in contrast to apartheid-dominated South Africa."[7] On August 9, 1971, ILO officials promised to help the Lesotho government with "experts in Labor Statistics and Manpower planning, cooperatives, small scale industries, [and] experts to help expand Lerotholi [Technical School]." It was the work of the UNDP envoy to Lesotho that brought the ILO officials to Maseru as part of their publication and formalization of "Country Programme, 1972–1976" to guide and prioritize international funding for Lesotho's development projects.[8] In September 1971, the resident UNDP representative also promised that a team from the IBRD would arrive by March 1972 "solely to assist the Government of Lesotho prepare in final form request for [the USAID-sponsored Thaba Bosiu] Agricultural project."[9]

Flush with the knowledge that international funding from non–South African sources was secure and imminent, the Jonathan regime could embark on a foreign policy that was more independent of South Africa. This included being more assertive in talks about the water project with the South African authorities. In 1971, a British consulting firm contracted by the UNDP completed a $2.7 million feasibility study of the project, and in the same year the Lesotho government requested that the World Bank "finance the final design stage."[10] South Africa did not want either organization involved with the water project. As early as August 1969, Prime Minister Vorster's top aide, Albie Burger, wrote to Prime Minister Jonathan to register the South African cabinet's disapproval of the involvement of both organizations. Burger noted that the United Nations had a "political vendetta against [Vorster's] Government" and that South African officials were suspicious of the political motivations of World Bank officials, fearing they were actively working to undermine the apartheid state.[11]

Prime Minister Jonathan's responses in the early 1970s differed markedly from those in the pre-coup period. In 1969, he had responded to criticisms with an apologetic tone, saying, "In our present financial and economic circumstances, we cannot expect to approach a project of this magnitude as completely free agents."[12] By 1972, the timidity was gone. Jonathan's government contacted the South African secretary for water affairs in March 1972, demanding a higher price for the water from the highlands scheme, using these funding agencies as cover. Jonathan noted that a return of R1 million ($1.34 million) on an investment of R75 million to R90 million ($100 million to $120 million) "would not be considered as adequate, either by the World Bank or any other bilateral or multilateral aid agencies which might consider providing funds to Lesotho for this project." He then escalated the rhetoric even further, accusing South Africa of asking Lesotho to "subsidize South African consumers of water."[13] This new assertiveness from the Lesotho government led to the

suspension of talks in March and the full diplomatic rupture that Jonathan's militantly anti-apartheid Independence Day speech in October
1972 caused. Both countries broke off official talks on the water project in
November 1972.[14]

Jonathan was, in effect, declaring that the days of his government
simply accepting any deal on development assistance offered by the South
African government were over. This marked a new phase in his government's attitude toward development. However, the freedom to reject inadequate aid was a direct result of the authoritarian consolidation of power.
No longer beholden to electoral concerns and propped up by security
forces bolstered by the apartheid regime itself, the Lesotho government
could be more selective in accepting aid since the short-term political imperative of getting immediate aid into the country was gone.

By 1972, the South African government had amply demonstrated to
Jonathan that it was interested only in helping him in such a way that Lesotho's development did not threaten the economic foundations of South
Africa. The South Africans had used their economic clout with major
multinational corporations to scuttle efforts to set up a Honda engine
manufacturing plant, an Italian shoe factory, and a West German televi-
sion factory in Lesotho by threatening the companies with loss of access
to South African markets if plans went forward.[15] Further, South Africa
devalued the rand in 1971 without consulting the other members of the
Southern African Customs Union, making the Jonathan government,
among others, feel impotent in its economic relations with South Africa.[16]
Added up, the ability to draw foreign funding in significant quantities, the
lack of direct funding from South Africa for development since independence, and the discomfort resulting from South African interference in
Lesotho's economy allowed Jonathan and the BNP regime by 1972 to feel
confident that it could at least survive, and perhaps even thrive, without
the support of Pretoria.

The diplomatic reaction of African states to Jonathan's shift on South
Africa was immediate and beneficial. In November 1972, a mere month
after Jonathan's Independence Day speech, Tanzania established formal
ties with Lesotho. Previously, Tanzania, like most African states, had shied
away from the country, seeing it as a puppet of the apartheid regime, little
better than the Bantustans. Almost immediately the imprimatur of President Nyerere's recognition paved the way for Lesotho to improve relations
with the OAU, as well as with Uganda, Swaziland, Rwanda, and Botswana.
Beyond the continent, Lesotho made more direct overtures to Israel and

established diplomatic links with Yugoslavia in February 1973.[17] These first tentative diplomatic relationships with the wider world were characterized at first by Jonathan's affinity for states in the Non-Aligned Movement. The success of these diplomatic ventures, and the very real possibility of obtaining significant quantities of aid from new sources, led the government by the late 1970s and early 1980s to throw all caution to the wind and establish full ties with East Germany, North Korea, and other communist states. These shifting policies, most of which are beyond the scope of this work, serve primarily as examples of how the imperative to secure development funding caused the Jonathan government to greatly broaden the diplomatic ties of the Lesotho government in the first decade of independence. Through the early and mid-1970s, however, the vast majority of Lesotho's development aid was still coming from Western sources like the United States, West Germany, Sweden, Denmark, Canada, and the United Kingdom.[18]

Of these, the continued support of the United Kingdom and the new sources of support from the United States were the most important for the Lesotho government. The vulnerability of the Jonathan government to a single donor in 1970 made top governmental officials wary of relying on a single funder, who then would be able to exert disproportionate control over domestic politics, policies, and projects. Aid missions from multiple countries and the opening of offices by various UN agencies in Maseru also confirmed the sovereignty of the Lesotho government. The various flags, new construction, and the presence of expatriate diplomats and technical experts were tangible reminders that life after colonialism and free from apartheid held the promise of real benefit for all Basotho.

In this period when American development aid to Lesotho increased, it was only partially about what the Lesotho government was doing: the logic of the international aid system also drove the uptick in assistance. Social comparison loomed large for some bureaucrats. USAID officials in 1972 noted that they "felt guilty" about not having yet funded a "capital project" in Lesotho, as they had in similar places like Botswana.[19] This fit in the context of U.S. policy during the presidency of Richard Nixon to continue to support independent states near South Africa as a way of demonstrating American commitment to racial equality and self-determination.[20] The American desire to support the Lesotho regime, however, also had Cold War implications. The Americans saw Lesotho as a bastion against communism because of Jonathan's hard line. Finally, but certainly not of least importance, was the ease with which the Americans could render assistance to Lesotho and reap a diplomatic reward. Lesotho, as a policy paper noted, was a place where "a small input of economic assistance . . . would reap returns far out of proportion to the actual cost and demonstrate tangibly our commitment to the development of stable African states which maintain the principle of racial equality."[21]

As further evidence of its commitment to the region, in June 1971, the United States upgraded diplomatic representation to Lesotho, Botswana, and Swaziland, jointly appointing Charles Nelson ambassador to all three countries. A career State Department official, Nelson's main experience was with USAID. The appointment highlighted the U.S. diplomatic strategy for the region: gain Cold War allies by providing aid for development.[22] Lesotho was also assisted by the U.S. Congress, which lifted USAID restrictions on starting new bilateral aid programs.[23]

For the Lesotho government, the promise of increased funding for development and the removal of electoral concerns meant that officials could better use aid and development for their own political purposes. This did not mean that contestations over aid were eliminated. Rather, they occurred within government ranks instead of between political parties. After purging the civil service, the BNP government struggled to implement projects since many of the best-educated civil servants either left or were forced out. The break with South Africa also meant that the government lost many of its top-level administrators who headed government offices like the High Court and the Department of Public Works. Infighting was rampant between various departments and the nascent Central Planning and Development Office (CPDO), which reported directly to the prime minister until 1970 and after 1970 to the minister of finance. The CPDO was, in theory, supposed to coordinate all aid for development, but ministries were loath to give up to the CPDO the power to solicit and disburse funds.[24]

The dysfunction within the civil service and the lack of trained local personnel with suitable political views meant that the government relied on short-term project managers from funding agencies and outside consultants. The decision to rely on outside experts was another outgrowth of Jonathan's efforts to place development beyond the reach of the political process, or at least beyond the reach of politics that did not align with BNP goals. Using outside consultants allowed the Jonathan government to start the process of depoliticization in the early 1970s. This was done in direct response to the fierce opposition that BCP and MFP politicians and supporters had mounted in the late 1960s to government development efforts.[25] The depoliticization of development and the push to rely almost solely on technocratic advice for project planning and implementation meant that the route to political legitimacy lay simply in project delivery rather than in the delivery of "successful" projects, as defined by local people and communities. For this, however, the continued ability of the government to secure funding from abroad to ensure project arrival and implementation was vital.

Debates over development funding and project implementation were fierce in the early 1970s, but they took place mainly within BNP government circles because of the authoritarian crackdown and the ban on political activity. During Jonathan's July 1972 trip to Denmark to solicit aid for Lesotho's dairy industry, he asked the Danish government to help him reduce dependence on South African assistance. On the one hand, it was a shrewd strategy as the Danes were early vocal critics of apartheid. On the other hand, the connection between anti-apartheid activism and the Danish government led by the left-leaning Social Democratic Party caused some in the BNP to worry that Jonathan was moving the party away from its strong anticommunist stance.[26] The split with South Africa led Anthony Clovis Manyeli, minister of education, to resign from the cabinet. Manyeli went on to start his own political party in 1975, the National Independent Party. While Manyeli was the only minister to resign in 1972, the most vocal anticommunist, conservative Roman Catholic faction of the party was not pleased with the South Africa split, or with the recognition of communist Yugoslavia that followed in 1973.

Undergirding Jonathan's ability to make the split with South Africa and buck the most conservative members of his cabinet was the advanced stage of negotiations with the United States and the IDA over the Thaba Bosiu Rural Development Scheme. While the Leribe Pilot Project, funded by the FAO, was already in operation in 1971, it was the promise of massive U.S. and World Bank aid that gave Jonathan the confidence to remake his country's foreign relations. A detailed examination of this particular project is, therefore, particularly germane.

AGRICULTURAL PROJECTS: THE THABA BOSIU RURAL DEVELOPMENT SCHEME

The idea of "improving" agriculture in order to enhance food security for rural Basotho, reduce national dependency on food imports, curb soil erosion, and boost exports of agricultural products as a means of raising rural household incomes was as old as the idea of development in Lesotho. Colonial-era projects had all shared these same goals, and had also aimed to reform the land tenure system. A shortage of arable land in Lesotho from the early twentieth century left most farmers either without enough land to support families or with multiple noncontiguous fields. A series of small fields often discouraged farmers from pursuing strategies like mechanization. Thus funding agencies made the consolidation of holdings central to independence-era projects like Thaba Bosiu. This seemingly simple technocratic solution was in practice much more difficult because land allocation was a highly complex and emotional issue. Consolidation meant that people had to be asked or forced to give up land their families had farmed in some cases for generations.

Despite the storied history of agricultural project failure in Lesotho, donors in the 1970s remained enamored with the idea of such schemes because there were seemingly no suitable large-scale development alternatives in the country. The stronger motivation for such projects, however, was a firm belief that technocratic and technological solutions could yet be found to make Lesotho's rural agriculture profitable. World Bank planners thought that the biggest impediment to agricultural projects was the resistance of Basotho farmers. Colonial planners would have recognized the World Bank appraisal from 1973 for the Thaba Bosiu Scheme that blamed Basotho farmers for their own poverty since "traditional land use and cultural habits inhibit change."[27]

Despite starting the project with this rather dismal outlook or, read alternatively, a naive optimism that the project could rapidly change "cultural habits," the discussions, planning, and project funding for the Thaba Bosiu Scheme came together relatively quickly from August 1970 to late 1972. This was because all the main actors—the IDA, the Lesotho government, and USAID—had compelling, though not always overlapping, motivations to get the program up and running quickly. For the IDA, World Bank president Robert McNamara set the goal of doubling loans to the Least Developed Countries in the five years after 1968, and the Lesotho project nicely met this remit. Therefore, the IDA eagerly plunged ahead with the project despite its expressed worries about Basotho buy-in and participation. The Lesotho government was eager, bordering on desperate, to have a major project funded by IDA and USAID, as discussed above. Finally, USAID officials had been endeavoring to expand their operations into Lesotho since at least 1970. Thus, even before Lesotho officials signed the final agreement on Thaba Bosiu, USAID officials in Washington in mid-1972 signaled their commitment to the future project by allocating an initial $1 million in support.[28]

The planners relied not just on prior development schemes in Lesotho as models, but they also looked at similar agricultural development projects in South Africa and the southern African region. The Thaba Bosiu Scheme was, in addition to being modeled on colonial-era projects in Lesotho like the Taung Scheme, strikingly similar to the "Betterment Schemes" South Africa ran in the nearby Transkei and Ciskei from the 1930s to the 1970s. These development continuities were not coincidences, as many former colonial officials made career moves to the staffs of the big international development agencies at independence.[29] The USAID and IDA planners working on the Thaba Bosiu Scheme specifically modeled their Lesotho efforts on the Lilongwe Project already in operation in Malawi. This project, funded by the same mix of USAID and IDA funds, was designed to invigorate local agriculture in ways similar to Thaba Bosiu.[30]

With $2.8 million in USAID grants and $5.6 million in IDA loans funding the project, the Thaba Bosiu Scheme was at the time of its inception the largest and most expensive the country had ever seen. Thaba Bosiu included credit provisions for farmers to purchase new "Green Revolution" hybrid seeds and fertilizers as well as stud bulls and sheep to improve the breeding stock. The project allowed the government to hire more agricultural extension officers to teach farmers new practices, build more connector roads from villages to the existent road system, and improve the marketing of local agricultural products. The project was designed to serve 12,000 households in 490 villages across an expanse of 121,000 hectares in the fertile lowland Maseru and Berea Districts, encompassing the entire drainage of the Phutiatsana River south and west of the capital, Maseru.[31]

From the inception of the project in the southern hemisphere winter of 1973, it was striking how little of the money went directly to farmers. The project was not a coordinated effort to provide direct assistance to rural Basotho farmers. Rather, it was a massive loan (repayable over fifteen years) from the IDA to the government of Lesotho to support an expansion of the civil service and its related infrastructure in the rural areas around Maseru. The loan designated $850,000 for fertilizers, seeds, and breeding animals, but this was less than the $950,000 budget for the salaries and travel of expatriate staff. A further $300,000 went to purchase vehicles, along with $1.6 million for local staff salaries and "project operations." Finally, a line item of $1 million was earmarked for "Civil Works." This included a sum designated for local road building, but the majority of the funds was earmarked for building offices and staff housing in Masianokeng, a small town about fifteen kilometers from Maseru that served as project headquarters.[32] Thus, the majority of the project money went to financing physical infrastructure primarily used by civil servants that undergirded the ability of the government to build a new network of politically trustworthy local and expatriate civil servants who owed their jobs not to meeting metrics of project success but simply to the continued operation of the project.

The project met the needs of all its partners, which, tellingly, did not include local communities. By 1975, the project employed 128 local staff members and twenty-two expatriates, with most of the latter occupying politically sensitive senior administrative positions in the technical departments.[33] This influx of personnel with ties to the Jonathan government depoliticized the project as administrators focused primarily on ensuring that the project hit benchmarks set by funding agencies, regardless of how these marks comported with local needs. The IDA could claim it was fulfilling its remit to help Basotho farmers produce for the regional and global agricultural market by pointing to the number of roads built and marketing campaigns created. USAID could claim successful assistance in an IDA project in one of the world's poorest countries, one that had never previously received a major USAID project. Strikingly, none of these metrics focused on direct poverty alleviation, so while the project never substantially raised rural incomes, institutionally it was a success.

A major goal of the Thaba Bosiu Scheme was to create local governance structures to complement the centralization the government had enacted. USAID's early planning documents from 1971 and 1972 noted that colonial development schemes failed because they did not center development on people: "Their participation and involvement in solutions and decision making . . . [were] not as a partnership between the people and their government for the benefit of the community."[34] By the time the project came to fruition, however, the Lesotho government, USAID, and the IDA had largely agreed to ignore this insight in favor of a model of community consultation that sought less a two-way conversation between communities and government officials than a venue for government officials to communicate project information to communities. In early 1973, the final IDA report prior to the release of funds noted that the project involved creating by statute a new body, the Thaba Bosiu Rural Development Authority, which "would be free from normal government regulations with respect to staff selection, salary scales, procurement and accounting principles" under the control of a project manager.[35]

This independence from the civil service, and the free hand it gave the government to consolidate authority in rural areas, was power the BNP government had sought as far back as 1965 when it first proposed the abolition of district councils. It was only with the advent of authoritarian rule and large-scale development efforts that the BNP government was able to see the goal come to fruition. In a nod to representative government and concerns expressed by USAID and other partners, the BNP proposed a series of development and advisory land distribution committees that could theoretically function as responsive bodies of local government at the village level, but in practice these boards became extensions of the party's structure.[36] The creation of these new administrative structures as a part of the Thaba Bosiu Scheme demonstrates the manner in which the BNP co-opted development projects to buttress its rule and consolidate rural authority during the 1970s.

Thaba Bosiu became the model for other large area-based agricultural projects in Lesotho in the 1970s. The visibility of Lesotho's rural poverty and the belief that small-scale agriculture represented the only viable economic strategy that could have an impact on large numbers of Basotho made agricultural projects popular with donors. While Thaba Bosiu was the first comprehensive project running at a large scale, a smaller initiative, the Leribe Pilot Project, ran from 1970 to 1975. Funded by UNDP and FAO, this project had similar goals but focused on a smaller area, and its project fields were noncontiguous. At the conclusion of its funding in 1975, the Lesotho government convinced the Swedish International Development Cooperation Agency (SIDA) and FAO to expand the geographical area and continue the work of the project. The Khomokhoana Rural Development Project, which ran from 1975 to 1980, eventually came to encompass 26,000 hectares primarily in the Leribe District. In the southern mountains, UNDP and FAO also collaborated to fund the Senqu River Agricultural Extension Project. Running from 1974 to 1977 and covering 140,000 hectares split into seven blocks, this project focused largely on providing better extension services to rural farmers.[37] Finally, the Thaba Tseka Mountain Development Project, funded primarily by the Canadian International Development Agency from 1975 to 1984, took the area-based agricultural project model to its logical bureaucratic conclusion. The project aimed to create a tenth government administrative district in the central mountains, and it brought into existence a full complement of government agency offices and services in the newly designated district headquarters town of Thaba Tseka.[38]

The Thaba Bosiu Scheme was especially important because it was close to Maseru, allowing it to be a showcase project for the government. USAID administrators noted in February 1973, prior to the official launch of the project, that it had "fervent support" from top administration officials in Maseru who had already "publicized the project extensively."[39] In addition, the project was located in an area that tended to strongly support the opposition, although the headquarters was located in a town right next to a major Roman Catholic mission. The BNP government hoped to neutralize opposition support with a combination of economic development and increased government authority.

By October 1972, the month in which Jonathan first clearly signaled his intention to radically rethink the Lesotho government's relations with the South African regime, project planning for the Thaba Bosiu Scheme was nearing completion. But delays that month in the finalization of the paperwork for the project were causing "concern to a number of people" in Maseru, according to American aid officials.[40] The documents were finally signed, but the worries of top government officials suggest the degree to which officials understood that the government's popularity was contingent on this and similar projects.

Though the Thaba Bosiu Scheme started only in 1973, barely a year later, in August 1974, the project's USAID evaluators were already concluding that it would miss its poverty alleviation goals. In their estimation, it was a "top-down operation in the sense that it has not made an effort to understand local situations and work through local institutions. . . . [T]he staff's philosophy is that good ideas will sell themselves."[41] The report acknowledged that this was not good practice, but the authors justified it by echoing colonial claims about Basotho resistance to development. They argued that Lesotho was a place "where it is not easy to promote an idea that will make things markedly better." On account of this supposed resistance, "only marginal changes for the better are possible" in the remaining four years of project funding.[42]

Blaming this specific failure on the local population seems like a rather calculated and cynical ploy to deflect responsibility from where it belongs: the alleviation of poverty was not a central objective of the project design. Jerome French, another USAID official writing in 1975, noted that he "doubt[ed] that the Project will have much of an impact on development within the area beyond the period of its own life cycle."[43] A couple of months later, a further USAID assessment—all, of course, paid for from project funds—admitted that the entrenchment of state power in the rural areas, the ability of the government to "reach and influence rural people to accept change," was the only result from the project that would outlast the funding.[44]

Basotho who lived in the project area were under no illusions that project failure was their fault, and they did not like the government giving over increased powers to project administrators. Even before the project began, local people anticipated that the project would serve primarily to strengthen government authority and control while having little impact on income or farming practices. A 1972 petition to project planners and officials from a group of residents who called themselves the Prominent Citizens Committee outlined the local objections. In addition to a detailed look at the specific grievances, the document nicely highlights the way in which people in rural Lesotho in the early 1970s viewed the concept of development. It provides evidence of just how badly project planners, local and overseas, misread the attitudes of rural Basotho to development and independence.

The petition was notable for its expressed support of the Lesotho government, particularly because it came from communities that largely supported the opposition. It was written in perfect English, suggesting that the authors were well educated and therefore that most of the members of the Prominent Citizens Committee were opposition supporters. The arguments they made suggest that despite the repressive measures taken by the BNP government, the petitioners still held to the belief that an efficient and effective national government—the dream of independence—was in their individual and collective interest. This belief in the potential efficacy of both government and development in general to improve life outcomes for Basotho flew in the face of assumptions made by non-Basotho planners. An anonymous USAID official noted in 1974 that "political divisions" hindered the project but did not expand on how these divisions were affecting the project.[45] However, a simplistic view from an outside consultant that dismissed project criticism as simply "politics" ignored the long history of contestation over development projects in Lesotho and the degree to which Basotho of all political persuasions supported the idea of "development."

It is worth quoting at length from the petition since this was a critical juncture when the first large-scale aid project arrived. The Prominent Citizens Committee remained anonymous, likely in an attempt to lessen the chance of retaliation by project and government personnel. Committee members also ran the risk of being accused of participating in a political act, an action banned under Jonathan's five-year politics "holiday." The petition started with the claim that the Thaba Bosiu project would have "disastrous effects on the Government of Lesotho" and continued:

> To give the project autonomy without the necessary safeguards would empower persons unversed with or opposed to the political policies of the Government, to embark on policies diametrically opposed to established policies in such fields as employment, Credit, Marketing and general execution. . . . A proper safeguard would be for Government to appoint the project manager and add to the proposed members of the project committee prominent citizens and representatives of the cooperatives and farmers' associations in the project area. This committee would have overall responsibility in the execution of the project. Only then could the project be given autonomy.[46]

Their ideas for local input would have allowed more Basotho at the grassroots to have a say in how and when farming inputs would be most useful to people in the project area. Proposing a consultative committee harkened back to the cooperative structures of *kopanos*, like the one in Mazenod ha Paki, a village that was on the edge of the project area. Of course, the committee members had the chance to benefit directly from the changes to the project they were proposing, but this should not detract from the legitimate criticism they leveled at the lack of local representation in project structures.

The Prominent Citizens Committee also criticized the financial provisions of the project for not prioritizing inputs going straight to local farmers and communities. They noted that only 18 percent of the total project budget went to direct farm assistance, with a further 6 percent allocated to provide credit to farmers. The petitioners contrasted this unfavorably with the 20 percent allocated to administration and 13 percent to roads. They asked the project planners to add more direct support to farmers by cutting the allocation for the construction of houses for administrators in Masianokeng. They also thought the "fantastically inflated salaries" of top Basotho and expatriate officials should be cut. Reappropriating more funds to farmers better "suited the needs and aspirations of the farming community in the order of priorities."[47]

In an effort to win support from Lesotho government officials, the petitioners made explicit appeals to the idea of a Basotho national community. They asked why the project headquarters were not located at King Moshoeshoe's mountain, Thaba Bosiu, for which the project was named. They argued that in addition to the deep symbolism of centering the project in the "cradle of the Basotho nation," the mountain was arguably closer to more lands under project jurisdiction.[48] Similarly, they drew on the common national sentiment of resistance to South African economic dominance when they asked whether the centralized marketing of the project (to be carried out through the South African Maize Board, an arm of the apartheid government) was going to be "exploitative" of both Basotho farmers and the Lesotho government since they were outsourcing control over this aspect of the project.

Tying together their strands of criticism, the petitioners warned that the scheme threatened to undermine the legitimacy of the Lesotho government in the eyes of rural Basotho farmers. Those who took out loans and ended up in debt might have their land confiscated by creditors—an unprecedented alienation of land within Lesotho.

> Who among our people would still feel well disposed towards the BNP Government if farmers were deprived of their sole means of livelihood including land as a result of the application of the severe penalties it is proposed be inflicted on the so-called delinquent borrowers by their own government and this be seen as a safe security of loans? The proposed marketing system is so exploitory [*sic*] that it is made absolutely impossible for farmers to ever manage to repay their loans, let alone ridiculing our Government in the eyes of the world?[49]

Emphasizing control of and access to land as being key to the economic self-sufficiency of rural households, the petitioners co-opted the government's language of development and played on BNP government insecurities in terms of how little development it had so far delivered in an effort to win support for more local project control. Throughout, the petitioners argued that the project was administratively top-heavy, lacked useful structures for getting local participation, offered little chance to incorporate local expertise, and generally needed to focus more on direct supports for farmers.

The strongest language in the petition linked these 1970s activists with the earlier rhetorical consensus on development. The petitioners wanted the project to "not only ensure improved agricultural production and marketing but also enhance and safeguard the interests of the farming communities and the Lesotho government."[50] They quite clearly spelled out their enthusiasm for this particular project, which is striking because, as already seen, their anger about the lack of local consultation was also present. The linkage of development outcomes with successful local communities and the power of the national government also hearkens back to the three-part vision for what many Basotho hoped development could bring at independence. Finally, the optimism implicit in the writing of the petition, especially in the face of an authoritarian crackdown, suggests that these particular Basotho were maintaining faith in development in the face of what they considered less-than-ideal local conditions.

The petitioners did not go completely unheard, though the international funding agencies ignored the bulk of their concerns. USAID planners did ask project personnel to hold more meetings with local communities during the late planning phases and early stages of project implementation. Athol Ellis, director of the USAID office for southern Africa, asked the IDA to investigate the technical claims made by the Prominent Citizens Committee.[51] Ellis, however, casually dismissed most of the complaints even as he passed along this recommendation, discrediting the petitioners because they were "members of the opposition party."[52] This comment shows that Ellis was at least cognizant of how politicized development had been in early independence Lesotho, but the petition was more striking for how substantially pro-government it was. Perhaps the pro-government message was merely a ploy to increase the petition's chances of falling on friendly ears, but such a cynical reading ignores how deeply Basotho, especially those involved in politics, had personally internalized the rhetoric of development and its connection to independence.

Much to the dismay, we can be sure, of the ignored petitioners, the Thaba Bosiu Scheme took the forms that they predicted. Outside experts and government civil servants entrenched themselves in new houses purpose-built in Masianokeng. The loan money from the World Bank financed a few roads and these houses and paid the salaries of Lesotho government employees, local and expatriate, for the five years of project operation, while Basotho citizen-farmers were left with the long-term tax bill. The project entrenched government representatives in the rural lowlands around Thaba Bosiu and Masianokeng and allowed the Lesotho government to further solicit development funds from abroad based on the perception of competency built by its ability to manage and complete such a large project.

CONTINUED SMALL PROJECTS

To some extent, the coup of 1970 and resulting authoritarian turn by the government dimmed some of the heady optimism of the late colonial and early independence periods. The sentiment that replaced this optimism included resignation in the face of political intransigence, but it also included a hopeful sense that finding personal, professional, and communal satisfaction was still possible, even if individual views and aspirations needed to be redefined for the postcoup era. In part, younger Basotho fueled their sense of hope by broadening the groups in which they claimed membership and their collective identities: the Basotho nation, the state of Lesotho, a Pan-African outlook, participants in the struggle against apartheid. But just as in the early independence period, young Basotho also nurtured faith in development by participating in and helping shape smaller community-based projects bringing incremental progress. They also found spaces within the larger development regime where they could personally benefit from the new conditions.

While the focus of the BNP government dramatically shifted to securing and administering large projects, the smaller community development projects of the early independence period continued. The BNP government in 1965–70 desired to bring development projects into a coherent program guided by the central government to ensure that these efforts resulted in desired political outcomes. The BNP loss in the 1970 elections underscored the party's failure to do so during that time period, but the BNP did a much better job of this by the early 1970s.

In 1971, the Lesotho government published its development plan in a booklet titled *The Development of Growth Centres in Lesotho* that spelled out the new coordinated strategy of community development the government hoped to deploy. The report identified five "primary centres," Maseru, Leribe, Mohale's Hoek, Mokhotlong, and Qacha's Nek; eleven "secondary centres," including the rest of the district capitals, Morija/Matsieng, Roma, Mapoteng, and Marakabei, among others; and thirty-five "tertiary centers" that included larger villages in the lowlands, foothills, and mountain regions around which development focused.[53] This did not supersede the ability of departments to organize and carry out projects outside these centers, but it did focus efforts: "Development at the village level (such as small village water schemes) will still of course continue, but priority will be given to providing services for the 'growth centres' which will serve the ward or other area in which they are situated." The government envisioned that the Department of Community Development would work primarily in the tertiary centers, while the "Ministries of Works and other professional ministries" would work in the larger centers. The hope was to coordinate these new divisions

> to ensure that development in the rural areas in particular is not as at present *haphazard and un-coordinated* but is channeled into selected 'growth centres' where the Department of Community Development will endeavor to provide, in conjunction with the Ministry of Works, water systems and other community services formerly provided by the now defunct District Councils. The community services must *not* be forced upon people but must be put in through the self-help scheme if the real needs of the people are to be properly met.[54]

The smaller projects did not attract as much new support or attention as the large area-based agricultural projects in the early 1970s, but they did see an increase in funding. Water projects had garnered $22,000 in U.S. support and R34,230 ($47,922) in Lesotho government support in 1968–69.[55] By 1971, the Lesotho government was budgeting R75,000 ($105,000) for pipes and materials and an additional R8,000 ($11,200) for building materials that helped complete fifty-two village water projects (fig. 5.1).[56] U.S. contributions to water projects increased substantially as well: $75,000 by the early 1970s and $114,000 by 1974. Most of the money was earmarked "to support water projects."[57]

The increased American money also went to a wider variety of small development projects run by the Lesotho government with various inter-

Figure 5.1 "Matheson, Alastair. Woman carrying irrigation pipe, ca. 1971." Africa America Institute Records (MS 849). Special Collections and University Archives, University of Massachusetts Amherst Libraries.

national partners. UNICEF helped support poultry cooperatives that were called Egg Circles, which helped supply school lunch programs (fig. 5.2). Peace Corps volunteer Noel Jackson, serving from 1969 to 1971, worked as an adviser to the Egg Circle groups. He reported they were popular because Basotho women could take initiative and play central roles in the groups. He helped arrange for the program to "import newborn chicks from South Africa," raise them for a few weeks, and then sell them to "the poultry farmers throughout the country."[58] This was a popular program, as evidenced by the 100,000 eggs that UNICEF gathered from the Egg Circles to distribute to schools in 1971.

The distribution of public works and development projects along political lines that was so prevalent in the 1960s continued unabated into the

Figure 5.2 "Matheson, Alastair. A woman egg producer at the Maseru Egg Circle waits, as clerk totes up payment due her. Every year about 100,000 eggs are given to schools as repayment of poultry equipment supplied by UNICEF, ca. 1971." Africa America Institute Records (MS 849). Special Collections and University Archives, University of Massachusetts Amherst Libraries.

1970s, so these benefits accrued unevenly across the country. Institutionally, Catholic missions had a particularly easy time gaining access to funds to expand their educational and social services. Sister Clara Rapholo recalled that the Jonathan government "started paying [for] more teachers" at Catholic St. Rodrigue Secondary School, where she was teaching, and then sometime in the 1970s she "went to the office of Leabua" to ask for money to build the mission's health clinic. She "just talked to the man there and we received about 20,000 rand to build it."[59] For those who were not Catholic, or BNP supporters, however, the entrenchment of autocratic power at the center meant that there were fewer opportunities to directly access state development projects.

Another program that favored those who supported the government was the Food-for-Work scheme. This program, in which the government "paid" volunteer laborers with food donations from abroad, played a key role for the Jonathan government. Food-for-Work focused primarily on the foothill and mountain residents whose support Jonathan and the BNP had largely lost in the 1970s elections. Catholics like Moeketsi Lesitsi remembered these programs as being "very popular" because people were working "preparing roads joining villages, working to contain soil erosion in dongas, making wells and other things like this."[60] By 1971, the program had constructed over four hundred miles of new roads in the mountains, including finally connecting the district headquarter towns of Qacha's Nek and Mokhotlong to the rest of the country (fig. 5.3). Residents and officials in these towns, as well as in many nearby villages, no longer had to fly or take a long, circuitous route through South Africa to reach the capital. Similarly, in the foothills, the program had constructed an additional eight hundred miles of new roads.[61]

By the early 1970s, the project was employing 6,625 volunteers a month on average. Each volunteer had to work a minimum of fifteen days

Figure 5.3 Rural Basotho working on self-help road construction, Mokhotlong District, late 1960s. Courtesy of Ted Nettelton, former district commissioner, Mokhotlong District.

in order to receive one hundred pounds of maize meal, twenty pounds of whole wheat flour, and two pounds of vegetable oil. As with the Egg Circle projects, the participants were mainly women—about 70 percent according to the former director's estimate.[62] While the assistance was provided primarily to villages that had supported the ruling party, the projects did important work by providing nutrition and sustenance to a hungry rural population subjected to the vagaries of Lesotho's often-dry weather.[63] They also gave many rural communities a taste of what development could do for their village in the short and long term—a taste of independence.

Like many of the other development programs, the visibility of the Food-for-Work program was as important to government officials as the tangible construction results (fig. 5.4). Officials made sure to distribute the food in its original bags, which came with large stamps reading, "Donated by the People of the United States of America," thereby making the point that Jonathan's engagement with the United States was paying dividends for ordinary Basotho that differed markedly from what had been on offer from the colonial regime. The contract for distributing the food went to Catholic Relief Services, a way of giving patronage opportunities to Jonathan's biggest political supporter, the Catholic Church.

The Lesotho Credit Union Scheme for Agriculture was another popular small rural development program that continued into the 1970s. Such programs had difficulty reaching all Basotho because of the absolute poverty of some residents, as one Peace Corps volunteer, Steve Goertz, recalled. Stationed in the poor, rural Mohale's Hoek District from 1969 to late 1970, he recalled that local people were not opposed to the idea of credit cooperatives to improve their farming practices, but many were "poor mountain people growing sorghum and raising a few animals. . . . [T]hey had a minimal amount of money, or none at all, to put into a credit union account."[64] Still, even under these conditions, the LECUSA branch that Goertz was sent to supervise operated among those who had a bit of cash to put into the cooperative. Those that operated in the northern lowlands in the relatively better watered areas in the Maseru and Mafeteng Districts, however, fared better.

LECUSA had started in 1968, and the first branches received extensive donations from abroad that included tractors, tillers, and planters, as well as funds for administrative support from the University of Botswana, Lesotho and Swaziland–based extension officers and planning personnel.

Figure 5.4 Delivery of food and material aid from the United States, no date. Courtesy of *Moeletsi oa Basotho*.

Funds came from a variety of governmental and nongovernmental orga-nizations, including OXFAM, USAID, the English Catholic Fund for Overseas Development, and the American Catholic Relief Services.[65] The tractor in each LECUSA branch was available for farmers to rent in order to plow their fields. The credit union was supposed to collect tractor fees and offer loans to finance "plowing, hybrid drought resistant seeds, fer-tilizer, and insecticide."[66]

There was, of course, a colonial history of projects using similar stra-tegies to improve plowing and planting, but the addition of university extension officers and Peace Corps volunteers was new. These individuals utilized the physical spaces and administrative structures of LECUSA branches to not only demonstrate new farming techniques but also to improve the skills of local managers in practical matters like bookkeeping.[67] By 1971, there were twenty LECUSA branches operating in every district of the country, excepting Mokhotlong.[68] The costs recouped through tractor rental and loans for seeds never outpaced expenses, however, and LECUSA branches remained overall a money-losing venture for the government. Total losses countrywide for the twenty chapters in 1971 were in the range of R8,000 ($11,200), which the government deemed a small price to pay for a rural development project that was relatively popular.[69]

LECUSA maintained its popularity with Basotho in spite of, or perhaps because of, the infusion of government cash that made it financially viable. Robert Warner, also working in the Mohale's Hoek District, reported that "cooperative members were getting much better results [in maize production] than the non-members." During his tenure, which lasted from 1971 to 1973, the LECUSA branch there "increased in size, [and] got more tractors and plows in place."[70] Clark Tibbits was in Lesotho from 1967 to 1969, serving as a Peace Corps volunteer with the LECUSA branch in the Roma valley. He reported the cooperatives were "very popular" when he served in the late 1960s, but unlike most other volunteers, Tibbits remained engaged in agricultural policy and research in Lesotho, returning to the country nine or ten times between his initial departure in 1969 and 2012. He assessed LECUSA through the 1970s and 1980s as "continuing for a long time, people still talk about it, but it gradually declined as there were not enough resources to sustain it."[71] The results that the LECUSA branches helped achieve certainly did not lead to massive increases in income for rural Basotho, but the organizational skills developed by midlevel managers turned out to be useful to them in other contexts. Both Warner and Tibbits noted that the informal classes they taught on bookkeeping, accounting, and other managerial tasks were among the best-received activities with which they assisted.

BASOTHO COMPROMISES

The demand from rural Basotho for classes on accounting and bookkeeping through LECUSA is representative of a larger 1970s trend of people in Lesotho making peace with the political status quo while also continuing to work for the changes they wanted to see in society. This was, in large part, a self-preservation strategy as individuals made the best of the opportunities that were in front of them, but on a broader scale it also meant readjusting visions of what independence and development could and should look like. A few case studies illustrate how Basotho of various educations and backgrounds shifted their conceptions of the benefits of independence in order to accommodate the new political realities of the 1970s and 1980s.

Selborne Mohlalisi was a longtime member of the civil service who, as discussed earlier, faced discrimination in his career because of his affiliation with the Lesotho Evangelical Church. He missed out on a chance to work in the prime minister's office in 1969 because his church affiliation made his political loyalties suspect. Still, he persisted in his civil service career, continuing in the Ministry of Education instead. There in the period 1973–76 he helped set up the pay department for teachers. Previously, the government had provided money to the educational secretariats for the three largest Christian missions, which then disbursed salaries to teachers in schools across the country. As Mohlalisi noted, "At the time it was unheard of for teachers to be paid by Government, [but] . . . there were problems" with secretariats at times withholding money during disputes over work conditions or political affiliations.[72] Mohlalisi was very proud of his efforts to set up direct payments, which allowed teachers greater freedom in their work and personal lives because it made them full-fledged civil servants instead of employees of the missions. Mohlalisi, still proud of this effort decades later, noted that his program was the "basis for what you see now is called the 'Teaching Service Department and Teaching Services Commission.'" As someone who had hoped independence would allow Basotho, and in particular the civil service, to "develop the country, be able to manage our own affairs and do what we thought was good as the people who were born in the country," Mohlalisi made the most of his employment situation. Denied the chance to move even closer to the seat of power, he found a way in the Ministry of Education to achieve some meaningful progress despite the politicization of the civil service.

Michael Mateka similarly fought for his own independence vision through his work. Mateka, who joined the Catholic Brothers of the Sacred Heart in 1959, started his teaching career in 1963. He taught high school at various Catholic schools until in 1971 he became principal of Christ the King High School in Roma, a position he held throughout the decade. When characterizing the period, he was highly critical of government efforts because the Ministry of Education was beholden to overseas funding for new initiatives in the schools. He noted that as funding agencies changed priorities or the source of money for schools shifted from one country to another, teachers, principals, and students experienced a "whole succession of ill-planned innovations that were never discussed and never evaluated. They kept displacing each other like water out of the tap and nobody ever doing anything."[73] The biggest frustration for Mateka, however, was that "with the introduction of these new things . . . you couldn't question." Even Mateka, principal of one of the top Catholic high schools in the country, was frustrated by his inability to have a meaningful role in the formulation or modification of government policy. The restriction, he believed, resulted largely from the Ministry of Education's reliance on development funding from abroad, which limited the ability of Basotho to have a meaningful voice in shaping policy.

Mateka did not give in to the urge to throw up his hands in the face of this intransigence from the ministry. Rather, he redoubled his efforts to bring about student-centered education in his own institution and later, in 1986, when he was appointed to the position of Catholic Education Secretary, to the entire system of Catholic schooling in Lesotho. He noted, "When you teach a student you teach a person, you don't teach the syllabus. . . . [T]he little I teach him or her, I hope it will last a lifetime to enable him to think himself out of a context and see the alternatives and decide."[74] This view of education as a means of empowerment was strikingly similar to that expressed by a wide range of Basotho students from across the political spectrum in the late 1960s. The similarities suggest that while Mateka found some of his avenues for improving the responsiveness of school administrations stymied by government efforts and the restrictions imposed by funding agencies, he was still able to work for his visions of independence in the day-to-day routines of the educational system.

Yet another civil servant working through challenging conditions for his vision of independence was Mohlalefi Moteane. An opposition supporter through high school and his university years, he hoped that independence would bring about a degree of economic self-sufficiency for Basotho. He articulated his independence vision as making Lesotho a place "for Basotho to be able to run their own affairs[,] . . . to rule ourselves, to be able to decide to belong to the UN institutions, to give freedom to the younger generations to be able to qualify and become doctors, engineers so that they come back and run their own affairs[,] . . . to give a chance for us to make matches. You understand what I mean? A box of matches."[75] This conception incorporated all three parts of the common independence vision that came about as part of the rhetorical consensus on development common to Basotho youth in the early independence period.

By the time Moteane qualified as a veterinarian and started work in the civil service in 1974, however, the authoritarian BNP government was deeply entrenched. This lack of democratic governance did not stop him from pouring himself into his work to further his visions to the extent possible. Working primarily on large animals, and thus with rural Basotho herders, Moteane "came into contact with the people and admired what people do[,] . . . what the Basotho farmers can do."[76] After he left government service in the 1980s, he started trading in wool and mohair in addition to practicing veterinary medicine privately. Getting involved in the trading side of farming gave him even more respect for the farmers, appreciating "their level of development" in terms of being savvy about marketing, pricing, and "how they . . . [managed] the animals." Moteane's work as a trader resulted in rural farmers having an additional outlet and helped them increase income by trading through a trusted, local veterinary provider. All of these efforts comported with Moteane's stated goals of promoting more Basotho self-sufficiency. While the lack of political change in the 1970s was disappointing in terms of his earlier vision for independence, he still found space within the political system through development efforts to work for and help bring about more economic opportunities in Lesotho.

It was not only in the economic realm that Basotho continued to carve out independence visions, as the political activities of Maleseko Kena during the 1970s show. Kena was politically active, as was her husband, Mokhafisi Jacob Kena, longtime general secretary of the Communist Party of Lesotho. Her vision for independence in Lesotho included the construction of more roads and schools and more development. "We hoped for more with independence," she said.[77] Kena was raising the seven children she had with Jacob in the rural southern district of Qacha's Nek, and it was difficult for them. Jacob was sent to prison after the coup of 1970 and then spent time in exile in the Eastern Bloc. Maleseko, meanwhile, was responsible for the small-scale economic activities that sustained the family and allowed her to send all seven of her children to school. She sold farm produce, peddled eggs from her chickens, maintained a small community grain mill, and sewed dresses for clients across Lesotho and South Africa, sending them the finished product by post. As a staunch ANC supporter, she found Lesotho's politics disheartening because of the strident anticommunist line of the BNP government in the 1960s and early 1970s and because the BCP was aligned with the PAC. Therefore, she discontinued her active involvement in Lesotho's domestic politics.

This did not mean she gave up on political work, however. She redoubled her efforts in the 1970s as her house functioned as a way station and safe house for ANC, PAC, "Steve Biko's group," and South African Communist Party members fleeing apartheid. Maleseko was the initial point of contact for those fleeing into Lesotho along the largely unguarded southern border: "They would come at Sehlabathebe, other border posts along here [Qacha's Nek] and even some just came across the mountains."[78] When they arrived at her house, she said, "I gave them money for transport. I gave them food and clothes. . . . I gave them what I had." She helped them get to the airport at Qacha's Nek; from there they flew to Maseru, where a larger network of activists, including Chris Hani from 1974 to 1982, helped them either settle in Lesotho or move farther north into independent states in Africa.[79] By playing an important role in the wider struggle against apartheid from her home in rural southern Lesotho, Maleseko was working for her vision of independence. She could not build the roads and infrastructure she hoped to see from formal independence in Lesotho, but she worked on a daily basis to ensure that her own children had access to the best education she could provide and, through her political work, tried to bring about the conditions for better governance in the region through the demise of the apartheid state.

Thabelo Kebise, born in Lesotho but raised for some years in South Africa, was in primary school at independence in 1966. He had, however, been at the independence ceremonies in Maseru and had been impressed by the orderly youth groups: "I saw the Cadets putting on their . . . colorful uniform, playing some drums and trumpets and bugles, and it was very interesting, I remember. And I joined the Cadets from that time."[80] In addition to being enthralled with the youth groups, Kebise kept coming back for Independence Day celebrations every year from his home in Motsekuoa, about an hour bus ride from Maseru. Through this he came to hope that independence would bring "some developments of the country whereby we could have sufficient food, agriculture, and the establishment of new factories in our country, and maybe we were expecting some trains to run through the country, maybe from Butha Buthe to Quthing [north to south] . . . also, the water, the Highlands Water Scheme had been talked about in Lesotho for *many, many* years." In addition to this developmentalist vision of independence, Kebise expected the return of the "Conquered Territories" of the Free State to Lesotho.

Kebise and his family, as detailed earlier, were staunch opposition supporters, so he knew that employment in Lesotho was not likely in 1975 when he finished high school. Therefore, he immediately set off to get a job in the Free State gold fields in Welkom.[81] He ended up scraping together enough money to go to driver's training school and passed his heavy truck drivers' exam in the late 1970s. When he moved back to Lesotho in the early 1980s, he first obtained a job working for the German Development Corporation (GTZ) on its Matelile Rural Development Project. From there, he managed to get work for a time on the initial stages of the Lesotho Highlands Water Project in the late 1980s and in a variety of private sector transport jobs during the 1990s. In June 2001, Kebise and his colleagues from all these jobs opened DEMOWU, the Driver's, Earth Moving Operators and Allied Workers Union, out of a small office in the Bus Stop area of central Maseru. Kebise had been trying to organize his peers into a union for ten years. Even when he was working on the Highlands Water Project, he had felt like "the drivers in Lesotho were very much oppressed and they were just paid by the way the owners could just think. There wasn't anything that has been there to say this is the procedure that should be followed."

Kebise's and the union's emphasis on procedures and organizing reflected their visions for corporatist development in the post-independence period. They wanted the fruits of independence to be broadly available to the drivers, as well as the owners, of the big construction firms that were garnering the contracts from the increasingly lucrative large development projects in Lesotho. It is important to note that in his development-oriented view of independence, which involved factories and trains and other symbols of modernity, Kebise started off by mentioning "sufficient food." This basic need was at the heart of his independence vision, and it was informed, at least in part, by his itinerant lifestyle, bouncing between Lesotho and South Africa. Kebise's life had been, like so many Basotho before and since, a series of moves between Lesotho and South Africa searching for work that provided enough money on which to live, as well as dignity and freedom. Kebise's jobs in South Africa and Lesotho were not purposeless wandering or necessarily the fault of oppressive economic structures—though the oppressive structures, particularly those erected by the apartheid state, were certainly present and limiting the choices he had for employment. They were also the result of Kebise's search for the jobs that fit with his visions of what employment should look like in the independence era: an acknowledged equality that gave people space to live up to their potential.

Individual Basotho and the country of Lesotho as a whole could never escape the shadow of apartheid South Africa in the 1970s. Some individuals like Kebise were lucky enough to find a skill that would translate into employment back home after a long stint working under apartheid labor rules. Kena made her own way, and actively took part in the resistance to the apartheid regime, even though she was confined to Lesotho because she was wanted by security forces in South Africa and would have been arrested had she attempted to officially cross the border. Still others, like Moteane, Mohlalisi, and Mateka, found their way into government work that allowed them to avoid direct contact with apartheid through most of their working years. All of these people shared, however, a changing vision of what development should look like and what independence should mean for Lesotho. In their own ways, they had to grapple with the fact that independence and development did not arrive in the exact forms and ways in which they had hoped during earlier times. They had to make compromises, and the combination of increased economic opportunities, more governmental services, and an increased say in governance almost never arrived simultaneously for anyone.

The compromises of individuals were mirrored, to some extent, in the compromises that the Lesotho government found it necessary to make in order to obtain the increased development funding that buttressed its limited popular support in the 1970s. The open break with the South African government in 1972, while opening the door to much broader international development funding, also meant foreclosing on the possibility of the grand Highlands Water Project coming to fruition anytime in the 1970s. While the long-term hope remained among government officials that the South Africans would eventually need Lesotho's water—as they indeed did—in the short term, losing this project was a blow to the BNP government, which had long promised this project to supporters and opponents alike.

Compromises in foreign policy and in individual expectations allowed the Lesotho government and Basotho respectively to make sense of and come to terms with the realities of the political situations they faced. In order to keep alive the hope of greater funding, officials of the Lesotho government had to trust they would see the fruits of their brave stand against apartheid through assistance from new and different international partners. Likewise, ordinary Basotho hoped that continuing to work for better local communities and for their own educational and career opportunities would bring about some of the changes they wanted to see from independence. Both of these compromises, however, led to the entrenchment of the developmentalist regime that emerged in Lesotho by the late 1970s whereby individuals had little to no say over the shape and form of projects and the government traded its hard-won power and sovereignty for large development projects run by outside technocratic "experts."

The developmentalist regime was the logical end of the rhetorical consensus on development that took root in colonial Basutoland and early independence Lesotho. Thus, it just "made sense," as Havel wrote, to both ordinary Basotho and to government officials that Lesotho needed to solicit development projects from any and all funders, no matter the cost. By their very nature, however, these projects could not bring about the full independence vision that the rhetorical consensus on development promised. This was largely because the projects operated on the logic of funders and donor agencies and thus were centralized and focused primarily on creating physical and bureaucratic structures. This, of course, is development as Ferguson's "anti-politics machine." Basotho did not have a choice about whether development brought about this state of affairs, but they could control, to some extent, their own reactions to it. By refocusing and refining their aspirations for the development they hoped to see from independence in light of the political realities of 1970s Lesotho, Basotho showed the resiliency of hope in the idea and practice of development.

CHAPTER 6

The Road to Development

In Antjie Krog's *Begging to Be Black*, her interlocutor on Lesotho is a young Mosotho university student studying in South Africa named Mannini Mokhothu. Krog asks how her experiences growing up in the rural Lesotho town of Semonkong, deep in the Maluti Mountains, affect how she sees and experiences life in urban South Africa. Mokhothu responds that she misses the connectedness that was so familiar in her Lesotho upbringing, a connectedness she still finds whenever she returns. The most damaging part of studying in South Africa, she reports, is that the uprootedness of the university left "an enormous and I think permanent scar" because she no longer had "the same kind of access to everybody's hearts and resources that I had in Semonkong."[1]

The types of communities that Basotho in Lesotho constructed were based, to a large extent, on being interconnected socially and economically in ways that development planners and Lesotho government officials were not willing or able to build into projects in the 1960s and 1970s. Mokhothu notes that at her house, "Nothing there belongs only to one person. Not even where you sleep. I had nothing that was solely my own; even my clothes belonged to or would go to somebody else."[2] But she also angrily rejects Krog's attempt to say that her ability to navigate with equal success posh Cape Town suburbs and poor, rural Lesotho communities made for a "double life." She also rejects the notion that her adaptations were to something called "modernity," because "if you say modernity you imply that I have a sense of self that is pre-modern, primitive."[3] Mokhothu's reflections on modernity reflect the same sensibilities that Basotho who lived in the independence era expressed. They saw themselves, and continue to see themselves, as full-fledged members of a national and global community fully engaged with ideologies of development and independence.

How people in Lesotho viewed themselves as organic and thickly connected members of multiple communities at the local, national, and international levels played a key role in how they internalized the rhetoric and practice of development and how they experienced development efforts of the independence era. The construction of the road linking Mokhothu's home community of Semonkong to Maseru and the rest of the lowlands illustrates the resilience of Basotho in the face of multiple development failures over decades. The project also suggests that the failure of planners and politicians alike to understand this sense of connectedness and community represents a missed opportunity to achieve fruitful development collaborations that could have meaningfully changed material circumstances for many Basotho.

Semonkong is situated at 2,275 meters (7,464 feet) above sea level in the far southeastern corner of the Maseru District. Basotho looking for a place of refuge from the violence of the Gun War with the Cape Colony founded the town in the 1880s. Today the town is a crown jewel of the tourism industry, with the spectacular 192-meter (630-foot) single-drop Maletsunyane Falls located just outside town. The paved road that today takes visitors and locals from Maseru to Semonkong was first proposed in the colonial era, but construction initially started through the initiative of local communities coming together to break a road with pick and shovel through the rocky mountains in the 1970s. Basotho from communities in and around Semonkong needed access to the lowland and foothill road system and were not seeing results from government efforts, so they took matters into their own hands: they ran their own self-help program.

Semonkong was geographically isolated until the road was finally built in stages from the 1980s to 2014, and it has undoubtedly increased the economic opportunities for Semonkong residents. The first vehicle to arrive in Semonkong was a tractor that locals hauled over the mountain passes by hand and with the assistance of a donkey cart in the early 1950s. Passenger air service started in 1952, giving residents much faster access to Maseru than the bridle path that connected the town to the roadhead at Ramabanta about 50 kilometers (31 miles) away over multiple mountain passes. Semonkong was the main commercial depot for the central Maluti Mountains, and thus building a road was long a priority for the government, but for years it remained stuck in the planning phase. The road was initially included in late colonial road-building plans and flagged as a key connector linking Maseru with the far southern district headquarters town of Qacha's Nek. Building this road was a necessary link in constructing a comprehensive road system in Lesotho. The colonial government and the first independent government of Lesotho both included this road in their requests for road funding to donor agencies in the late 1960s. The Lesotho government finally financed and completed the road between Ramabanta and Semonkong, with the assistance of international donors, in a vast and costly project in the early 1980s.[4] The last segment of the road—the connection southward to connect Semonkong with Qacha's Nek—was not completed until 2014.

While the road was part of government plans, it came to fruition largely because local communities along the route took the initiative when project planning stalled. By 1971, residents of the mountain communities that would be served by a road completed the first rough track that allowed four-wheel-drive vehicles to travel all the way from Maseru to Semonkong.[5] The road was notable because it was done completely on the initiative of the local communities along the route and was not part of the official self-help program that funneled food aid to communities working on road projects. The informal construction process meant, however, that the road was dangerously rough. Faced with a fait accompli of a completed, if dangerous, road in 1972, the Lesotho cabinet supported an immediate upgrade through the formal Food-for-Work scheme. Bogged down in the politics of postcoup development, however, funding for even this relatively simple upgrading effort remained stalled in the Ministry of Works for years.

With the road seemingly stalled indefinitely in 1972–73, residents formed a local committee to keep pressure on the government to fund the work. The committee also organized continued maintenance in villages along the route to ensure that it remained passable to four-wheel-drive vehicles. Committee members successfully solicited funds for the construction efforts as well. They raised over R1,000 ($1,340) from local donors including the Anglican Church, the Catholic Church, St. Leonard's

Catholic Mission in Semonkong, and the prime minister himself. They also appealed to the American embassy to fund the estimated R17,000 ($22,780) it would take to upgrade the road to the standards demanded by the Food-for-Work program.[6] In short, the economic and social benefits of the road were such that local community members were willing to volunteer their own time, money, and labor to construct and maintain it.

In 1975, after three more years of inaction, the Central Planning Office decided to radically change course and build a paved road over the route to Semonkong. They put together a comprehensive plan for mountain development that included roads in the northern mountains that might be useful for future dam projects along with the road to Semonkong. They applied to the African Development Bank (ADB) for R3.5 million ($4.69 million) to fund the roads, which would be built by contractors. Since the estimates for the cost of a Food-for-Work program road were around R30,000 ($40,200), the new plans represented over a hundred-fold increase in the funds needed to construct the road.[7] The road also represented a significantly larger burden for Basotho taxpayers, who would have to repay the loan. In addition, the Food-for-Work plan could have had the road completed by 1972 or 1973, whereas with the ADB loan the road remained a rough four-wheel-drive-only track until the early 1980s. While the paved road made vehicle access to Semonkong even easier, the initial request and subsequent pleas from local communities along the road played very little role in the form that the project eventually took.

How the road was eventually built between Ramabanta and Semonkong, however, is but one story of development along this representative pathway, as the length of the road from Maseru to Semonkong is littered with the remains of development efforts attempted since independence. Driving out of Maseru on the main south highway, the turn for Semonkong is at Masianokeng, which served as the project headquarters for the Thaba Bosiu Rural Development Scheme. The houses built at such great cost with IDA loans in the early 1970s sit on a little hill overlooking the road, in a state of repair similar to that of the privately constructed homes in the town. At the road junction, there is an abandoned building that once housed the asparagus-canning factory that was supposed to offer an alternative cash crop for rural Basotho farmers as part of the scheme, but it failed to capture enough Basotho farmers or a market for canned asparagus. Today it sits abandoned and forlorn.

Fifteen kilometers farther up, the road narrows and has noticeably more potholes. This happens right after the turnoff for Thaba Tseka and the access road to Mohale Dam, the second catchment dam completed in the early 2000s during Phase IB of the Lesotho Highlands Water Project. The road to Mohale Dam continues on to Thaba Tseka, the administrative capital of the central mountain district, constructed with funding from the Canadian government as part of an area-based agricultural scheme in the late 1970s and early 1980s.[8] The Lesotho Highlands Water Project, which only started in 1986 after the apartheid regime supported a military coup against Prime Minister Jonathan, is ongoing. Construction on the third major dam, Polihali, started in the mid-2010s, and the road to Thaba Tseka is receiving further upgrades to support the expected transport of construction supplies. Polihali is scheduled for completion in the early 2020s. While the project brings in a significant percentage of government revenue at present, it has displaced large numbers of people from their homes and communities. There have been allegations of bribery, kickbacks, and other forms of fraud associated with the project, and the project comes in for criticism during dry periods for selling Lesotho's water to South Africa while Basotho struggle to meet their own local needs.[9]

Around the next bend of the Semonkong road and up a hill through the dense residential community of Roma, the road passes the main campus of the National University of Lesotho. The university received significant donor assistance from USAID, the Canadian government, and the Ford Foundation as it transitioned from a Catholic institution to a regionally known research and teaching institution. These days, the university dominates the higher education scene in Lesotho but struggles to secure government funding, and many top Basotho students attempt to gain access to South African institutions offering a wider range of degrees and certificate programs. There is also the perception that graduating from a South African institution proffers more postgraduate employment opportunities. The rest of the town of Roma is dominated by the Catholic Church, and in particular its social service institutions in the fields of education and health. There are a series of primary schools, two high schools, the major seminary that trains Basotho priests, and St. Joseph's Hospital. Roma illustrates the extent to which churches and other voluntary organizations still carry out significant development work in Lesotho side-by-side with governmental institutions.

Just past Roma, the road climbs precipitously as it leaves the lowlands for the foothills. The villages are farther apart, with swift, shallow streams cutting through the beautiful valleys. The road winds up, down, and around the larger hills. At the road junction town of Moitsupeli, where the paved road ended until the mid-2000s, stands the abandoned Thabana-li-Mele Craft Center. Funded by the Swedish International Development Agency in 1968–70, 1972–79, and 1982–85, the center started as a cooperative *kopano* producing woven mohair rugs for sale to tourists. When that model did not prove profitable enough for local people or the donors, the center tried to reinvent itself as an education center for women, but when this last effort failed in the mid-1980s, the center closed its doors.[10]

The last foothills town is Ramabanta, which was until the late 1960s the roadhead. The town contains the Fatima pilgrimage site that annually attracts thousands of Catholic Basotho, as well as a tourist lodge that does a brisk business in governmental and development conferences during the week and South African off-road bike and 4x4 enthusiasts on the weekends. Ramabanta has managed to capitalize, to some degree, on Lesotho's burgeoning tourism sector, though most residents of the town do not see much benefit from it because it remains confined to one small lodge.

Beyond Ramabanta, the road climbs a series of switchbacks into the high mountains. With the land primarily used for summer grazing, there are few villages here. Arriving in Semonkong, it is clear the town has captured the tourist market to an even greater extent. Semonkong advertises its monthly horse races, held on an open plain not far from town, and annually hosts the culminating stage of a multiday mountain bike race that finishes overlooking the Maletsunyane Falls—surely one of the most spectacular finishes in the world. The town has a frontier vibe, touted in the professional promotional literature as being based around people from surrounding communities who still arrive to do business on horseback. Despite the presence of the road, most town shops still retain a collection of hitching posts in front of their stores to accommodate their equestrian customers. The town, however, has a dusty and quiet feel, with the tourist lodge near the waterfalls rarely at capacity because of how far up in the mountains Semonkong is and because there are none of the large game animals common to the southern African region that attract overseas tourists in large numbers.

For all the failed projects that dot the highways and byways of Lesotho, there have been some improvements in the quality of life since independence in Semonkong. The 2014 completion of the southern portion of the road between Semonkong and Qacha's Nek means that the town now serves as the primary taxi waypoint for travelers between that southern district and Maseru. This gives more people the chance to earn cash as small-scale traders in the informal economy that clusters around the bus and taxi stops. The presence of a steady, if not massive, number of tourists from South Africa and abroad means an infusion of cash and jobs at the local lodge and the ability of those who own horses to hire them out for pony treks to the waterfall.

Further, there is the chance, however small, that local students might meet a foreign benefactor willing to pay for school tuition, as happened with Mannini Mokhothu. This is how she was able to attend the University of Western Cape outside Cape Town.[11] Mokhothu envisioned the promises of development and independence on the individual level, to be sure, but also for communities as a whole. Asked whether she was living a new life outside of Semonkong, Mokhothu responded that even when she left Semonkong, she was still a member of the community. "I haven't changed," she said, and people in the community "respect the old Mannini as being a real person" despite living far away and having access to academic and economic opportunities others in Semonkong and Lesotho do not.[12] The thickness of the community lives on, even in the hopes and dreams of those who might move away for studies or work. Mokhothu's journey from the mountains of Lesotho to Cape Town was facilitated by the markers of economic progress—roads, improved educational systems, tourism—that have come fitfully to Lesotho since the 1960s, but it was the embeddedness of individuals that made the community persevere in endeavors like building the road that allowed Semonkong residents to access the rest of Lesotho and the wider world. This was true across Lesotho as individuals and communities worked for development within their local, embedded frameworks.

The rhetorical consensus on development continues to live on in Lesotho, over fifty years after the formal transfer of power. The return of multiparty democracy in Lesotho since 1993 has brought about a renewed focus on the delivery and optics of community development, harkening back to the contestations over development in the early independence period, from 1965 to 1970. In May 2016, Prime Minister Pakalitha Mosisili was in the foothills of the Maseru District in the Makhaleng constituency, a good two-and-a-half-hour drive from Maseru. He was there to inaugurate a new police post that he lauded as a "center of development" in the community that would attract more satellite government offices: "Soon, other ministries like Home Affairs will bring their national identity and civil registration services here," he said.[13]

Mosisili, despite coming from a party that in earlier iterations was part of the opposition to Prime Minister Jonathan, used the speech as an opportunity to make an appeal that Jonathan would have recognized: unity through development. He even indirectly mentioned Jonathan, claiming "there is no single government which can boast that it developed this country single-handedly since independence."[14] Again, hearkening back to the independence era, Mosisili argued that only his party at the time, the Democratic Congress (DC), was fully "committed to improving the lives of Basotho [through] effective and efficient service-delivery."[15] With their political base in the rural areas, Mosisili and the DC needed to bring development projects to their constituencies to make the case for continued electoral support.

While poverty remains endemic in Lesotho, employment opportunities are scarce, and government so often seems to benefit only those who can get into an elected position in Parliament, the resiliency of the independence era and the optimism of the population in Lesotho are still alive. Afrobarometer data from surveys conducted in 2014 showed that 52 percent of Basotho thought that the country was "going in the wrong direction," while only 39 percent said it was "going in the right direction."[16] Similarly, 59 percent of the respondents thought that the economic situation in Lesotho was either "very bad" or "fairly bad," and only 25 percent thought it was "very good" or "fairly good." The statistics go on. Fifty percent of Basotho reported "never" having enough clean water in their homes, and 40 percent reported "never" having enough to eat. And yet, despite these oppressive material conditions and a political system that seems designed primarily for turmoil, Basotho are optimistic and hopeful for the future. When asked what they thought economic conditions would be like a year in the future, 62 percent thought they would be "better" or "much better." This optimism, which can be traced back to the independence era, is Havelian. It is not borne out by the economic, material, or political conditions in Lesotho, which are often bleak, but rooted in a deep-seated hope that one day, someday, people working individually and in community can bring about development and independence in the Mountain Kingdom.

NOTES

Introduction

1. Those who reside in Lesotho are collectively Basotho. The singular is Mosotho. *Lesotho* translates directly as "the land of the Sotho," and Basotho have referred to the land by this term since the nineteenth century. This book respects that usage and uses the colonial name Basutoland only when making explicit reference to the colonial government. The first language of most Basotho is Sesotho.

2. Interview, Thabelo Kebise, Maseru Bus Stop, April 1, 2008.

3. James Ferguson, *The Anti-Politics Machine: "Development," Depoliticization, and Bureaucratic Power in Lesotho* (New York: Cambridge University Press, 1990), 3–8.

4. Ibid., xiv.

5. Frederick Cooper, *Africa since 1940: The Presence of the Past* (Cambridge: Cambridge University Press, 2002).

6. John Aerni-Flessner, "Development, Politics, and the Centralization of State Power in Lesotho, 1960–1975," *Journal of African History* 55, no. 3 (2014): 401–21.

7. Charles Piot, *Nostalgia for the Future: West Africa after the Cold War* (Chicago: University of Chicago Press, 2010), 20.

8. Robert M. Ahearne, "Development and Progress as Historical Phenomenon in Tanzania: 'Maendeleo? We Had That in the Past,'" *African Studies Review* 59, no. 1 (2016): 83; J. S. Hogendorn and K. M. Scott, "The East African Groundnut Scheme: Lessons of a Large-Scale Agricultural Failure," *African Economic History* 10 (1981): 81–115.

9. They were either unwilling or unable to acknowledge that Judith Van Allen's concept "bad future things" was possible and that rural Basotho could conceive of these outcomes as well as see the positive vision. Judith Van Allen, "'Bad Future Things' and Liberatory Moments: Capitalism, Gender and the State in Botswana," *Radical History Review* 76 (2000): 136–68.

10. Frederick Cooper, "Writing the History of Development," *Journal of Modern European History* 8, no. 1 (2010): 10.

11. Joey Power, *Political Culture and Nationalism in Malawi: Building Kwacha* (Rochester, NY: Rochester University Press, 2010); Susan Geiger, *TANU Women: Gender and Culture in the Making of Tanganyikan Nationalism, 1955–1965* (Portsmouth, NH: Heinemann, 1997); Kelly Michelle Askew, *Performing the Nation: Swahili Music and Cultural Politics in Tanzania* (Chicago: University of Chicago Press, 2002); Marissa Jean Moorman, *Intonations: A Social History of Music and Nation in Luanda, Angola, from 1945 to Recent Times* (Athens: Ohio University Press, 2008).

12. David Coplan, *In the Time of Cannibals: The Word Music of South Africa's Basotho Migrants* (Chicago: University of Chicago Press, 1994), xvi.

13. L. B. B. J. Machobane, *Government and Change in Lesotho, 1800–1966: A Study of Political Institutions* (New York: Cambridge University Press, 1990), 23.

14. Sandra Wallman, "Lesotho's *Pitso*: Traditional Meetings in a Modern Setting," *Canadian Journal of African Studies* 2, no. 2 (1968): 170.

15. Mischa Honeck and Gabriel Rosenberg, "Transnational Generations: Organizing Youth in the Cold War," *Diplomatic History* 38, no. 2 (2014): 239.

16. Donald A. Ritchie, *Doing Oral History* (New York: Twayne Publishers, 1995), 12–13.

17. George K. Kieh, *Beyond State Failure and Collapse: Making the State Relevant in Africa* (Lanham, MD: Lexington Books, 2007); Jean-Philippe Platteau, "Institutional Obstacles to African Economic Development: State, Ethnicity and Custom," *Journal of Economic Behavior and Organization* 71 (2009): 669–89. Leslie Bank, interestingly, argues the flip side of this argument in the South African context, namely, that the state role in building ethnic nationalisms has been overstated while the role of clan and politics has been underrated. The effect is the same: the role of individuals in building nationalisms has been understated by much of the scholarship. Leslie Bank, "The Failure of Ethnic Nationalism: Land, Power and the Politics of Clanship on the South African High Veld 1860–1990," *Africa* 65, no. 4 (1995): 565–91.

18. Frederick Cooper called nationalism "thin" in "Possibility and Constraint: African Independence in Historical Perspective," *Journal of African History* 49, no. 2 (2008): 187; Crawford Young calls this a "discourse of protest" in *The African Colonial State in Comparative Perspective* (New Haven, CT: Yale University Press, 1994), 238; Young, again, calls it "banal" in "Nation, Ethnicity, and Citizenship: Dilemmas of Democracy and Civil Order in Africa," in *Making Nations, Creating Strangers*, ed. Sara Dorman, Daniel Hammett, and Paul Nugent (Boston: Brill, 2007), 248; Mahmood Mamdani calls nationalism the "social and ideological glue" in *Citizen and Subject: Contemporary Africa and the Legacy of Late Colonialism* (Princeton, NJ: Princeton University Press, 1996), 290.

19. Andrew Bowman, "Mass Production or Production by the Masses? Tractors, Cooperatives, and the Politics of Rural Development in Post-Independence Zambia," *Journal of African History* 52, no. 2 (2011): 201–21; Christophe Bonneuil, "Development as Experiment: Science and State Building in Late Colonial and Postcolonial Africa, 1930–1970," *Osiris* 15 (2000): 258–81; Christophe Bonneuil, "Penetrating the Natives: Peanut Breeding, Peasants and the Colonial State in Senegal (1900–1950)," *Science, Technology and Society* 4, no. 2 (1999): 273–302; Priya Lal, "Militants, Mothers, and the National Family: *Ujamaa*, Gender, and Rural Development in Postcolonial Tanzania," *Journal of African History* 51, no. 1 (2010): 1–20.

20. Kara Moskowitz, "'Are You Planting Trees or Are You Planting People?' Squatter Resistance and International Development in the Making of a Kenyan Postcolonial Political Order (c. 1963–78)," *Journal of African History* 56, no. 1 (2015): 99–118; Ahearne, "Development and Progress," 77–96.

21. One work that ties development to democratization in Lesotho is Khabele Matlosa, "Aid, Development and Democracy in Lesotho, 1966–1996" (Unpublished paper, Center for Southern African Studies, University of Western Cape, 1999).

22. Gregory Mann, *From Empires to NGOs in the West African Sahel: The Road to Nongovernmentality* (New York: Cambridge University Press, 2014), 6.

23. James C. Scott, *Seeing Like a State: How Certain Schemes to Improve the Human Condition Have Failed* (New Haven, CT: Yale University Press, 1998), 190–91.

24. Kate B. Showers, *Imperial Gullies: Soil Erosion and Conservation in Lesotho* (Athens: Ohio University Press, 2005); Sandra Wallman, *Take Out Hunger: Two Case Studies of Rural Development in Basutoland* (London: Athlone Press, 1969); Marc Epprecht and Andrea Nattrass, *"This Matter of Women Is Getting Very Bad": Gender, Development and Politics in Colonial Lesotho* (Pietermaritzburg: University of Kwa-Zulu Natal Press, 2000); Marc Epprecht, "Domesticity and Piety in Colonial Lesotho: The Private Politics of Basotho Women's Pious Associations," *Journal of Southern African Studies* 19, no. 2 (1993): 202–24.

25. Oscar Mwangi, "Hydropolitics, Ecocide, and Human Security in Lesotho: A Case Study of the Lesotho Highlands Water Project," *Journal of Southern African Studies* 33, no. 1 (2007): 3–17; Oscar Mwangi, "Environmental Change and Human Security in Lesotho: The Role of the Lesotho Highlands Water Project in Environmental Degradation," *African Security Review* 17, no. 3 (2008): 58–70; Mabusetsa Lenka Thamae and Lori Pottinger, eds., *On the Wrong Side of Development: Lessons Learned from the Lesotho Highlands Water Project* (Maseru: Transformation Resource Center, 2006); Femi Akindele and Relebohile Senyane, *The Irony of the "White Gold"* (Maseru: Transformation Resource Center, 2004).

26. Monica M. van Beusekom, *Negotiating Development: African Farmers and Colonial Experts at the Office du Niger, 1920–1960* (Portsmouth, NH: Heinemann, 2002); Jamie Monson, *Africa's Freedom Railway: How a Chinese Development Project Changed Lives and Livelihoods in Tanzania* (Bloomington: Indiana University Press, 2009); Allen F. Isaacman and Barbara Isaacman, *Dams, Displacement, and the Delusion of Development: Cahora Bassa and Its Legacies in Mozambique, 1965–2007* (Athens: Ohio University Press, 2013).

27. Leander Schneider, *Government of Development: Peasants and Politicians in Postcolonial Tanzania* (Bloomington: Indiana University Press, 2014); Priya Lal, *African Socialism in Postcolonial Tanzania: Between the Village and the World* (New York: Cambridge University Press, 2015).

28. Joanna Tague, "Before Asylum and Expert Witness: Mozambican Refugee Settlement and Rural Development in Southern Tanzania, 1964–75," in *African Asylum at a Crossroads: Activism, Expert Testimony, and Refugee Rights*, ed. Iris Berger et al. (Athens: Ohio University Press, 2015).

29. A case study that looks at this type of small-scale project is Ben Jones, *Beyond the State in Rural Uganda* (Edinburgh: Edinburgh University Press, 2009).

30. Piot, *Nostalgia*, 152.

31. Nick Cullather, "Development? It's History," *Diplomatic History* 24, no. 4 (2000): 642; see also Michael E. Latham, "Introduction: Modernization, International History and the Cold War World," in *Staging Growth: Modernization, Development and the Global Cold War*, ed. David C. Engerman et al. (Boston: University of Massachusetts Press, 2003).

32. Walter Rostow, *Stages of Growth: A Non-Communist Manifesto* (New York: Cambridge University Press, 1960).

33. Larry Grubbs, *Secular Missionaries: Americans and African Development in the 1960s* (Boston: University of Massachusetts Press, 2009), 38.

34. Joseph Hodge, "British Colonial Expertise, Post-Colonial Careering and the Early History of International Development," *Journal of Modern European History* 8, no. 1 (2010): 39–40.

35. Joseph Hodge and Gerald Hödl, "Introduction," in *Developing Africa: Concepts and Practices in Twentieth-Century Colonialism*, ed. Joseph Hodge, Gerald Hödl, and Martina Kopf (Manchester: Manchester University Press, 2014), 2.

36. Thanks to Motlatsi Thabane of the National University of Lesotho, Department of Historical Studies, for consulting on the translation of this term. Errors of interpretation, of course, lie with the author.

37. Hunter has examined shifts in the meaning of the Swahili word for development, *maendeleo*, arguing that its meaning shifted over the course of the twentieth century from "going on" or "advance" to "community development." In Sesotho similar conceptions came to be melded into *tsoela-pele*, but the older meanings remained, too. Emma Hunter, "A History of *Maendeleo*: The Con-

cept of 'Development' in Tanganyika's Late Colonial Public Sphere," in Hodge, Hödl, and Kopf, *Developing Africa*, 87.

38. For just a few of the works that have cited Ferguson in global context, see Stuart Corbridge, Glyn Williams, Manoj Srivastava, and Rene Veron, *Seeing the State: Governance and Governmentality in India* (New York: Cambridge University Press, 2005); Lucia da Corta, "The Political Economy of Agrarian Change: Dinosaur or Phoenix?," in *The Comparative Political Economy of Development: Africa and South Asia*, ed. Barbara Harriss-White and Judith Heyer (New York: Routledge, 2010); Joel Wainwright, *Decolonizing Development: Colonial Power and the Maya* (Malden, MA: Wiley-Blackwell, 2008).

39. San Marino and the Vatican are the only other UN-recognized states that are complete enclaves. Entities like tribal nations in the United States also have similar claims, though they do not have formal UN recognition.

40. Basotho politicians, even today, call for the return of land claimed by Lesotho in the Free State Province, which is known in Lesotho as the "Conquered Territories." David Coplan, "A River Runs through It: The Meaning of the Lesotho–Free State Border," *African Affairs* 100, no. 398 (2001): 81–116.

41. The best accounts of the life of Moshoeshoe come from dueling biographies published in 1975: Peter Sanders, *Moshoeshoe, Chief of the Sotho* (London: Heinemann, 1975); Leonard Thompson, *Survival in Two Worlds: Moshoeshoe of Lesotho, 1786–1870* (Oxford: Clarendon Press, 1975). A later work that critiques some of their arguments is Scott Rosenberg, *Promises of Moshoeshoe: Culture, Nationalism, and Identity in Lesotho* (Roma, Lesotho: Institute of Southern African Studies, 2008).

42. This time is nicely chronicled in Norman Etherington, "A Tempest in a Teapot? Nineteenth Century Contests for Land in South Africa's Caledon Valley and the Invention of the Mfecane," *Journal of African History* 45, no. 2 (2004): 203–19.

43. Martin Moloantoa Lelimo, *The Question of Lesotho's Conquered Territory: It's Time for an Answer* (Morija, Lesotho: Morija Museum and Archives, 1998).

44. The Protestant mission archives at Morija, Lesotho, contain many works on this time period, most coming from early missionary accounts: R. C. Germond, *Chronicles of Basutoland: A Running Commentary on the Events of the Years 1830–1902* (Morija, Lesotho: Morija Sesuto Book Depot, 1967); Eugene Casalis, *The Basutos, or Twenty-Three Years in Southern Africa* (Morija, Lesotho: Morija Museum and Archives, 1992) (orig. pub. 1861); D. F. Ellenberger and J. C. Macgregor, *History of the Basuto: Ancient and Modern* (Morija, Lesotho: Morija Museum and Archives, 1992) (orig. pub. 1912); Thomas Arbousset, *Missionary Excursion into the Blue Mountains: Being an Account of King Moshoeshoe's Expedition from Thaba-Bosiu to the Source of the Malibamatso River in the Year 1840* (Morija, Lesotho: Morija Museum and Archives, 1991).

45. Machobane, *Government and Change*, 5–10.

46. David B. Coplan and Timothy Quinlan, "A Chief by the People: Nation versus State in Lesotho," *Africa: Journal of the International African Institute* 67, no. 1 (1997): 31–32.

47. Motlatsi Thabane, *Who Owns the Land in Lesotho? Land Disputes and the Politics of Land Ownership in Lesotho* (Roma, Lesotho: Institute of Southern African Studies, 1998), 1.

48. Coplan and Quinlan, "Chief," 32.

49. Lord Hailey popularized the term *parallel rule* in *An Africa Survey Revised 1956: A Survey of Problems Arising in Africa South of the Sahara* (New York: Oxford University Press, 1957), 272. Today there are ten administrative districts in Lesotho, eight of which have the same administrative headquarters as in the colonial period: (from north to south) Leribe (Hlotse), Teyateyaneng (TY), Maseru, Mafeteng, Mohale's Hoek, Quthing, Qacha's Nek, and Mokhotlong. Butha Buthe became a separate district in the 1920s, and the 10th district, Thaba Tseka, was created in the 1970s and 1980s through the funding of Canadian development efforts.

50. Peter Sanders, *"Throwing Down White Man": Cape Rule and Misrule in Colonial Lesotho, 1871–1884* (Pontypool, Wales: Merlin Press, 2011); Elizabeth Eldredge, *Power in Colonial Africa: Conflict and Discourse in Lesotho, 1870–1960* (Madison: University of Wisconsin Press, 2008); Coplan and Quinlan, "Chief," 32–33; Sandra Burman, *Chiefdom Politics and Alien Law: Basutoland under Cape Rule, 1871–1884* (New York: Africana, 1981); Colin Murray and Peter Sanders, *Medicine Murder in Colonial Lesotho: The Anatomy of a Moral Crisis* (Edinburgh: Edinburgh University Press, 2005).

51. Machobane, *Government and Change*, 20–21.

52. Casalis, *The Basutos*; Germond, *Chronicles*; Michael Seeiso Sekoati, *The History of the Roman Catholic Church in Lesotho: 1862–1989* (Pretoria: UNISA Press, 2001); Epprecht and Nattrass, *"This Matter of Women."*

53. T. H. Mothibe, "Lesotho: Historical Legacies of Nationalism and Nationhood," in *Southern Africa after Apartheid: Prospects for the Inner Periphery in the 1990s*, ed. Sehoai Santho and Mafa Sejanamane (Harare: SAPES Trust, 1991), 188–93; Stimela Jason Jingoes, J. G. Perry, and Cassandra Perry, *A Chief Is a Chief by the People: The Autobiography of Stimela Jason Jingoes* (New York: Oxford University Press, 1975).

54. Murray and Sanders, *Medicine Murder*.

55. T. W. K. 'Mote, "Native Demands under the Banner of the ICU," *Naledi ea Lesotho* (Mafeteng), March 6, 1925; Robert Vinson, *The Americans Are Coming! Dreams of African American Liberation in Segregationist South Africa* (Athens: Ohio University Press, 2011); Amanda D. Kemp and Robert Vinson, "'Poking Holes in the Sky': Professor James Thaele, American Negroes, and Modernity in 1920s Segregationist South Africa," *African Studies Review* 43, no. 1 (2000): 141–59.

56. David Ambrose, *Naledi ea Lesotho, the Basutoland Star* (Roma, Lesotho: House 9 Publications, National University of Lesotho, 2007).

57. Edwin W. Smith, *The Mabilles of Basutoland* (Morija, Lesotho: Morija Museum and Archives, 1996) (orig. pub. 1939), 128, 223; Daniel P. Kunene, "'Leselinyana la Lesotho' and Sotho Historiography," *History in Africa* 4 (1977): 150; Ambrose, *Naledi ea Lesotho*. For example, Josiel Modise, Letter to the Editor, "The Shame of the United States of America," November 28, 1924; "Visit of Dr. Landes from America," January 29, 1926; and "Death of Mrs. Washington," August 7, 1925.

58. The classic text on the role of print in the building of nationalism is, of course, Benedict Anderson, *Imagined Communities: Reflections on the Origin and Spread of Nationalism* (London: Verso, 1983), but the literature on this in southern Africa is substantial as well. For a South African overview, see Peter Limb, *The ANC's Early Years: Nation, Class and Place in South Africa before 1940* (Pretoria: UNISA Press, 2010); for Lesotho, see Kunene, "Leselinyana la Lesotho"; G. M. Haliburton, "Walter Matitta and Josiel Lefela: A Prophet and a Politician in Lesotho," *History of Religion in Africa* 7, no. 2 (1975): 111–31.

59. Peter Delius, *The Land Belongs to Us: The Pedi Polity, the Boers, and the British in the Nineteenth-Century Transvaal* (Berkeley: University of California Press, 1984), 64–65; Eldredge, *Power*, 34; Judith M. Kimble, *Migrant Labour and Colonial Rule in Basutoland, 1890–1930* (Grahamstown, South Africa: Institute of Social and Economic Research, 1999); J. M. Mohapeloa, *Tentative British Imperialism in Lesotho, 1884–1910: A Study in Basotho–Colonial Office Interaction and South Africa's Influence on It* (Morija, Lesotho: Morija Museum and Archives, 2002).

60. David Turkon, "Commoners and Kings and Subaltern: Political Factionism and Structured Inequality in Lesotho," *Political and Legal Anthropology Review* 31 (2008): 203; Robert Rotberg, *Peacekeeping and Peace Enforcement in Africa: Methods of Conflict Prevention* (Washington, DC: Brookings Institution Press, 2010), 98.

61. Burman, *Cape Rule*, 45.

62. Elizabeth Eldredge, *A South African Kingdom: The Pursuit of Security in Nineteenth-Century Lesotho* (New York: Cambridge University Press, 1993); A. C. A. van der Wiel, *Migratory Wage Labour: Its Role in the Economy of Lesotho* (Mazenod, Lesotho: Mazenod Book Centre, 1977); Eddy Tshidiso Maloka, *Basotho and the Mines: A Social History of Labour Migrancy in Lesotho and South Africa, c. 1890–1940* (Dakar: CODESRIA, 2004); Colin Murray, *Families Divided: The Impact of Migrant Labour in Lesotho* (New York: Cambridge University Press, 1981).

63. Coplan, *In the Time of Cannibals*; Clive Glaser, *Bo-Tsotsi: The Youth Gangs of Soweto, 1935–1976* (Portsmouth, NH: Heinemann, 2000).

64. Jeff Guy and Motlatsi Thabane, "Technology, Ethnicity and Ideology: Basotho Miners and Shaft Sinking on the South African Gold Mines," *Journal of Southern African Studies* 14, no. 2 (1988): 257–78; Gary Kynoch, *We Are Fighting the World: A History of the Marashea Gangs of South Africa, 1947–1999* (Athens: Ohio University Press, 2005).

65. Alan R. Booth, "Lord Selborne and the British Protectorates, 1908–1910," *Journal of African History* 10, no. 1 (1969): 147.

66. Joel Bolnick, "Potlako Leballo: The Man Who Hurried to Meet His Destiny," *Journal of Modern African Studies* 29, no. 3 (1991): 413–42; Arianna Lissoni, "The PAC in Basutoland, c. 1962–1965," *South African Historical Journal* 62, no. 1 (2010): 54–77.

67. Coplan, *In the Time of Cannibals*, 260.

68. Guy and Thabane, "Shaft Sinking."

69. Richard Weisfelder, "Early Voices of Protest in Basutoland: The Progressive Association and Lekhotla la Bafo," *African Studies Review* 17, no. 2 (1974): 397–409; Robert Edgar, *Prophets with Honour: A Documentary History of Lekhotla la Bafo* (Johannesburg: Ravan Press, 1988).

70. Epprecht and Nattrass, *"This Matter of Women."*

71. Showers, *Imperial Gullies*, 63; Malijeng Ngqaleni, "A Review of Lesotho's Agricultural Policies and Strategies for the 1990s," in Santho and Sejanamane, *Southern Africa after Apartheid*, 130–32. For the regional roots of such projects, see C. J. de Wet, *Moving Together, Drifting Apart: Betterment Planning and Villagisation in a South African Homeland* (Johannesburg: Witwatersrand University Press, 1995); Jacob Tropp, "The Contested Nature of Colonial Landscapes: Historical Perspectives on Livestock and Environments in the Transkei," *Kronos* 30 (2004): 118–37; P. A. McAllister, "Resistance to 'Betterment' in the Transkei: A Case Study from Willowvale District," *Journal of Southern African Studies* 15, no. 2 (1989): 346–68.

CHAPTER 1   Political Changes and Basotho Responses, 1950s to Independence

1. Jay Straker, *Youth, Nationalism and the Guinean Revolution* (Bloomington: Indiana University Press, 2009); Jean Allman, "The Youngmen and the Porcupine: Class, Nationalism and Asante's Struggle for Self-Determination, 1954–57," *Journal of African History* 31, no. 2 (1990): 263–79; Power, *Political Culture and Nationalism*; Mueni Wa Muiu, *The Pitfalls of Liberal Democracy and Late Nationalism in South Africa* (New York: Palgrave Macmillan, 2008); Geiger, *TANU Women*; Askew, *Performing the Nation*.

2. Lelimo, *Conquered Territory*, 200–205.

3. Maloka, *Basotho and the Mines*; Kimble, *Migrant Labour*, 53–55.

4. Machobane, *Government and Change*, 71.

5. Hailey, *Africa Survey Revised*, 272–74.

6. Rosenberg, *Promises*, 39–40; Eldredge, *Kingdom*, 195–96.

7. "The Failure of Unity," *Naledi*, December 24, 1926.

8. Lord Hailey, *An African Survey: A Study of Problems Arising in Africa South of the Sahara* (New York: Oxford University Press, 1938), 399.

9. Showers, *Imperial Gullies*, 181, 257; William Beinart, "Soil Erosion, Conservationism and Ideas About Development: A Southern African Exploration, 1900–1960," *Journal of Southern African Studies* 11, no. 1 (1984): 60–61. The history of this anti-erosion campaign is explored in more detail in chapter 3.

10. *Financial and Economic Position of Basutoland: Report of the Commission Appointed by the Secretary of State for Dominion Affairs* (hereafter Pim Report), presented by the Secretary of State for Dominion Affairs to Parliament by Command of His Majesty, May 1935, 183–86.

11. John Iliffe, *A Modern History of Tanganyika* (Cambridge: Cambridge University Press, 1979), 436.

12. Pim Report, 180–83.

13. Ibid.

14. Machobane, *Government and Change*, 220–27.

15. Murray and Sanders, *Medicine Murder*, 3.

16. Ibid., 284.

17. National Archives of the United Kingdom (hereafter TNA) CAB 129/45 Memo Visit by the Secretary of State for Commonwealth Relations to the Union of South Africa, Southern Rhodesia and the Three High Commission Territories of Basutoland, the Bechuanaland Protectorate and Swaziland, April 16, 1951, 6.

18. TNA CAB 129/45 Secretary of State Visit to South Africa, 6.

19. Lord Hailey, *Native Administration in the British African Territories: Part V. The High Commission Territories: Basutoland, the Bechuanaland Protectorate and Swaziland* (London: Her Majesty's Stationery Office, 1953), 140.

20. Machobane, *Government and Change*, 82.

21. Ibid., 240.

22. *Proceedings of the 48th Session of the Basuto National Council, 13th September 1952* (Maseru: Government Printing, 1953); *Proceedings of the 49th (1953) Session of the Basuto National Council, 26 September 1953* (Maseru: Government Printing, 1954).

23. *Basutoland Report of the Administrative Reforms Committee* (Maseru: Government Printing, 1954), 1.

24. Interview, Tšeliso Ramakhula, Maseru, Lower Thamae, March 1, 2009.

25. "Komiti E Kholo Ea Nchafatso Ea Puso Lesotho" (The Committee on Government Reform in Lesotho, trans. by author), *Moeletsi oa Basotho*, May 15, 1954; Z. S. Thole, "Komiti ea Nchafatso ea Puso" (Government Reform Committee, trans. by author), *Moeletsi oa Basotho*, June 26, 1954; Kaizer Mohlakola, "Administrative Reform in Basutoland and the Commission of Sir Henry Moore," *Leselinyana la Lesotho*, May 23, 1955.

26. Chaka Ntsane, for one, remembered newspapers being delivered to mission stations and then being read aloud for those who were not literate. Interview, Chaka Ntsane, Maseru, February 24, 2009.

27. TNA CAB 128/27 Notes of Cabinet Meeting, Incorporation of High Commission Territories, July 6, 1954.

28. John Darwin, *The Empire Project: The Rise and Fall of the British World System, 1830–1970* (New York: Cambridge University Press, 2009), 607–9.

29. *Basutoland: Report on Constitutional Discussions Held in London in November and December 1958* (London: Her Majesty's Stationery Office, 1959).

30. The BPA also went by its Sesotho abbreviation, KTP, which stood for Kopano ea Tsoela-pele. Edgar, *Prophets*; Weisfelder, "Protest in Basutoland," 399–400.

31. Vinson, *The Americans Are Coming!*

32. National Archives of South Africa, Pretoria (hereafter NASA, PT), BAO 3232 C43/3/7 BCP and Labour Recruitment 1967, Correspondence between Bekker, Secretary of Foreign Affairs and Commissioner South African Police, June 1967, trans. Faith Cranfield.

33. Mangaliso R. Sobukwe, "The Dog and the Wolf," *Mohlabani* 4 (July 1958); Clive Glaser, *The ANC Youth League* (Athens: Ohio University Press, 2012), 58–60; Lissoni, "PAC in Basutoland."

34. Tom Lodge, *Sharpeville: An Apartheid Massacre and Its Consequences* (New York: Oxford University Press, 2011), 198.

35. Weisfelder, *Political Contention*, 13.

36. Lissoni, "PAC in Basutoland," 58.

37. Stephen J. Gill, *A Short History of Lesotho* (Morija, Lesotho: Morija Museum and Archives, 1993), 204.

38. *Report of the Commission Enquiring into the Disturbances at the Lerotholi Technical School and Basutoland High School 1960* (Maseru: Government Printing, 1960).

39. Duncan, the son of the British governor-general of South Africa, was involved in politics in Lesotho as his South African politics gradually radicalized in the 1950s and 1960s. When he was editor of the Liberal Party newspaper, *Contact*, he arranged for the BCP newspaper, *Mohlabani*, to be printed in Cape Town after it was banned from Lesotho in 1955. In 1963 he joined the PAC, its first member of European descent, and played a role in the increasingly radical connections between the BCP and the PAC's armed wing, Poqo. He purchased two trading stores in the remote southern Quthing District of Lesotho in the hope of using them as bases for Poqo guerrilla missions into the Transkei. C. J. Driver, *Patrick Duncan: South African and Pan-African* (London: Heinemann, 1980).

40. Marc Epprecht, "Women's 'Conservatism' and the Politics of Gender in Late Colonial Lesotho," *Journal of African History* 36, no. 1 (1995): 47; Weisfelder, *Political Contention*, 28–31.

41. Succession to the monarchy in Lesotho in the twentieth century was a controversial process because of the various factions within the senior chieftaincy. The fact that 'Mantsebo was a woman further complicated the debates around succession, and it is hard to untangle where the gendered nature of the

opposition bled into the personality conflicts and divisions within the senior chieftaincy. These lines often correlated with descent from the various sons of Moshoeshoe I. The most concise explanation is in Murray and Sanders, *Medicine Murder*, 34–36.

42. Weisfelder, *Political Contention*, 18–20.

43. Ibid., table I(B).

44. Interview, Alexander Sekoli, St. David's Mission, Berea, November 25, 2008.

45. Interview, Moeketsi Lesitsi, St. Monica's Mission, Leribe, November 26, 2008.

46. Weisfelder, *Political Contention*, 18.

47. Machobane, *Government and Change*, 263; Weisfelder, *Political Contention*, 20–21.

48. TNA CAB 129/98 *Africa: The Next Ten Years*, Memorandum from Secretary of State for Foreign Affairs, July 2, 1959.

49. Kunene, "Leselinyana la Lesotho," 150.

50. "The Mission Press of Basutoland," *Basutoland Witness* 3, nos. 4–5 (1949).

51. Interview, Chaka Ntsane, Maseru, February 24, 2009; interview, Tšeliso Ramakhula, Maseru, Lower Thamae, March 1, 2009.

52. There is no comprehensive history of the newspapers of Lesotho, but Stephen Gill has a short section in *A Short History of Lesotho*, 192–96; David Ambrose has some scattered information in *Maseru: An Illustrated History* (Morija, Lesotho: Morija Museum and Archives, 1993). A more comprehensive look at the early nonmission papers is in Ambrose's *Naledi ea Lesotho, the Basutoland Star*. These accounts, however, focus on the religious press and early secular papers. For political papers, see the longtime *Mohlabani* editor B. M. Khaketla's *Lesotho 1970: An African Coup under the Microscope* (London: C. Hurst & Co., 1971), even if its information, too, is scattered throughout the book.

53. Lodge, *Sharpeville*, 163–64.

54. Kwandiwe Kondlo, *In the Twilight of Revolution: The Pan Africanist Congress of Azania (South Africa), 1959–1994* (Basel: Basler Afrika Bibliographien, 2009), 103–10, 236–39.

55. TNA DO 35/7426 Refugees Airlift from High Commission Territories, Telex High Commissioner Pretoria, to Colonial Office, June 7, 1960.

56. TNA DO 35/7356 Basutoland Entry and Residence Proclamation.

57. Robert Edgar, *The Making of an African Communist: Edwin Thabo Mofutsanyana and the Communist Party of South Africa 1927–1939* (Pretoria: UNISA, 2005); Robert Edgar, personal correspondence.

58. TNA DO 35/7171 Disturbances at Leloaleng Technical School Quthing, Report District Commissioner Quthing to Government Secretary Maseru, March 24, 1958.

59. Interview, Motsapi Moorosi, Maseru East, March 12, 2009.

60. Zakes Mda, *Sometimes There Is a Void: Memoirs of an Outsider* (New York: Farrar, Straus and Giroux, 2012), 101–2; Mark Gevisser, *Thabo Mbeki: The Dream Deferred* (Johannesburg: Jonathan Ball, 2007), 447.

61. Medard Rwelamira, *Refugees in a Chess Game: Reflections on Botswana, Lesotho and Swaziland Refugee Policies* (Uppsala: Scandinavian Institute of African Studies, 1990), 30.

62. The institution changed its name to the University of Botswana, Lesotho and Swaziland (UBLS) in 1966, before becoming the National University of Lesotho (NUL) in an acrimonious split in 1975.

63. Interview, Marie Selena, Hlotse, November 26, 2008.

64. All of these are discussed in more detail in chapter 2.

65. Matlosa, "Aid, Development and Democracy," 5.

66. This is discussed more fully in chapter 2.

67. *Basutoland Constitutional Conference: Presented to Parliament by the Secretary of State for the Colonies by Command of Her Majesty May 1964* (London: Her Majesty's Stationery Office, 1964).

68. Interviews, Armelina Tsiki, St. Rodrigue, May 7, 2009; Chaka Ntsane, Maseru, February 24, 2009; Selborne Mohlalisi, Morija, November 10, 2008; Mohlalefi Moteane, Maseru, May 27, 2009; Clara Rapholo, Roma, May 5, 2009.

69. Interview, Raphael Leseli, Roma, January 15, 2009.

70. Interview, Chaka Ntsane, Maseru, February 24, 2009.

71. Interview, Selborne Mohlalisi, Morija, November 10, 2008.

72. Interview, Moeketsi Lesitsi, St. Monica's Mission, Leribe, November 26, 2008.

73. Interview, Raphael Leseli, Roma, January 15, 2009.

74. Interview, Michael Mateka, Sacred Heart High School, Leribe, November 26, 2008.

75. Lissoni, "PAC in Basutoland," 73; Robert Edgar, "The Lesotho Coup of 1986," *South African Review* 4 (1988): 374–75.

76. This is examined more in chapter 4 in discussions of how young Basotho deployed development rhetoric and practice to argue for their vision of the nation in the late colonial and early independence periods.

77. Interview, Moeketsi Lesitsi, St. Monica's Mission, Leribe, November 26, 2008.

78. Anonymous interview, Rothe, Mafeteng, April 6, 2009.

79. Interview, Tšeliso Ramakhula, Maseru, Lower Thamae, May 1, 2009.

80. Interview, Mohlalefi Moteane, Maseru, May 27, 2009.

81. Interview, Motsapi Moorosi, Maseru East, March 12, 2009.

82. *Annual Report by the Director of Education for the Year 1951* (Maseru: Government Printing, 1951); *Annual Report of the Permanent Secretary for the Year 1966 and a General Survey of Progress and Development in the Triennium*

1964–66 (Maseru: Government Printing, 1967); *Annual Report of the Ministry of Education and Culture, 1970/72* (Maseru: Government Printing, 1972).

83. Interview, Chaka Ntsane, Maseru, February 24, 2009.

84. Interview, Chaka Ntsane, Maseru, February 24, 2009.

85. Interview, Mohlalefi Moteane, Maseru, May 27, 2009.

86. N. Kaul, *Report on Local Government in Lesotho* (Maseru: Government Printing, 1966), 22.

87. Weisfelder, *Political Contention*, table I(B); TNA CO 1048/897 Basutoland Independence Conference.

88. Weisfelder, *Political Contention*, 107–8.

89. TNA CO 1048/867 Visit of Basutoland Delegation to London Nov. 1965 for Constitutional Talks (November 22 to December 1, 1965), "Briefing for Secretary of State for Colonies," November 22, 1965.

90. "The Prime Minister's Independence Broadcast to the Nation," *Lesotho Quarterly* 1, no. 4 (1966): 2.

CHAPTER 2   The Colonial Era and the Rhetorical Consensus on Development

1. TNA OD 31/169 Lesotho Post-Independence Aid, recorded conversation between High Commissioner Maseru and Prime Minister Jonathan, February 9, 1967.

2. National Archives at College Park, College Park, MD (hereafter NACP), RG 490 Records of the Peace Corps, Office of International Operations, Country Plans 1966–85, Lesotho, Box 54, Lesotho 1966–71 9224, Lesotho: Program Summary Forecast, October 6, 1966.

3. Hodge and Hödl, "Introduction," 14.

4. Latham, "Modernization," 6.

5. Cullather, "Development," 641.

6. NACP, RG 59 General Records of the Department of State, Bureau of African Affairs, Records of the Bureau of African Affairs, 1958–66, Box 55, 1958–66, Folder: General Political, High Commission Territories, 1963–65, Memo, January 6, 1964.

7. NASA, PT, EAE 299 EA 4/3/2 Economic Assistance 1967, Help for Lesotho; trans. Faith Cranfield.

8. Darwin, *Empire Project*, 577–78; Grubbs, *Secular Missionaries*, 20–21.

9. William Easterly, *The Tyranny of Experts: Economists, Dictators, and the Forgotten Rights of the Poor* (New York: Basic Books, 2013), 30.

10. Easterly, *Tyranny of Experts*, 81.

11. Hodge and Hödl, "Introduction," 5–9.

12. Murray, *Families Divided*, 86, 171.

13. Beinart, "Soil Erosion," 80–81.

14. The latter studies marked the start of the Lesotho Highlands Water Project. The consulting engineers, Ninham Shand and Graeme Walker, who proposed and carried out the early studies, would win key contracts in the construction of Phase I in the 1980s and 1990s.

15. Molapo, quoted in *1957 Basutoland National Council.*

16. Matlosa, "Aid, Development and Democracy," 7.

17. TNA CO 1048/892 Basutoland: Final Report Before Independence, British Government Representative to Secretary of State for the Colonies, October 3, 1966.

18. Interview, Tšeliso Ramakhula, Maseru, Lower Thamae, March 1, 2009.

19. Kaul, *Local Government*, 22.

20. Aerni-Flessner, "Development and Politics," 407–8.

21. World Bank, *Lesotho: A Development Challenge* (Washington, DC: World Bank, 1975), 1.

22. Murray and Sanders, *Medicine Murder*, 16–19; Kimble, *Migrant Labour*, 5; Eldredge, *South African Kingdom*, 11; Motlatsi Thabane, "Aspects of Colonial Economy and Society, 1868–1966," in *Essays on Aspects of the Political Economy of Lesotho 1500–2000*, ed. Motlatsi Thabane and Neville Pule (Roma, Lesotho: Department of History, 2000), 112.

23. Pim Report, 183–86.

24. Showers, *Imperial Gullies*, 155.

25. Ibid., 175.

26. de Wet, *Betterment Planning.*

27. Showers, *Imperial Gullies*, 178.

28. Thabane, "Colonial Economy," 128–29.

29. While the first subventions were delivered in 1871, it was only after the Colonial Office regained direct responsibility for Basutoland in 1885 that these payments became regularized. *Annual Report by the Director of Education for the Year 1951* (Maseru: Government Printers, 1952).

30. *Annual Report of the Director of Education for the Year 1954* (Maseru: Government Printing, 1955).

31. Derek R. Peterson, *Creative Writing: Translation, Bookkeeping, and the Work of Imagination in Colonial Kenya* (Portsmouth, NH: Heinemann, 2004), esp. ch. 6.

32. T. Dunbar Moodie and Vivienne Ndatshe, *Going for Gold: Men, Mines, and Migration* (Berkeley: University of California Press, 1994); Murray, *Families Divided.*

33. *Education Annual Report 1954; The Annual Report of the Ministry of Education and Culture 1969* (Maseru: Government Printing, 1970).

34. Interview, Armelina Tsiki, St. Rodrigue, May 7, 2009.

35. *Basutoland: Report of the Commission Appointed by His Majesty's Secretary of State for Dominion Affairs to Enquire into and Make Recommendations upon Education in Basutoland* (Pretoria: Government Printer, 1946).

36. *Annual Report of the Ministry of Education and Culture, 1970/72* (Maseru: Government Printer, 1972).

37. *Colonial Reports, Basutoland 1952* (Maseru: Government Printing, 1953).

38. Martin Thomas, "Contrasting Patterns of Decolonization: Belgian and Portuguese Africa," in *Crises of Empire: Decolonization and Europe's Imperial States, 1918–1975*, ed. Martin Thomas, Bob Moore, and L. J. Butler (London: Hodder Education, 2008), 385.

39. Interviews, Simon Phafane, Maseru, November 3, 2008; Clara Rapholo, Roma, May 5, 2009; Maleseko Kena, Tsoelike Auplas, March 17, 2009; Raphael Leseli, Roma, January 15, 2009.

40. Alvord, quoted in E. Kushinga Makombe, "Developing Rural Africa: Rural Development Discourse in Colonial Zimbabwe, 1944–79," in Hodge, Hödl, and Kopf, *Developing Africa*, 155, 159.

41. Figures on mining from Jonathan Crush and Belinda Dodson, *Migration, Remittances and "Development" in Lesotho* (Cape Town: Idasa, 2010), 9.

42. Epprecht, "Women's 'Conservatism,'" 34.

43. Epprecht and Nattrass, *"This Matter of Women,"* 176–87.

44. Epprecht, "Women's 'Conservatism,'" 29–31.

45. Ibid., 54.

46. *Annual Report by the Director of Education for the Year 1954* (Maseru: Government Printers, 1955).

47. Figures from *Annual Report on Basutoland for the Year 1954* (London: Her Majesty's Stationery Office, 1955); Epprecht, "Domesticity," 211.

48. Interview, Maleseko Kena, Tsoelike Auplas, March 17, 2009.

49. TNA FCO 141/293 Basutoland Cooperatives 1946–60, Memo, Resident Commissioner to Registrar of Cooperative Societies, March 30, 1961.

50. TNA DO 35/7384 Community Development in the HCT 1957–60, Report from District Commissioner Conference, 1959.

51. A. F. Robertson, "Popular Scientist: James Jacob Machobane and 'Mantsa Tlala,'" *African Affairs* 93, no. 370 (1994): 99–121.

52. National University of Lesotho Archives Leribe Collection (hereafter NULA LC) 37/2 1936–1958 Agricultural General and Monthly Reports, January 1954–February 1957, Letter J. J. Machobane to Venn, Soil Fertility Officer Maseru Experimental Station, May 10, 1957.

53. J. J. Machobane, *The Machobane Mass Agricultural and Development Foundation College: Prospectus* (Nqechane, Lesotho: Self-published, 1961), 1.

54. NULA LC 37/2 1936–1958 Agricultural General and Monthly Reports, January 1954–February 1957, Letter Senior Agricultural and Livestock

Officer to Director of Livestock and Agricultural Services Maseru, December 31, 1955.

55. Robertson, "Popular Scientist," 108.

56. J. J. Machobane and Robert Berold, *Drive Out Hunger: The Story of J. J. Machobane of Lesotho* (Johannesburg: Jacana Media, 2005), 43–62, 70–73, 109–10.

57. Frederick Cooper, *Decolonization and African Society: The Labor Question in French and British Africa* (New York: Cambridge University Press, 1996).

58. Rosaleen Smyth, "The Roots of Community Development in Colonial Office Policy and Practice in Africa," *Social Policy and Administration* 38, no. 4 (2004): 219.

59. TNA DO 35/7384 Community Development in the HCT 1957–60, Report from District Commissioner Conference, 1959.

60. TNA DO 35/7384 Community Development in the HCT 1957–60, Report from District Commissioner Conference, 1959.

61. TNA DO 35/7384 Community Development in the HCT 1957–60, Report from District Commissioner Conference, 1959. For British West African worries, see Victoria Tashjian and Jean Allman, *"I Will Not Eat Stone": A Women's History of Colonial Asante* (Portsmouth, NH: Heinemann, 2000).

62. TNA DO 35/7384 Community Development in the HCT 1957–60, Report from District Commissioner Conference, 1959.

63. Motlatsi Thabane, *"Liphokojoe* of Kao: A Study of a Diamond Digger Rebel Group in the Lesotho Highlands," *Journal of Southern African Studies* 26, no. 1 (2000): 105–6.

64. Murray and Sanders, *Medicine Murder*, 30–36.

65. *Sekama* was the Sesotho word for weathered kimberlite—the rock formation in which most diamonds are found. It was used by some of the clans in Lesotho as part of youth initiation ceremonies, so individuals and communities clearly knew where to find this type of rock. I owe a debt of gratitude to Kabi Kolobe, Maele Neko, and Thoora Semela for the twitter conversation in which they explained this to me.

66. 1954 and 1957 Paramount Chief's Circulars, Circular No. 12, June 25, 1956.

67. *1956 Basutoland Council.*

68. Poka, quoted in *1956 Basutoland Council.*

69. Councilor Sekhonyana Molapo, quoted in *1957 Basutoland Council.*

70. Councilors Gabriel Manyeli and Ntsu Mokhehle, quoted in *1957 Basutoland Council.*

71. Motlatsi Thabane, *Individual Diamond Digging in Lesotho, 1955–1970: A Study of an Aspect of the Social and Economic History of Lesotho*, Trondheim Studies in History No. 8 (Trondheim, Norway: The University, 1995), 3.

72. Ibid., 44.

73. NULA LC 4 1954–59 Arms and Ammunition Permits, Letter Jonathan Mathealira, Chief of Tsikoane to District Commissioner Leribe, May 15, 1959.

74. TNA FCO 141/481 Elias Monare Case, Note on Monare Commissioner of Police, July 4, 1960.

75. TNA FCO 141/556 Force Requirements in HCT 1965.

76. Thabane, "*Liphokojoe* of Kao," 120–21.

77. TNA CAB 129/45 Secretary of State Memo to Cabinet, April 16, 1951.

78. NULA LC 26 1931–57 Caledon River Gauging and Silt Sampling.

79. NULA LC 26 1931–57 Caledon River Gauging and Silt Sampling.

80. NASA, PT BES 7 10/7A Caledon River Project Purchases of Land in Basutoland, Letter Prime Minister Smuts to British High Commissioner Pretoria, December 23, 1942.

81. Lefela, quoted in *1954 Basutoland Council.*

82. Molapo, quoted in *1954 Basutoland Council.*

83. Ferguson, *Anti-Politics Machine*, 273–75.

84. Joann McGregor, *Cross the Zambezi: The Politics of Landscape on a Central African Frontier* (Rochester: Boydell & Brewer, 2009), ch. 6.

85. Ibid., 108.

86. *1957 Basutoland National Council.*

87. Councilor Maqoaelane Hlekane, quoted in *1957 Basutoland National Council; World Bank, Staff Appraisal Report Lesotho Highlands Water Project (Phase 1A)*, 1991, 8.

88. Boipuso, "The Burden of Self-Rule," *Mohlabani*, October 1958, 11.

89. Molapo, quoted in *1957 Basutoland Council.*

90. Selemo, quoted in *1957 Basutoland Council.*

91. Mwangi, "Hydropolitics and Human Security," 3–17.

92. TNA CAB 129/45 Secretary of State Memo to Cabinet, April 16, 1951.

93. NULA LC 8 Official Visits 1943–58; Chris Conz, "'Wisdom Does Not Live in One House': Compiling Environmental Knowledge in Lesotho, Southern Africa, c. 1880–1965" (PhD diss., Boston University, 2017), ch. 6.

94. Interview, Peter Millin, Clarens, RSA, March 6, 2009.

95. Akinagum Fidelis Esenjor, "A Community Based Conservation Programme for the Management and Conservation of Land Resources in Lesotho" (PhD diss., University of the Free State, 2004), 121.

96. Thabane, "Colonial Economy," 118.

97. Showers, *Imperial Gullies*, 227.

98. 1962 Colonial Annual Report of the Agricultural Department, quoted in Showers, *Imperial Gullies*, 59.

99. Wallman, *Take Out Hunger*, 83.

100. Leslie Bank, "The Janus-Face of Rural Class Formation: An Economic and Political History of Traders in QwaQwa, 1960–1985" (Unpublished paper, University of Witwatersrand History Workshop, 1990); D. A. Kotze, "The Witzieshoek Revolt 1940–1950," *African Studies* 41, no. 1 (1982): 127–41.

101. TNA FCO 141/887 Subversive Organizations, Memo District Commissioner Butha Buthe to Government Secretary Maseru, October 18, 1951.

102. D. R. Mochecko, "Lesotho le Tsoela-pele," *Moeletsi oa Basotho* 22, no. 973 (August 21, 1954): 3; trans. author.

103. S. Lepolesa, "Lesotho le Tsoela-pele," *Moeletsi oa Basotho* 22, no. 977 (September 18, 1954): 3; trans. author.

104. Bank, "QwaQwa," 1; de Wet, *Betterment Planning*.

105. Showers, *Imperial Gullies*, 178.

106. Wallman, *Take Out Hunger*, 90–91.

107. Ibid., 83.

108. TNA FCO 141/481 Elias Monare Case, Memo District Commissioner Mohale's Hoek to Resident Commissioner Maseru, April 26, 1961.

109. TNA FCO 141/481 Elias Monare Case, Notes for Meeting on Taung and Monare, May 18, 1961.

110. Conz, "'Wisdom Does Not Live in One House,'" 362–81.

111. Richard Weisfelder, "Power Struggle in Lesotho," *Africa Report* 12, no. 1 (1967): 5–6.

112. RG 59 General Records of the Department of State, Bureau of African Affairs, Office of Eastern and Southern African Affairs, Records Relating to South Africa, 1959–65, Records Relating to South West Africa, 1957–63, Box 3, Folder: Basutoland 1958–59, Memo about Constitutional Change in Basutoland.

113. Philip E. Muehlenbeck, *Betting on the Africans: John F. Kennedy's Courting of African Nationalist Leaders* (New York: Oxford University Press, 2014), 44–57.

114. John F. E. Ohiorhenuan, "Don't Cry for Me Africa," *Transition* 102 (2010): 140.

115. TNA CO 1048/284 Visit by Paramount Chief of Basutoland to the United Kingdom, United States and Canada, 1962, Memo High Commissioner Ottawa to Secretary of State for the Colonies, February 28, 1962.

116. TNA CO 1048/284 Visit by Paramount Chief of Basutoland to the United Kingdom, United States and Canada, 1962 Memorandum to the United States Government on Basutoland and Its Immediate Needs, from Moshoeshoe II, February 1962.

117. NACP RG 59 General Records of the Department of State, Bureau of African Affairs, Records of the Bureau of African Affairs, 1958–66, Box 54, Folder: Political Relations and Affairs, HCT 1964 and back, Confidential

Briefing Paper, no date; Box 55, Folder: General Political, HCT 1963–65, Note January 6, 1964.

118. TNA CO 1048/284 Visit by Paramount Chief, Memo Colonial Office to Secretary of State for Colonies, February 7, 1962.

119. TNA FCO 141/456 Basutoland: Delegation to USA, Memo Resident Commissioner Chaplin to High Commissioner, February 16, 1961.

120. All quotations in this paragraph are from TNA CO 1048/281 Paramount Chief of Basutoland: Petition to High Commissioner about Development of Basutoland, May 25, 1962.

121. TNA CO 1048/281 Paramount Chief of Basutoland: Petition to High Commissioner about Development of Basutoland, May 25, 1962.

122. Gabriele Winai Ström, *Development and Dependence in Lesotho: The Enclave of South Africa* (Uppsala: Scandinavian Institute of African Studies, 1978), 60.

123. TNA FCO 141/842 Official Visitors to Basutoland, Notes on Basutoland for Eirene White, Under-Secretary of State for the Colonies Visit, March 1965.

124. Interview, Tšeliso Ramakhula, Maseru, Lower Thamae, May 1, 2009.

125. Interview, Mohlalefi Moteane, Maseru, May 27, 2009.

126. Interview, Thabelo Kebise, Maseru Bus Stop, April 1, 2009.

127. Interview, Raphael Leseli, Roma, January 15, 2009.

128. Interview, Chaka Ntsane, Maseru, February 24, 2009.

129. Interviews, Tšeliso Ramakhula, Maseru, Lower Thamae, March 1, 2009; Michael Mateka, Sacred Heart High School, Leribe, November 26, 2008.

130. Interview, Selborne Mohlalisi, Morija, November 10, 2008.

131. Interview, Moeketsi Lesitsi, St. Monica's Mission, Leribe, November 26, 2008.

132. Interview, Selborne Mohlalisi, Morija, November 10, 2008.

133. Interview, Scott Brumburgh, telephone, August 6, 2012.

134. All Verwoerd quotations from TNA CAB 129/101 Prime Minister's African Tour, Report April 12, 1960, 147–48.

135. Lelimo, *Lesotho's Conquered Territory*, 203–5.

136. TNA CO 1048/38 Basutoland Development Plan 1963–68, Notes on BAFED 1962.

137. The post-independence smaller factories are discussed in more detail in chapter 5.

138. Z. A. Konczacki, Jane Parpart, and Timothy Shaw, eds., *Studies in the Economic History of Southern Africa*, vol. 2: *South Africa, Lesotho and Swaziland* (Hoboken, NJ: Routledge, 1990), 153.

139. NACP RG 59 General Records of the Department of State, Bureau of African Affairs, Records of the Bureau of African Affairs, 1958–66, Box 4, Folder: AID US, South Africa, 1965, Letter Jesse MacKnight, no date.

140. TNA OD 31/219 South African Assistance to Lesotho, 1967–69, Memo High Commissioner Maseru to the Commonwealth Office, October 17, 1968.

141. World Bank Archives, Washington, DC (hereafter WBA), 1859610 Roads Project, Lesotho/Basutoland, Negotiations, Vol. 1: 1961–65, Outline of Road Situation in Basutoland (prepared by Basutoland Government), March 22, 1961.

142. WBA 1859610 Roads Project, Lesotho/Basutoland, Negotiations, Vol. 1: 1961–65, *Report on Visit*, April 25, 1961.

143. WBA 1859610 Roads Project, Lesotho/Basutoland, Negotiations, Vol. 1: 1961–65, Letter H. J. van Helden, IDA to Barnes, Public Works Department, March 21, 1962.

144. WBA 1859610 Roads Project, Lesotho/Basutoland, Negotiations, Vol 1: 1961–65, Appraisal Visit May 18–22, 1963, H. R. Young.

145. WBA 1859610 Roads Project, Lesotho/Basutoland, Negotiations, Vol. 1: 1961–65, Letter Barnes to Cope, IDA, January 23, 1964.

146. Interview, Selborne Mohlalisi, Morija, November 10, 2008.

147. John Aerni-Flessner, "Self-Help Development Projects and Conceptions of Independence in Lesotho, 1950s–1970s," *International Journal of African Historical Studies* 50, no. 1 (2017): 11–33.

THREE   Working for Development

1. Charles Maier, *In Search of Stability: Explorations in Historical Political Economy* (New York: Cambridge University Press, 1987), 130.

2. Grubbs, *Secular Missionaries*, 69, 76.

3. Kaul, *Local Government*, Annexure: Local Government Policy.

4. "Community Development in Lesotho," *Basutoland Quarterly* 3, no. 1 (1966): 16–17.

5. "Let Us Take along the Lamps of Wisdom," *Lesotho News* (Ladybrand), March 18, 1966, 2.

6. Ibid.

7. Ström, *Development and Dependence*, 91–92.

8. Wallman, *Take Out Hunger*, 135.

9. "New Political Parties, Their Manifestos," *Mohlabani* 4 (August 1958): 8–9.

10. Ibid., 10–11.

11. "Basutoland Congress Manifesto," *Mohlabani* 4 (December 1958): 3; original emphasis.

12. John Motloheloa, "Lesotho's Road to Independence—The Founding of the Communist Party of Lesotho (Basutoland)," *African Communist* 10 (July–August 1962): 23.

13. Latham, "Modernization," 6.

14. Epprecht and Nattrass, *This Matter of Women*," 4–5.

15. Interview, Peter Khamane, Ha QhuQhu, October 29, 2008.

16. Interview, Gabriel Tlaba, Lesotho College of Education, October 7, 2008.

17. Epprecht, "Domesticity," 214, 218, 222–23.

18. *Report of the Commission Enquiring into the Disturbances at the Lerotholi Technical School and Basutoland High School 1960* (Maseru: Basutoland Government, 1960).

19. Moodie and Ndatshe, *Going for Gold*, 16–22; Murray, *Families Divided*, 175–76.

20. TNA DO 35/7171 Disturbances at Leloaleng Technical School Quthing Report from the Resident Commissioner, Basutoland on Leloaleng Disturbances, June 14, 1958.

21. TNA FCO 141/853 Passports and Visas Note, Immigration Office, Maseru, March 1963.

22. TNA FCO 141/456 Basutoland: Delegation to USA Memo Resident Commissioner Maseru to High Commissioner Pretoria, February 16, 1961.

23. TNA CO 1048/931 Student Passports Used in Travel in Unauthorized Countries, Colonial Office Memo Markham to Stonehouse, April 13, 1966.

24. Interview, Mohlalefi Moteane, Maseru, May 27, 2009.

25. Interview, Simon Phafane, Maseru, November 3, 2008.

26. TNA FCO 141/456 Basutoland: Delegation to USA Government Secretary Maseru to Government House, Nairobi June 8, 1961.

27. TNA FCO 141/456 Basutoland: Delegation to USA Executive Council, "Aims of Tour," July 13, 1961.

28. TNA FCO 141/456 Basutoland: Delegation to USA Executive Council, "Aims of Tour," July 13, 1961.

29. TNA FCO 141/456 Basutoland: Delegation to USA Executive Council, Note High Commissioner Pretoria to Resident Commissioner Maseru, October 12, 1961.

30. TNA DO 35/7384 Community Development in the HCT 1957–60, Memo Resident Commissioner Basutoland to Commonwealth Relations Office, May 19, 1960.

31. Wallman, *Take Out Hunger*, 119.

32. WBA 1591147 Roads Project Reports and Studies 1960–62, *Report on Soil Conservation Scheme, Estimates for Period 1/4/60–31/3/64.*

33. WBA 1591147 Roads Project Reports and Studies 1960–62, *Report on Soil Conservation Scheme, Estimates for Period 1/4/60–31/3/64.*

34. Kaul, *Local Government*, 22.

35. WBA 1859610 Roads Project, Lesotho/Basutoland, Negotiations Vol. 1 1961–65, Letter H. J. van Helden, IDA, to Barnes, Department of Public Works, March 21, 1962.

36. In October 1966 it became the University of Botswana, Lesotho and Swaziland. The three governments jointly ran it until 1975 when Lesotho pulled out, forming the National University of Lesotho on the Roma campus. For more on this, see Mothusi T. Mashologu, *A Broken Reed: The Traumatic Experience of the Last Day of the University of Botswana, Lesotho and Swaziland, and Its Aftermath* (Morija, Lesotho: Phafa Publishers, 2006).

37. NACP RG 286 Agency for International Development Central Subject Files, 1968–73, Bureau for Africa/Office for Southern Africa Regional Coordination, Box 3, Folder PRM 3, Regional Activities–Lesotho FY 69, Note Hugh McCubbin World Food Program to A. Howard, U.S. Embassy Maseru, August 7, 1968—History of WFP Assistance in Lesotho.

38. Local Government Proclamation, 1959 (No. 52 of 1959), in *Basutoland Constitutional Handbook: Containing the Basutoland (Constitution) Order in Council, 1959, and Related Legislation and Reports* (Maseru: Government Printing, 1960).

39. Ström, *Development and Dependence*, 60.

40. Wallman, *Take Out Hunger*, 132; interview, Michael Mateka, Sacred Heart High School, Leribe, November 26, 2008.

41. Interview, Peter Millin, Clarens, RSA, March 6, 2009.

42. Mann, *Empires to NGOs*, 9.

43. TNA CAB 129/101 Development Policy: Memorandum by the Chancellor of the Exchequer, March 28, 1960, 2.

44. TNA CAB 129/98 *Africa: The Next Ten Years*, Memorandum from Secretary of State for Foreign Affairs, July 2, 1959.

45. TNA CAB 129/114 Valedictory Despatch, Sir John Maud to Lord Home, May 20, 1963, 8.

46. TNA FCO 141/839 Financial Implications of Constitutional Development, Note from High Commissioner Cape Town to Colonial Office London, March 13, 1964; original emphasis.

47. Weisfelder, *Political Contention*, 64; Monson, *Freedom Railway*, 6–7.

48. Weisfelder, *Political Contention*, 67–68.

49. NACP RG 59 General Records of the Department of State, Bureau of African Affairs, Office of Southern African Affairs, Box 54, Letter B.M. Khaketla to Kenneth Snyder, Bureau of Cultural and Educational Affairs, Department of State, April 30, 1962.

50. Weisfelder, *Political Contention*, 69.

51. Ibid., 67.

52. Interview, Moeketsi Lesitsi, St. Monica's Mission, Leribe, November 26, 2008.

53. Interview, Armelina Tsiki, St. Rodrigue High School, May 7, 2009.

54. Interview, Mohlalefi Moteane, Maseru, May 27, 2009.

55. Interview, Michael Mateka, Sacred Heart High School, Leribe, November 26, 2008.

56. BNP Deputy Leader Sekhonyana 'Maseribane, thus, was the first prime minister of Basutoland from May 1965.

57. Gabriele Winai Ström, *Migration and Development: Dependence on South Africa: A Study of Lesotho* (Uppsala: Scandinavian Institute of African Studies, 1986), 49.

58. TNA FCO 141/851 Oxfam, Telegram British Government Representative Maseru to Secretary of State, June 10, 1965.

59. Khaketla, *African Coup*, 32.

60. TNA FCO 141/851 Oxfam, letter BCP to British Government Representative, June 11, 1965; "Grain Gift from South Africa," *Lesotho Times* (Mazenod), June 18, 1965.

61. "Grain for Basutoland, the Prime Minister's Conference," *Lesotho Times* (Mazenod), July 9, 1965.

62. "Basutoland Government Proceeds with Grain Distribution," *Lesotho Times* (Mazenod), August 13, 1965

63. "Opening of Hlotse Bridge, PM's Speech," *Basutoland Times* (Mazenod), August 26, 1966.

64. "Second Self-Help Programme for Lesotho" and "Six-Month Self Help Campaign Starts Soon," *Lesotho News* (Ladybrand), April 25, 1967, 1; "Girls' Hostel Opened at Butha Buthe Secondary School," *Lesotho News* (Ladybrand), June 27, 1967, 4.

65. S. M. Letsie, quoted in Basutoland Government, *Parliamentary Debates (Hansard): Official Report First Series, Volume 1*, 1335.

66. Interview, Raphael Leseli, Roma, January 15, 2009.

67. TNA FCO 141/916 Central Intelligence Committee Reports, 1966, March 1966, Central Intelligence Committee Report.

68. TNA FCO 141/916 Central Intelligence Committee Reports, 1966, March 1966, Central Intelligence Committee Report.

69. TNA FCO 141/916 Central Intelligence Committee Reports, 1966, April 1966, Central Intelligence Committee Report.

70. "King and Premier to Lead Tree-Planting," *Lesotho News* (Ladybrand), August 6, 1968, 1.

71. Interview, Michael Mateka, Sacred Heart High School, Leribe November 26, 2008.

72. TNA OD 31/170 Lesotho Post-Independence Aid, Telegram British Embassy Vienna to High Commissioner Maseru, April 12, 1967.

73. Carol Lancaster, *U.S. Aid to Sub-Saharan Africa: Challenges, Constraints, and Choices* (Washington, DC: Center for Strategic and International Studies, 1982), 173.

74. NASA, PT EAE 299 EA 4/3/2 Economic Assistance 1967, Secretary of Foreign Affairs, Economic Division, Memo: Plans for the Economic Development of Lesotho, Botswana, and Swaziland; trans. Faith Cranfield.

75. NASA, PT WW 404 K25/3/1 Water Issues 1967, Technical Discussions with Lesotho about the Oxbow Scheme, December 19, 1966; trans. Faith Cranfield.

76. Lesotho Government, *Parliamentary Debates: Official Report (Hansard)* (Maseru: Government Printing, 1967), May 11, 1967.

77. Department of International Relations and Cooperation Archives, Pretoria (hereafter DIRCO) BTS 1/159/6/1 Oxbow and Kau Hydroelectric Schemes (Vol. 4), Letter Lord Fraser of Londale to Vorster, February 5, 1969.

78. TNA FCO 141/976 Famine Relief, British Government Representative to Foreign and Commonwealth Office, March 8, 1966.

79. TNA FCO 141/169 Post Independence Aid to Lesotho, conversation between Prime Minister Jonathan and British High Commissioner Maseru, February 9, 1967.

80. Interview, Motsapi Moorosi, Maseru East, March 12, 2009.

81. Lesotho Government, *Parliamentary Debates: Official Report (Hansard)* (Maseru: Government Printing, 1967).

82. NACP RG 59 General Records of the Department of State, Office of the Secretary/Office Chief of Protocol, Files of Visits by Heads of Government, Dignitaries and Delegations, 1928–76, Visit Files, Folder V-42 Visit of PM Jonathan of Lesotho, September 22, 1967, and Record of Conversation between Secretary of State Dean Rusk and Jonathan, September 29, 1967.

83. "Ma-America a 70 a Fihla Lesotho" (70 Americans Arrive in Lesotho), *Moeletsi oa Basotho* (Mazenod), January 6, 1968.

84. *Parliamentary Debates of the National Assembly, Hansard, Official Report, 30th Oct. 1967* (Maseru: Government Printing, 1967), speech by Mokhehle, November 2, 1967.

85. *Parliamentary Debates of the National Assembly, Hansard, Official Report, 30th Oct. 1967* (Maseru: Government Printing, 1967), speech by Mokhehle, November 2, 1967.

86. N. Mokhehle, "The American Peace Corps (part I)," *The Commentator* (August 1968): 21–23.

87. Interview, Dennis Caspe, telephone, July 10, 2012.

88. Julius A. Amin, *The Peace Corps in Cameroon* (Kent, OH: Kent State University Press, 1992), 135, 185; J. Larry Brown, *Peasants Come Last: A Memoir of the Peace Corps at Fifty* (Sunnyvale, CA: Lucita Publishing, 2011), 4–6; Elizabeth Cobbs Hoffman, *All You Need Is Love: The Peace Corps and the Spirit of the 1960s* (Cambridge, MA: Harvard University Press, 1998), 160.

89. Thabane, *Who Owns the Land*, 4–6.

90. "Voluntary Service in Quthing," *Moeletsi oa Basotho* (Mazenod), August 10, 1968; "International Voluntary Service," *Leselinyana la Lesotho* (Morija), June 1967; interview, Chaka Ntsane, Maseru, February 24, 2009; interview, Don Allen, email, March 2013.

91. Interview, Mohlalefi Moteane, Maseru, May 27, 2009.

92. Mda, *Sometimes There Is a Void*, 135–36.

93. Interview, Dennis Caspe, telephone, July 10, 2012.

94. NACP RG 490 Records of the Peace Corps, Office of International Operations, Country Plans 1966–1985, Lesotho, *Lesotho 1968–71 Program Memorandum*.

95. All information in this paragraph is from Wallman, *Take Out Hunger*, 118–20, 129–30, 132–35.

96. TNA FCO 141/795 Mafeteng District Council Tractor Scheme, Letter District Commissioner Mafeteng to Government Secretary Maseru, April 16, 1964.

97. Wallman, *Take Out Hunger*, 132.

98. TNA FCO 141/795 Mafeteng District Council Tractor Scheme, Letter Permanent Secretary for Local Government to Government Secretary Maseru, May 5, 1964.

99. Interview, Clark Tibbits, telephone, July 19, 2012.

100. Interview, Dennis Caspe, telephone, July 2012; interview, Clark Tibbits, telephone, July 19, 2012.

101. Department of Information, *Lesotho 1971* (Maseru: Department of Information, 1971).

102. Interview, Ted Hochstadt, email, July 2012.

103. Interview, Ted Hochstadt, email, July 2012.

104. All quotations are from interview, Ted Hochstadt, email, July 2012.

105. Interview, Ted Hochstadt, email, July 2012.

106. TNA FCO 141/932 Joint Territorial Intelligence Security Committee Conferences, 1962–65, September 1962 Minutes of Meeting; October 1964 Minutes of Meeting.

107. TNA FCO 141/369 Basutoland Papers from BCP File, Note July 6, 1961.

108. "Youth Rally a Success," *Lesotho News* (Ladybrand), April 21, 1967.

109. Lesotho National Archives (hereafter LNA), S3/12/3/13 Boy Scout Movement, 1914; for more on the Boy Scouts and Pathfinders in British colonial Africa, see Timothy Parsons, *Race, Resistance, and the Boy Scout Movement in British Colonial Africa* (Athens: Ohio University Press, 2004).

110. Basutoland Government, *Annual Report by the Director of Education for the Year 1951* (Maseru: Government Printing, 1952); *Annual Report of the Permanent Secretary for Education for the Year 1963 and a General Survey of Progress and Development in the Triennium 1961–63* (Maseru: Government Printers, 1964).

111. Interview, Peter Khamane, Ha QhuQhu, October 29, 2008. Peter leveraged his contacts in the schools and his work as a Boy Scout organizer to lay the groundwork for the foundation of the BNP and its associated Youth

Wing by the 1960s. He was one of the most polarizing figures of the independence era as his brand of militant anticommunism did not sit well with the BCP, whose Youth Wing destroyed his van in Maseru in 1961.

112. Interview, Gabriel Tlaba, Lesotho College of Education, October 7, 2008.

113. Anonymous interview, Rothe, Mafeteng, April 6, 2009.

114. Interview, Alexander Sekoli, St. David's Mission, Berea, November 13, 2008.

115. All quotations are from interview, Armelina Tsiki, St. Rodrigue High School, May 7, 2009.

116. J. Zimmerman, "The Church and Youth," *Basutoland Witness* (Morija) 11, no. 3 (1957): 3.

117. Morija Museum and Archives (hereafter MMA), *Mophato oa Morija*, unpublished history of the Mophato, no date, translated by Teboho Mokotjo; "Youth Leaders' Course at Morija," *Lesotho News* (Ladybrand), July 9, 1968.

118. Ruth Schoch, "SCM Easter Conference," *Basutoland Witness* (Morija) 67 (August 1964): 14.

119. Daniel R. Magaziner, *The Law and the Prophets: Black Consciousness in South Africa, 1968–1977* (Athens: Ohio University Press, 2010), 9, 73–74, 161–63.

120. All information on Tlaba is from interview, Gabriel Tlaba, Lesotho College of Education, October 28, 2008.

121. Interview, Chaka Ntsane, Maseru, February 24, 2009.

122. Interview, Chaka Ntsane, Maseru, February 24, 2009; interview, Don Allen, email, 2013.

123. Interview, Chaka Ntsane, Maseru, February 24, 2009.

124. R. Drew Smith and Stephanie C. Boddie, "Civic Service in Lesotho: Local Sources and US Connections," CSD Research Report 08-34 (2008), 11. Available at https://csd.wustl.edu/publications/documents/rp08-34.pdf.

125. All quotations are from interview, Maleseko Kena, Tsoelike Auplas, March 17, 2009.

126. Epprecht, "Domesticity," 204; Epprecht and Nattrass, *"This Matter of Women,"* 212–13. See also Bernice Mohapeloa, "Basutoland Homemakers Association," *Basutoland Witness* (Morija) 7, no. 1 (1953): 5–6.

127. John Aerni-Flessner, "Homemakers, Communists, and Refugees: Smuggling Anti-Apartheid Refugees in Rural Lesotho in the 1960s and 1970s," *Wagadu: A Journal of Transnational Women's and Gender Studies* 13 (2015): 183–209.

128. Interview, Gilbert Ramatlapeng, Maseru, June 12, 2015.

129. Interview, Clara Rapholo, Roma, May 5, 2009.

130. TNA FCO 141/1016 External Aid and Assistance 1965–66, Letter Ministry of Local Government to Ministry of Overseas Development, Local Government Adviser, August 31, 1965.

131. TNA FCO 141/988 Visit of ODM Mission October 1965, Memo ODM Mission Team to Government of Basutoland, October 28, 1965.

132. TNA OD 31/172 Lesotho Post-Independence Aid, Letter Prime Minister Jonathan to Prime Minister Wilson, March 4, 1968.

133. J. W. Biemanns, *Lesotho, an Uphill Road* (Maseru: Government Printing, 1968), 5.

134. D. Hirschmann, *Administration of Planning in Lesotho* (Manchester: University of Manchester Press, 1981), 15.

135. Ström, *Development and Dependence*, 93.

FOUR   The Internationalization of Lesotho's Development

1. TNA FCO 141/975 Water Resources in Basutoland, Leabua Jonathan to Sir Alexander Giles, July 16, 1965.

2. TNA FCO 141/975 Water Resources in Basutoland, Secretary of State for the Colonies to British Government Representative Maseru, August 6, 1965.

3. TNA FCO 141/975 Water Resources in Basutoland, Jonathan to Secretary of State for the Colonies, April 29, 1966.

4. NASA, PT WW K25/3/1 Water Issues 1967 Technical Discussions with Lesotho about the Oxbow Scheme, December 19, 1966.

5. DIRCO BTS 1/159/6/1 Oxbow and Kau Hydroelectric Schemes, *Pretoria News*, "South Africa, Lesotho Principle of Oxbow Plan," February 23, 1968.

6. *Speech by the Honourable Prime Minister of Lesotho Moving the 1968/69 Development Fund Estimates of Revenue and Expenditure in the House of Assembly on Wednesday, 20th, March 1968* (Maseru: Government Printing, 1968), 3.

7. Jonathan, *Development Speech*, 3.

8. Ibid., 6.

9. "New Project Announced at 'Leabua Highway' Opening," *Lesotho Times*, July 2, 1968; "It Will Be Leabua Jonathan Airport," *The Friend*, December 20, 1968. This was not a semantic one-off with no staying power, as some Basotho in interviews in 2008–9 still referred to the road as the Leabua Highway, over twenty years after he lost power.

10. Jonathan, *Development Speech*, 11.

11. See, e.g., Emma Hunter, "Dutiful Subjects, Patriotic Citizens, and the Concept of 'Good Citizenship' in Twentieth-Century Tanzania," *Historical Journal* 56, no. 1 (2013): 272–73.

12. NASA, PT EAE 299 EA 4/3/2 Economic Assistance 1967, Letter, Cowen and Horwood to Anton Rupert, January 11, 1967.

13. Interview, Clara Rapholo, Roma, May 5, 2009.

14. NASA, PT BAO 3232 C43/3/8 Vol. 1, Department of Foreign Affairs, Memo, "BCP—Activities with Regard to the Recruiting of Workers in Lesotho," August 9, 1967; trans. Faith Cranfield.

15. Interview, Tšeliso Ramakhula, Maseru, Lower Thamae, March 1, 2009.

16. Interview, Selborne Mohlalisi, Morija, November 10, 2008.

17. NACP RG 490 Records of the Peace Corps, Office of International Operations, Country Plans 1966–1985, Lesotho, Lesotho 1968–71: Program Memorandum.

18. W. J. A. Macartney, "The Lesotho General Election of 1970," *Government and Opposition* 8, no. 4 (1973): 494.

19. Interview, Peter Khamane, Ha QhuQhu, October 29, 2008.

20. "Lesotho Youth Service Takes Shape," *Lesotho Times*, November 10, 1967.

21. Cati Coe, *Dilemmas of Culture in African Schools: Youth, Nationalism and the Transformation of Knowledge* (Chicago: University of Chicago Press, 2005), 65–70; John McCracken, *A History of Malawi, 1859–1966* (Rochester, NY: James Currey, 2012), 371; Jeffrey Ahlman, "A New Type of Citizen: Youth, Gender, and Generation in the Ghanaian Builders Brigade," *Journal of African History* 53, no. 1 (2012): 87–105.

22. All information on Khamane is from interview, Peter Khamane, Ha QhuQhu, October 29, 2008.

23. The Catholic Church was the key supporter, both rhetorically and financially, of the BNP so this pipeline was especially strong at Catholic secondary and high schools. Interview, Gabriel Tlaba, Lesotho College of Education, October 7, 2008.

24. Interview, Gabriel Tlaba, Lesotho College of Education, October 28, 2008.

25. South African Democracy Education Trust, *The Road to Democracy in South Africa, Volume 2 (1970–1980)* (Pretoria: UNISA Press, 2006), 107–8.

26. "Students Given Lesotho Warning," *Rand Daily Mail* (Johannesburg), December 10, 1968.

27. Ibid.

28. 1965 and 1970 BCP Manifestos, in W. J. A. Macartney, ed., *Readings in BOLESWA Government: Select Documents on the Government and Politics of Botswana, Lesotho and Swaziland* (Roma, Lesotho: UBLS Printing Unit, 1971).

29. Ström, *Development and Dependence*, 69–70.

30. All quotations from the 1970 BNP Manifesto, in Macartney, *BOLESWA Government*.

31. "St. Rodrigue Library to Be Opened on March 16th," *Lesotho News* (Ladybrand), March 11, 1969, 3; "Water Supply Scheme," *Lesotho News* (Ladybrand), July 29, 1969, 1; "Letsie Opens Bokoro Water Supply Scheme," *Lesotho News* (Ladybrand), August 19, 1969, 1.

32. NACP RG 286 Agency for International Development P 907 Central Subject Files, 1968–1973, Bureau for Africa/Office for Southern Africa Regional Coordination, Box 5, *Special Self-Help Fund Annual Report FY1969*, July 21, 1969.

33. This changed after 1971, a shift that is documented and discussed in more detail in chapter 6.

34. Macartney, "Lesotho General Election 1970," 489.

35. "Support Me or Else . . . Jonathan," *Rand Daily Mail* (Johannesburg), October 25, 1969.

36. "Development Will Come to Winning Constituencies—Premier Jonathan," *Lesotho News* (Ladybrand), December 2, 1969, 3.

37. TNA OD 31/320, Lesotho National Development Corporation, Memo High Commissioner Maseru to Board of Trade London, February 12, 1969.

38. Jonathan, quoted in Khaketla, *Lesotho 1970*, 189.

39. Macartney, "Lesotho General Election 1970," 485.

40. RG 59 General Records of the Department of State, Executive Secretariat, Visit Files, 1966–70, Box 33, Folder V-42 Visit of PM Jonathan of Lesotho, Talking Points for Meeting with Jonathan, September 22, 1967.

41. Interviews, Frank Phillips, telephone, July 9, 2012; Tom Carroll, telephone, July 30, 2012; Bill Reed, telephone, August 3, 2012.

42. NACP RG 59 General Records of the Department of State, Bureau of African Affairs, Office of Southern African Affairs, Records Relating to Botswana, Lesotho and Swaziland, 1969–75 Box 1, Folder: PER 4: Staffing Lesotho, 1967–68, Letter Richard St. F. Post to Edward Clark Department of State, November 21, 1967.

43. TNA FCO 141/958 UN Personnel in HCT, Telex Embassy Pretoria to Ministry of Overseas Development, September 8, 1965; NASA, PT BAO 4102 C166/9/1916 Border Control 1967–73, Report on meeting between Prime Minister Jonathan and Muller Secretary for Foreign Affairs, May 1, 1967.

44. Macartney, "Lesotho General Election 1970," 481.

45. NASA PT EAE 299 EA 4/3/2 Customs Union, Department of Foreign Affairs memo, "Help for Lesotho," February 1967; trans. Faith Cranfield.

46. NASA PT EAE 299 EA 4/3/2 Customs Union, Department of Foreign Affairs memo, "Help for Lesotho," February 1967; trans. Faith Cranfield.

47. NASA PT EAE 299 EA 4/3/2 Customs Union, Department of Foreign Affairs memo, "Help for Lesotho," February 1967; trans. Faith Cranfield.

48. James Barber, *South Africa's Foreign Policy 1945–1970* (New York: Oxford University Press, 1973), 247–49.

49. NASA, PT EAE 299 EA 4/3/2 Economic Assistance 1967, "Notes for Talks," January 1967.

50. NASA, PT EAE 299 EA 4/3/2 Customs Union, Department of Foreign Affairs Memo, Capital Projects in Lesotho-Botswana-Swaziland, November 18, 1966; trans. Faith Cranfield.

51. TNA OD 31/170 Lesotho Post-Independence Aid, Notes on meeting King Moshoeshoe II, Minister of Overseas Development and Government of Lesotho, July 26–28, 1967.

52. TNA OD 31/169 Lesotho Post-Independence Aid, High Commissioner Maseru to Commonwealth Office, February 17, 1967.

53. Vorster, quoted in James Barber and John Barratt, *South Africa's Foreign Policy: The Search for Status and Security 1945–1988* (New York: Cambridge University Press, 1990), 134.

54. Macartney, "Lesotho General Election 1970," 480.

55. For instance, Leo McDuling, "Uneasy Choice before Lesotho," *Rand Daily Mail* (Johannesburg), January 23, 1970; Matthew White, "South Africa Role in Lesotho General Election," *The Star* (Johannesburg), January 23, 1970; "Leabua Faces a Strong Threat," *Weekend World* (Johannesburg), December 14, 1969. On contemporary reporting, John Aerni-Flessner, Charles Fogelman, and Jeffrey Smith, "Pierce Lesotho's Fog with Facts," *Mail and Guardian* (Johannesburg), February 27, 2015.

56. Macartney, "Lesotho General Election 1970," 484.

57. Summary of the conduct of the election and its results from Macartney, "Lesotho General Election 1970," 484–85, 489.

58. NACP RG 59 General Records of the Department of State, Bureau of African Affairs, Office of Southern African Affairs, Records Relating to Botswana, Lesotho and Swaziland, 1969–75, Box 1, Letter Stephen Gebelt, Charge d'Affaires Maseru to Horace Byrne Department of State, February 2, 1970; personal correspondence with Richard Weisfelder; interview, Timothy Carney, East Lansing, March 18, 2016.

59. Interview, Simon Phafane, Maseru, November 3, 2008.

60. OD 45/490 Financial Assistance to Lesotho from SA, Memo High Commissioner Maseru to Embassy Cape Town, September 16, 1970.

61. TNA OD 31/219 South African Assistance to Lesotho 1967–69, Note High Commissioner Maseru, to Foreign and Commonwealth Office, September 26, 1969.

62. TNA OD 31/371 British Aid to Lesotho 1971/72 and 1972/73, Comments on Budget, High Commissioner Maseru to Office of Development Administration and Foreign and Commonwealth Office, December 24, 1970.

63. FCO 45/467 Coup by PM of Lesotho, Telex Maseru to Foreign and Commonwealth Relations Office, March 3, 1970.

64. FCO 45/467 Coup by PM of Lesotho, Telex Maseru to Foreign and Commonwealth Relations Office, March 3, 1970.

65. Khaketla, *Lesotho 1970*, 266–71.

66. Thabane, "*Liphokojoe* of Kao," 107–8.

67. TNA OD 31/169 Lesotho Post-Independence Aid, Telex High Commissioner Maseru, to Overseas Development Ministry, February 10, 1967.

68. TNA OD 31/174 Lesotho Post-Independence Aid, Notes on Meeting on Financial Discussions London, December 8–10, 1969, and Memo on Aid 1970/71, December 10, 1969.

69. TNA OD 31/174 Lesotho Post-Independence Aid, Telex High Commissioner Maseru, to Overseas Development Ministry, January 15, 1970.

70. NACP RG 59 General Records of the Department of State, Bureau of African Affairs, Office of Southern African Affairs, Records Relating to Botswana, Lesotho and Swaziland, 1969–75, Box 1, Telegram, Secretary of State Washington to Maseru, February 7, 1970.

71. TNA FCO 45/487 Financial Position of Lesotho Government, March 1970, Memorandum from Working Committee on Reexamination of Budget for 1970/71 in Light of Aid Suspension, no date.

72. TNA FCO 45/490 Financial Assistance to Lesotho from South Africa Telex, High Commissioner Maseru to Foreign and Commonwealth Office, March 2, 1970.

73. USNA RG 59 General Records of the Department of State, Bureau of African Affairs, Office of Southern African Affairs, Records Relating to Botswana, Lesotho and Swaziland, 1969–75, Box 1, Telegram Embassy Maseru to Secretary of State Washington, March 25, 1970.

74. NACP RG 59 General Records of the Department of State, Bureau of African Affairs, Office of Southern African Affairs, Records Relating to Botswana, Lesotho and Swaziland, 1969–75, Box 1, Telegram Embassy Maseru to Secretary of State Washington, March 26, 1970.

75. Anonymous interview, email, August 2012.

76. Interview, William Lockhart, email, August 2012.

77. Interview, Timothy Carney, East Lansing, MI, March 18, 2016.

78. NACP RG 59 General Records of the Department of State, Bureau of African Affairs, Office of Southern African Affairs, Records Relating to Botswana, Lesotho and Swaziland, 1969–75, Box 1, Folder: Lesotho Govt Emergency 1970, Telegram Sec State Wash to Embassy Maseru, February 9, 1970.

79. NACP RG 59 General Records of the Department of State, Bureau of African Affairs, Office of Southern African Affairs, Records Relating to Botswana, Lesotho and Swaziland, 1969–75, Box 1, Folder: AID-1, General, BLS Memo: AID to Botswana, Lesotho, Swaziland, February 13, 1970.

80. NACP RG 286 Agency for International Development P 907 Central Subject Files, 1968–1973, Bureau for Africa/Office for Southern Africa Regional Coordination, Box 5, Folder: Assistance Plans, Letter Charles Campbell Regional Activities Coordinator to Steven Gebelt Maseru, February 27, 1970, and Trip Report, May 1970.

81. Khaketla, *Lesotho 1970*, 299–308.

82. Ibid., 304.

83. NACP RG 59 General Records of the Department of State, Bureau of African Affairs, Office of Southern African Affairs, Records Relating to Botswana, Lesotho and Swaziland, 1969–75, Box 1, Folder: AID-1, Gen'l, BLS, Memo Samuel C. Adams, Jr., Assistant Administrator for Africa (AID) to David Newsom, Asst Sec for African Affairs, Dept. of State, April 6, 1970, and Memo Charles Campbell, Office of Southern Africa Regional Activities Coordination to Harvey Nelson Jr., Outline AID Current and Planned Regional Activities for Southern Africa, April 14, 1970.

84. TNA FCO 45/466 Coup d'état by PM of Lesotho Minutes of Meeting on Help for Lesotho at Foreign and Commonwealth Office, February 19, 1970.

85. TNA FCO 45/468 Coup by PM of Lesotho, Letter Jonathan to Minister of Foreign Affairs, March 6, 1970.

86. TNA FCO 45/468 Coup by PM of Lesotho, Memo High Commissioner Maseru to Foreign and Commonwealth Office, March 17, 1970.

87. TNA FCO 45/487 Financial Position of Lesotho Government March 1970, Note on Meeting at Overseas Development Ministry with Mr. Glaze, formerly Deputy Financial Secretary, Ministry of Finance Lesotho, April 1, 1970.

88. TNA PREM 13/3297 Lesotho Coup, Memo Gaborone to Foreign and Commonwealth Office, June 9, 1970.

89. TNA FCO 45/468 Coup by PM of Lesotho, Telex High Commissioner Maseru to Foreign and Commonwealth Office, March 6, 1970.

90. TNA CAB 129/149 Cabinet Memo Secretary of State for Foreign and Commonwealth Affairs, April 14, 1970.

91. John E. Bardill and James Cobbe, *Lesotho: Dilemmas of Dependence in Southern Africa* (Boulder, CO: Westview Press, 1985), 137.

92. The next chapter explores the project particulars. NACP RG 59 General Records of the Department of State, Bureau of African Affairs, Office of Southern African Affairs, Records Relating to Botswana, Lesotho and Swaziland, 1969–75, Box 1, Folder: Lesotho Government Emergency 1970, Conversation between Tim Thahane and Peter Jones, Administrative Officer Bureau of Economic Affairs, May 29, 1970.

93. TNA CAB 128/45/17 Cabinet Minutes, April 16, 1970; TNA PREM 13/3297 Lesotho Coup, Memo to Prime Minister, April 15, 1970.

94. TNA PREM 13/3297 Lesotho Coup, Khama quoted in Memo Gaborone to Foreign and Commonwealth Office, June 9, 1970.

95. "Recognition by Her Majesty's Government," *Lesotho Times* (Ladybrand), March 17, 1970.

96. TNA PREM 13/3297 Lesotho Coup, Cabinet Secretary to Overseas Development Ministry, June 11, 1970.

97. "Leabua Is Aiming for National Unity," *The World* (Johannesburg), March 13, 1970.

98. World Bank, Eastern Africa Department, *Current Economic Position and Prospects of Lesotho*, September 27, 1971, 1.

99. Central Planning and Development Office, *Lesotho First Five-Year Development Plan 1970/71–1974/75* (Maseru: Kingdom of Lesotho, 1970), xiii.

100. Interview, Alexander Sekoli, St. David's Mission, Berea, November 13, 2008.

101. All quotations in this paragraph are from interview, Alexander Sekoli, St. David's Mission, Berea, November 13, 2008.

102. This statement should not be surprising, but in light of how writers still discuss nationalism and political involvement as being the preserve only of economic and social elites or confined to urban areas, it is still important to make. Kieh, *State Failure*; Platteau, "Institutional Obstacles"; Cooper, "Possibility and Constraint"; Young, *African Colonial State*; Mamdani, *Citizen and Subject*.

103. Interview, Gabriel Tlaba, Lesotho College of Education, October 28, 2008.

104. Interview, Tšeliso Ramakhula, Maseru, Lower Thamae, March 1, 2009.

105. Interview, Thabelo Kebise, Maseru Bus Stop, April 1, 2009; interview, Selborne Mohlalisi, Morija, November 10, 2008.

106. Ström, *Development and Dependence*, 69.

107. Mamapele Chakela, *The People Always Win* (Florida Hills, South Africa: Vivalia Publishers, 2006), 66, 68, 78.

108. Interview, Raphael Leseli, Roma, January 15, 2009.

109. All quotations in this paragraph are from interview, Raphael Leseli, Roma, January 15, 2009.

110. Interview, Raphael Leseli, Roma, January 15, 2009.

111. Anonymous interview, Rothe, Mafeteng, April 6, 2009.

112. Interview, Gabriel Tlaba, Lesotho College of Education, October 28, 2008; original emphasis.

113. Interview, Michael Mateka, Sacred Heart High School, Leribe, November 26, 2008.

114. Khabele Matlosa and Neville Pule, "The Military in Lesotho," *African Security Review* 10, no. 2 (2001): 62–74; T. H. Mothibe, "The Military and Democratization in Lesotho," *Lesotho Social Science Review* 5, no. 1 (1999): 47–63; Turkon, "Commoners, Kings, and Subaltern," 203–23.

115. Interview, Selborne Mohlalisi, Morija, November 10, 2008.

116. Interview, Chaka Ntsane, Maseru, February 24, 2009.

117. Interview, Mohlalefi Moteane, Maseru, May 27, 2009.

118. Interview, Gabriel Tlaba, Lesotho College of Education, October 28, 2008.

119. Interview, Raphael Leseli, Roma, January 15, 2009.

120. Interview, Gabriel Tlaba, Lesotho College of Education, October 28, 2008.

121. Interview, Michael Mateka, Sacred Heart High School, Leribe, November 26, 2008.

122. Interview, Chaka Ntsane, Maseru, February 24, 2009.

123. Interview, Mohlalefi Moteane, Maseru, May 27, 2009.

124. Moorosi would go on to be the first-ever Mosotho Olympian when he represented Lesotho in athletics at the 1972 Summer Games in Munich, West Germany. Interview, Motsapi Moorosi, Maseru East, March 12, 2009.

125. Interview, Moeketsi Lesitsi, St. Monica's Mission, Leribe, November 26, 2008.

126. TNA PREM 13/3297 Lesotho Coup, Memo Maseru to FCO, February 3, 1970.

127. Calvin Woodward, "Not a Complete Solution: Assessing the Long Years of Foreign Aid to Lesotho," *Africa Insight* 12, no. 3 (1982): 175.

128. Interview, Moeketsi Lesitsi, St. Monica's Mission, Leribe, November 26, 2008.

129. Ferguson, *Anti-Politics Machine*, 254–56.

FIVE   Authoritarianism, Aid, and the Anti-Politics Machine, 1970–1975

1. Aerni-Flessner, "Development and Politics," 403.

2. *Speeches by His Majesty the King and the Right Honourable the Prime Minister on the Occasion of the Sixth Anniversary of Independence* (Maseru: Government Printing, 1972), 8.

3. Jonathan speech, quoted in *Annual Report of the Ministry of Education and Culture, 1970/72.*

4. DIRCO BTS 1/159/6/1 Oxbow and Kau Hydroelectric Schemes (vol. 5), Meeting Minutes, July 9, 1971.

5. *Speech by the Right Honourable the Prime Minister on the Occasion of the Fifth Anniversary of Independence* (Maseru: Government Printing, 1971), 7–8.

6. *Manifesto on Southern Africa, Proclaimed by the Fifth Summit Conference of East and Central African States, 14th–16th April, 1969, Lusaka, Zambia,* http://africanactivist.msu.edu/document_metadata.php?objectid=32-130 -714. Accessed February 2, 2017.

7. NACP RG 59 General Records of the Department of State, Bureau of African Affairs, Office of Southern African Affairs, Records Relating to Botswana, Lesotho and Swaziland, 1969–75, Box 1, Folder: Basic Policies, Lesotho 1970, Policy Guidelines, Lesotho: updated August 27, 1970; Talking Points for Newsom Department of State for Meeting with Prime Minister, October 1970.

8. NACP RG 286 Agency for International Development P 907 Central Subject Files, 1968–73, Bureau for Africa/Office for Southern Africa Regional Coordination, Box 14, Folder: UNDP Lesotho FY72, Outline of Possible ILO Technical Assistance to Lesotho—additional working paper presented at the preliminary meeting held on 9 August 1971 at the School of Agriculture Maseru, in connection with the UNDP Country Programming, 1972–76.

9. NACP RG 286 Agency for International Development P 907 Central Subject Files, 1968–73, Bureau for Africa/Office for Southern Africa Regional Coordination, Box 12, Telegram Maseru to Washington, September 21, 1971.

10. World Bank, Eastern Africa Department, *Current Economic Position and Prospects of Lesotho*, September 27, 1971, 23.

11. DIRCO BTS 1/159/6/1 Oxbow and Kau Hydroelectric Schemes (vol. 5), Letter Albie Burger to Prime Minister Jonathan, August 4, 1969.

12. DIRCO BTS 1/159/6/1 Oxbow and Kau Hydroelectric Schemes (vol. 5), Letter Leabua Jonathan to Muller Department of Foreign Affairs, August 14, 1969.

13. DIRCO BTS 1/159/6/1 Oxbow and Kau Hydroelectric Schemes (vol. 5), Letter J. T. Mapetla Office of the Prime Minister to Jacques Kriel Secretary for Water Affairs, March 24, 1972.

14. DIRCO BTS 1/159/6/1 Oxbow and Kau Hydroelectric Schemes (vol. 6), Notes on Lesotho Malibamtso Scheme 1974/5.

15. TNA OD 31/219 South African Assistance to Lesotho 1967–69, Note High Commissioner Maseru to Foreign and Commonwealth Relations Office, October 29, 1968; Ström, *Development and Dependence*, 115.

16. John Bardill, "Destabilization: The Lesotho Case," *Collected Seminar Papers, Institute of Commonwealth Studies* 37 (1988): 192.

17. Jacqueline Audrey Kalley, Elna Schoeman, and Lydia Eve Andor, *Southern African Political History: A Chronology of Key Political Events from Independence to Mid-1997* (Westport, CT: Greenwood Press, 1999), 124–25.

18. World Bank, *Report and Recommendation of the President to the Executive Directors on a Proposed Development Credit to the Kingdom of Lesotho for the Thaba Bosiu Rural Development Project*, February 9, 1973, 2.

19. NACP RG 286 Agency for International Development P 907 Central Subject Files, 1968–73, Bureau for Africa/Office for Southern Africa Regional Coordination, Box 14, Folder: UNDP Lesotho FY72, Telegram USAID Washington to Embassy Maseru, September 30, 1972.

20. Eric J. Morgan, "Our Own Interests: Nixon, South Africa, and Dissent at Home and Abroad," *Diplomacy and Statecraft* 17, no. 3 (2006): 476–77.

21. NACP RG 59 General Records of the Department of State, Bureau of African Affairs, Office of Southern African Affairs, Records Relating to Botswana, Lesotho and Swaziland, 1969–75, Box 1, Folder: Basic Policies, Lesotho 1970, Policy Guidelines, Lesotho: updated August 27, 1970.

22. NACP RG 59 General Records of the Department of State, Bureau of African Affairs, Office of Southern African Affairs, Records Relating to Botswana, Lesotho and Swaziland, 1969–75, Box 2, Folder: Accreditation Amb. Nelson, June 11, 1971.

23. NACP RG 286 Agency for International Development P 907 Central Subject Files, 1968–73, Bureau for Africa/Office for Southern Africa Regional Coordination, Box 14, Folder: UNDP Lesotho FY72, Telegram USAID Washington to Embassy Maseru, September 30, 1972, and Telegram Embassy Maseru to USAID Washington, June 14, 1973.

24. Hirschmann, *Administration of Planning*, 28–31.

25. Ström, *Migration and Development*, 96.

26. "Lesotho Sees Freedom in Aid," *Rand Daily Mail* (Johannesburg), July 6, 1972.

27. World Bank, *Appraisal of the Thaba Bosiu Rural Development Scheme*, January 24, 1973, i.

28. NACP RG 286 Agency for International Development P 907 Central Subject Files, 1968–73, Bureau for Africa/Office for Southern Africa Regional Coordination, Box 8, Note Roy Stacey to Wesley Smith, US Embassy Maseru, February 8, 1972.

29. Joseph Hodge, *Triumph of the Expert: Agrarian Doctrines of Development and the Legacies of British Colonialism* (Athens: Ohio University Press, 2007).

30. NACP RG 286 Agency for International Development, USAID/Bureau for Technical Assistance/Office of Rural Development, 1970–76, Box 6, Folder: Area Programs—Lesotho, 1972–74, Thaba Bosiu Project, Background information, no date.

31. NACP RG 286 Agency for International Development, USAID/Bureau for Technical Assistance/Office of Rural Development, 1970–76, Box 6, Folder: Area Programs—Lesotho, 1972–74, Thaba Bosiu Project, Background information, no date.

32. All figures from World Bank, *Development Credit Agreement (Thaba Bosiu Rural Development Scheme) between Kingdom of Lesotho and International Development Association*, March 23, 1973, 17.

33. Lesotho Minister of Agriculture, Cooperatives, and Marketing, *Thaba Bosiu Rural Development Project: Annual Report, No. 2: 1 April 1974–31 March 1975*, June 1975, 3.

34. NACP RG 286 Agency for International Development, USAID/Bureau for Technical Assistance/Office of Rural Development, 1970–76, Box 6, Folder: Area Programs—Lesotho, 1972–74, Thaba Bosiu Project, Background information, no date.

35. World Bank, *Report and Recommendation of the President to the Executive Directors on a Proposed Development Credit to the Kingdom of Lesotho for the Thaba Bosiu Rural Development Project*, February 1973, 7.

36. Ström, *Development and Dependence*, 93–94; Matlosa, "Aid, Development and Democracy," 7.

37. For more on each of these projects, see Matlosa, "Aid, Development and Democracy," 9–10.

38. This project was the focus of Ferguson's *Anti-Politics Machine*.

39. NACP RG 286 Agency for International Development, USAID/Bureau for Technical Assistance/Office of Rural Development, 1970–76, Box 6, Folder: Area Programs—Lesotho, 1972–74, Deputy Secretary, International Development Association Memo on Thaba Bosiu Rural Development Project, February 9, 1973.

40. NACP RG 59 General Records of the Department of State, Bureau of African Affairs, Office of Southern African Affairs, Records Relating to Botswana, Lesotho and Swaziland, 1969–75, Box 2, Folder: Malibamatso Project, Lesotho 1972, Charles Nelson Ambassador to Richard Dols Department of State, October 12, 1972.

41. NACP RG 286 Agency for International Development, USAID/Bureau for Technical Assistance/Office of Rural Development, 1970–76, Box 6, Folder: Area Programs—Lesotho, 1972–75, Memo: Thaba Bosiu Project, August 1974.

42. NACP RG 286 Agency for International Development, USAID/Bureau for Technical Assistance/Office of Rural Development, 1970–76, Box 6, Folder: Area Programs—Lesotho, 1972–75, Memo: Thaba Bosiu Project, August 1974.

43. NACP RG 286 Agency for International Development, USAID/Bureau for Technical Assistance/Office of Rural Development, 1970–76, Box 6, Folder: Area Programs—Lesotho, 1972–75, Memo Jerome French Acting Direction Office of Development Administration to Victor Burke, June 13, 1975.

44. James B. Davis, James J. Acres, William A. Daley, USAID, and US Soil Conservation Service, *An Evaluation of the Thaba Bosiu Rural Development Project in Lesotho* (Maseru: USAID, 1975), 15.

45. NACP RG 286 Agency for International Development, USAID/Bureau for Technical Assistance/Office of Rural Development, 1970–76, Box 6, Folder: Area Programs—Lesotho, 1972–75, Memo: Thaba Bosiu Project, August 1974.

46. All quotations in this paragraph are from NACP RG 286 Agency for International Development P 907 Central Subject Files, 1968–73, Bureau for Africa/Office for Southern Africa Regional Coordination, Box 12, Petition, January 7, 1972.

47. NACP RG 286 Agency for International Development P 907 Central Subject Files, 1968–73, Bureau for Africa/Office for Southern Africa Regional Coordination, Box 12, Petition, January 7, 1972.

48. NACP RG 286 Agency for International Development P 907 Central Subject Files, 1968–73, Bureau for Africa/Office for Southern Africa Regional Coordination, Box 12, Petition, January 7, 1972.

49. NACP RG 286 Agency for International Development P 907 Central Subject Files, 1968–73, Bureau for Africa/Office for Southern Africa Regional Coordination, Box 12, Petition, January 7, 1972.

50. NACP RG 286 Agency for International Development P 907 Central Subject Files, 1968–73, Bureau for Africa/Office for Southern Africa Regional Coordination, Box 12, Petition, January 7, 1972.

51. NACP RG 286 Agency for International Development P 907 Central Subject Files, 1968–73, Bureau for Africa/Office for Southern Africa Regional Coordination, Box 12, Memo Athol Ellis Director Office of Southern African Affairs Bureau for Africa to Robert Dean Division Chief Eastern Africa, International Bank for Reconstruction, January 28, 1972.

52. NACP RG 286 Agency for International Development P 907 Central Subject Files, 1968–73, Bureau for Africa/Office for Southern Africa Regional Coordination, Box 12, Memo Athol Ellis Director Office of Southern African Affairs, Bureau for Africa to Robert Dean Division Chief Eastern Africa, International Bank for Reconstruction, January 28, 1972.

53. All quotations in this paragraph are from Ministries of Agriculture and Community Development, *Development of Growth Centres in Lesotho*, June 15, 1971.

54. Ministries of Agriculture and Community Development, *Development of Growth Centres in Lesotho*, June 15, 1971.

55. NACP RG 286 Agency for International Development P 907 Central Subject Files, 1968–73, Bureau for Africa/Office for Southern Africa Regional Coordination, Box 5, Folder: Assistance Plans Special Self-Help Fund Annual Report FY1969, July 21, 1969.

56. Ministries of Agriculture and Community Development, *Development of Growth Centres in Lesotho*, June 15, 1971.

57. NACP RG 286 Agency for International Development P 907 Central Subject Files, 1968–73, Bureau for Africa/Office for Southern Africa Regional Coordination, Box 18, Folder: ACSL Architecture and Construction Society (Lesotho) Telegram Maseru to Washington, July 1, 1974.

58. Interview, Noel Jackson, email, August 2012.

59. Interview, Clara Rapholo, Roma, May 5, 2009.

60. Interview, Moeketsi Lesitsi, St. Monica's Mission, Leribe, November 26, 2008.

61. Department of Information, *Lesotho 1971* (Maseru: Government Printing, 1971).

62. Interview, Ted Nettelton, email, June 2016.

63. NACP RG 286 Agency for International Development, USAID/ Bureau for Africa, Office of Eastern and Southern Africa, Closed Subject Files of the Southern Africa Regional Activities Coordination, 1969–73, Box 4,

Folder: Regional Activities (Lesotho) FY71 Report on Work-for-Food program administered by CRS, February 4, 1971.

64. Interview, Steve Goertz, email, July 2013.

65. NACP RG 286 Agency for International Development P 907 Central Subject Files, 1968–73, Bureau for Africa/Office for Southern Africa Regional Coordination, Box 6, Folder: Non-Government (CRS re LECUSA), Memo on LECUSA, no date.

66. Interview, William Lockhart, email, August 1, 2012.

67. Interview, Clark Tibbits, telephone, July 19, 2012.

68. Department of Information, *Lesotho 1971* (Maseru: Government Printing, 1971).

69. Ibid.

70. Interview, Robert Warner, telephone, July 29, 2012.

71. Interview, Clark Tibbits, telephone, July 19, 2012.

72. All quotations in this paragraph from interview, Selborne Mohlalisi, Morija, November 10, 2008.

73. All quotations in this paragraph from interview, Michael Mateka, Sacred Heart High School, Leribe, November 26, 2008.

74. Interview, Michael Mateka, Sacred Heart High School, Leribe, November 26, 2008.

75. Interview, Mohlalefi Moteane, Maseru, May 27, 2009.

76. All quotations in this paragraph from interview, Mohlalefi Moteane, Maseru, May 27, 2009.

77. All information and quotations in this paragraph from interview, Maleseko Kena, Tsoelike Auplas, March 17, 2009.

78. All information and quotations in this paragraph, unless otherwise noted, from interview, Maleseko Kena, Tsoelike Auplas, March 17, 2009.

79. The key role played by the Kena family in this network was noted in Mokhafisi Jacob Kena's 2016 obituary by the South African Communist Party, "The SACP Dips the Red Banner to a Fallen Hero, Comrade Mokhafisi Jacob Kena, aka Zukhov, aka Jeremiah Mosotho," *Umsebenzi Online* 15, no. 33 (September 28, 2016), http://www.sacp.org.za/pubs/umsebenzi/2016/vol15-33 .html. Accessed October 6, 2017.

80. All quotations and information in this paragraph from interview, Thabelo Kebise, Maseru Bus Stop, April 1, 2009.

81. All quotations and information in this paragraph from interview, Thabelo Kebise, Maseru Bus Stop, April 1, 2009.

SIX   The Road to Development

1. Mannini Mokhothu, quoted in Antjie Krog, *Begging to Be Black* (Cape Town: Random House Struik, 2009), 215.

2. Mokhothu, quoted in Krog, *Begging*, 216.

3. Mokhothu, quoted in Krog, *Begging*, 217.

4. All of the details of the 1960s to early 1980s projects are from D. Hirschmann, "The Ramabanta-Semonkong Road Project in Lesotho: A Case Study on Community Development and National Planning," *Humanitas* 9, no. 2 (1983): 135–40.

5. All details come from Hirschmann, "Ramabanta-Semonkong Road."

6. Figures from Hirschmann, "Ramabanta-Semonkong Road," 139.

7. Figures from Hirschmann, "Ramabanta-Semonkong Road," 139.

8. See Ferguson, *Anti-Politics Machine*.

9. Mwangi, "Hydropolitics"; John Hatchard, "Recent Developments in Combating the Bribery of Foreign Public Officials: A Cause for Optimism," *University of Detroit Mercy Law Review* 85 (2007): 1–28; National Public Radio, "Planet Money Podcast," Episode 706: "Water's Worth," June 17, 2016, http://www.npr.org./sections/money/2016/06/17/482459229/episode-806 -waters-worth, accessed February 15, 2017; "Nomvula Mokoyane's Watergate," *City Press* (Johannesburg), July 10, 2016.

10. Tyrell Duncan, Frank Baffoe, and Karin Metell, *Support against Apartheid: An Evaluation of 28 Years of Development Assistance to Lesotho* (Stockholm: SIDA, 1994), 61–62.

11. Krog, *Begging*, 179–80.

12. Ibid., 217.

13. All quotations in this paragraph from Pascalinah Kabi, "Mosisili Mocks Colonial Rule," *Lesotho Times* (Maseru), May 27, 2016, http://lestimes .com/mosisili-mocks-colonial-rule/.

14. All quotations in this paragraph from Kabi, "Mosisili Mocks Colonial Rule."

15. Mosisili was a BCP member in the 1960s, and he spent time in jail after the 1970 coup. Upon the return of democratic government in 1993, he served in the first BCP government under Prime Minister Ntsu Mokhehle. Most of the BCP members left the party in 1998, forming the Lesotho Congress for Democracy (LCD). Mosisili became head of that party before the 1998 elections, leading it to victory. He served as prime minister from 1998 to 2012, but in 2012, after losing a factional fight, Mosisili led an exodus from the LCD to form the Democratic Congress (DC). After being in opposition from 2012 to 2015, Mosisili served again as prime minister from March 2015 to June 2017 at the head of a seven-party coalition led by the DC.

16. All statistics in this paragraph from Advision Lesotho, "Summary of Results: Afrobarometer Round 6, Survey in Lesotho," http://afrobarometer .org/sites/default/files/publications/Summary%20of%20of%20results/les_r6 _sor_en.pdf; accessed February 14, 2017.

BIBLIOGRAPHY

ARCHIVAL COLLECTIONS

Institute of Southern African Studies (ISAS), National University of Lesotho
    Institute of Education Collection (IE)
Lesotho National Archives (LNA)
Lesotho Parliamentary Archives
Moeletsi oa Basotho Archives
Morija Museum and Archives (MMA)
    General Collection
    Mabille Collection
    Van Nispen Collection (VNC)
National Archives of South Africa, Pretoria (NASA, PT)
    Decisions of the Executive Council (URU)
    Department of Health (GES)
    Department of Native Affairs and Development/Bantu Administration
    (BAO)
    Economic Advisor to the Prime Minister (EAE)
    Prime Minister (PM)
    Private Secretary of the Minister of Economic Affairs (MES)
    Secretary of Native Affairs (NTS)
National Archives of the United Kingdom, Kew, London (TNA)
    Cabinet Office (CAB)
    Colonial Administration Archives (Migrated Archives)
    Colonial Office Files (CO)
    Dominions Office (DO)
    Foreign and Commonwealth Office (FCO)
    Home Office (HO)
    Overseas Development (OD)
    Prime Minister's Office (PREM)

National Archives of the United States, College Park, MD (NACP)
    CIA Files
    Record Group 59: Records of the State Department
    Record Group 286: Records of the United States Agency for International
    Development (USAID)
    Record Group 490: Records of the Peace Corps
National University of Lesotho Archives (NULA)
    General Collection
    Leribe Collection (LC)
Rhodes House Collections, Oxford
    Africa Bureau Collection (ABC)
        Joint Commission on the High Commission Territories
    Anti-Apartheid Movement Collection (AAM)
South African Democracy Education Trust
    Online Interview Collections
South Africa: Department of International Relations and Cooperation Archives
    (DIRCO)
    Private Secretary of the Minister of Lands and Water Affairs (WW)
    Secretary of Foreign Affairs (BTS)
Stellenbosch University Archives
    Walton Collection
Struggles for Freedom in Southern Africa
    Aluka Collection Interviews
World Bank Archives, Washington DC (WBA)

NEWSPAPERS, PERIODICALS, AND PODCASTS

BANTA Echoes/LANTA Echoes (Maseru)
Basutoland News/Lesotho News (Ladybrand/Maseru)
Basutoland Witness (Morija)
City Press (Johannesburg)
The Commentator (Maseru)
The Friend (Bloemfontein)
Leselinyana la Lesotho (Morija)
Lesotho Quarterly (Maseru)
Lesotho Times (Ladybrand)
Lesotho Times (Maseru)
Mail and Guardian (Johannesburg)
Makatolle (Maseru)
Mesa Mohloane (Mazenod)
Moeletsi oa Basotho (Mazenod)
Mohlabani (Maseru)
Naledi ea Lesotho (Mafeteng)

Nketu (Maseru)
Planet Money Podcast, National Public Radio (NPR) (Washington, DC)
The Post (Johannesburg)
Rand Daily Mail (Johannesburg)
South African Financial Gazette (Johannesburg)
The Star (Johannesburg)
Sunday Times (Johannesburg)
Umsebenzi Online (Johannesburg)
Weekend World (Johannesburg)

INTERVIEWS

Lesotho and South Africa

Anonymous, Rothe, Mafeteng, April 6, 2009
Cairns, Graham, Malealea, June 2, 2007
Jobo, Tlareng, Ha Jobo, January 20, 2009; trans. Kennedy Matsepe
Kebise, Thabelo, Maseru Bus Stop, April 1, 2009
Kena, Maleseka, Tsoelike Auplas, March 17, 2009
Khamane, Peter, Ha QhuQhu, October 29, 2008
Lerotholi, Mrs., Tsoelike Auplas, March 17, 2009
Leseli, Raphael, Roma, January 15, 2009
Lesitsi, Moeketsi, St. Monica's Mission, Leribe, November 26, 2008
Maimai, Mr., Ha Jobo, January 20, 2009; trans. Kennedy Matsepe
Mateka, Michael, Sacred Heart High School, Leribe, November 26, 2008
Mda, Zakes, email, January 8, 2016
Millin, Peter, Clarens, Republic of South Africa, March 6, 2009
Mohlalisi, Selborne, Morija, November 10, 2008
Moorosi, Motsapi, Maseru East, March 12, 2009
Moteane, Mohlalefi, Maseru, May 27, 2009
Nettelton, Ted, email, 2015 and 2016
Ntsane, Chaka, Maseru, February 24, 2009
Phafane, Simon, Maseru, November 3, 2008, and January 28, 2009
Ramakhula, Tšeliso, Maseru, Lower Thamae, March 4, 2009
Ramatlapeng, Gilbert, Maseru, June 12, 2015
Rapholo, Clara, Roma, May 5, 2009
Sekoli, Alexander, St. David's Mission, Berea, November 13, 2008
Selena, Marie, Hlotse, November 26, 2008
Taxi driver, Maseru, March 11, 2009
Tlaba, Gabriel, Lesotho College of Education, Maseru, October 7 and 28, 2008
Tourist Center employee, Thaba Bosiu, February 10, 2009
Tsiki, Armelina, St. Rodrigue High School, May 7, 2009
Turner, Stephen, Maseru, May 28, 2009

American Volunteers and Diplomats

Allen, Don, email, March 2013
Anonymous, email, August 2012
Bowne, Gary, email, July 2012
Brumburgh, Scott, telephone, August 6, 2012
Bullock, James, email, July 10, 2013
Carney, Timothy, East Lansing, MI, March 18, 2016
Carroll, Tom, telephone, July 30, 2012
Caspe, Cheryl, telephone, July 10, 2012
Caspe, Dennis, telephone, July 10, 2012
Goertz, Steve, email, July 2013
Hochstadt, Ted, email, July 2012
Jackson, Noel, email, August 2012
Lockhart, William, email, August 2012
Mayo, Douglas, email, August 2012
Phillips, Frank, telephone, July 9, 2012
Reed, Bill, telephone, August 3, 2012
Scieszka, Greg, North Syracuse, NY, August 1, 2012
Scieszka, Marjorie, telephone, August 2012
Sebatane, Lois, email, September 2012
Tibbits, Clark, telephone, July 19, 2012
Tibbits, Peggy, telephone, July 19, 2012
Warner, Robert, telephone, June 29, 2012
Wohlgehagen, Kathleen, email, July 2012

OFFICIAL REPORTS

Afrobarometer Data, Lesotho, Round 6, 2014. Available at http://www.afro
barometer.org.
Annual Report of the Director of Education for the Year 1929. Maseru: Government
Printing, 1929.
Annual Report of the Director of Education for the Year 1951. Maseru: Government
Printing, 1951.
Annual Report of the Director of Education for the Year 1954. Maseru: Government
Printing, 1955.
Annual Report of the Ministry of Education and Culture 1968. Maseru: Govern-
ment Printing, 1969.
Annual Report of the Ministry of Education and Culture 1969. Maseru: Govern-
ment Printing, 1970.
Annual Report of the Ministry of Education and Culture 1970/72. Maseru: Gov-
ernment Printing, 1972.

Annual Report of the Permanent Secretary for the Year 1966 and a General Survey of Progress and Development in the Triennium 1964–66. Maseru: Government Printing, 1967.

Annual Report on Basutoland for the Year 1954. London: Her Majesty's Stationery Office, 1955.

Basutoland Constitutional Conference: Presented to Parliament by the Secretary of State for the Colonies by Command of Her Majesty May 1964. London: Her Majesty's Stationery Office, 1964.

Basutoland Constitutional Handbook: Containing the Basutoland (Constitution) Order in Council, 1959, and Related Legislation and Reports. Maseru: Government Printing, 1960.

Basutoland 1956 Population Census, April 8, 1956. Maseru: Basutoland Government, 1958.

Basutoland Report of the Administrative Reforms Committee. Maseru: Government Printing, 1954.

Basutoland: Report of the Commission Appointed by His Majesty's Secretary of State for Dominion Affairs to Enquire into and Make Recommendations upon Education in Basutoland. Pretoria: Government Printer, 1946.

Basutoland: Report on Constitutional Discussions Held in London in November and December 1958. London: Her Majesty's Stationery Office, 1959.

Colonial Reports, Basutoland 1952. Maseru: Government Printing, 1953.

Current Economic Position and Prospects of Lesotho, World Bank, Eastern Africa Division, September 27, 1971.

Development of Growth Centres in Lesotho. Maseru: Ministries of Agriculture and Community Development, June 15, 1971.

Financial and Economic Position of Basutoland: Report of the Commission Appointed by the Secretary of State for Dominion Affairs. Presented by the Secretary of State for Dominion Affairs to Parliament by Command of His Majesty, May 1935.

Kingdom of Lesotho 1966 Population Census Report. Vol. 1. Morija, Lesotho: Morija Printing Works, 1969.

Lesotho First Five-Year Development Plan 1970/71–1974/75. Maseru: Kingdom of Lesotho, 1970.

Lesotho 1971. Maseru: Department of Information, 1971.

Machobane, J. J. *The Machobane Mass Agricultural and Development Foundation College: Prospectus.* Nqechane, Lesotho: Self-published, 1961.

Manifesto on Southern Africa, Proclaimed by the Fifth Summit Conference of East and Central African States, April 14–16, 1969, Lusaka, Zambia. Accessed at http://africanactivist.msu.edu/document_metadata.php?objectid =32-130-714.

Mophato oa Morija. Unpublished history of the Mophato, no date. Translated by Teboho Mokotjo.

Parliamentary Debates of the National Assembly, Hansard, Official Report, October 30, 1967. Maseru: Government Printing, 1967.

Parliamentary Debates: Official Report (Hansard). Maseru: Government Printing, 1967.

Proceedings of the 48th Session of the Basuto National Council, September 13, 1952. Maseru: Government Printing, 1953.

Proceedings of the 49th (1953) Session of the Basuto National Council, September 26, 1953. Maseru: Government Printing, 1954.

Proceedings of the 52nd (1956) Session of the Basutoland Council, September 29– October 24, 1956. Vol. 1. Maseru: Government Printing, 1956.

Proceedings of the Special (1956) Session of the Basutoland Council, May 7–23, 1956. Maseru: Government Printing, 1956.

Proceedings of the Special (1957) Session of the Basutoland Council, May 1957. Maseru: Government Printing, 1957.

Report of the Commission Enquiring into the Disturbances at the Lerotholi Technical School and Basutoland High School 1960. Maseru: Government Printing, 1960.

Report on Disturbances in Secondary Schools. Maseru: Government Printing, 1978.

Second Five-Year Development Plan. 1975/76–1980/81. Maseru: Government Printing, 1981.

Speech by the Honourable Prime Minister of Lesotho Moving the 1968/69 Development Fund Estimates of Revenue and Expenditure in the House of Assembly on Wednesday, March 20, 1968. Maseru: Government Printing, 1968.

Speech by the Right Honourable the Prime Minister on the Occasion of the Fifth Anniversary of Independence. Maseru: Government Printing, 1971.

Speeches by His Majesty the King and the Right Honourable the Prime Minister on the Occasion of the Sixth Anniversary of Independence. Maseru: Government Printing, 1972.

Thaba Bosiu Rural Development Project: Annual Report, No. 2: 1 April 1974–31 March 1975. Lesotho Minister of Agriculture, Cooperatives, and Marketing. June 1975.

World Bank. *Appraisal of the Thaba Bosiu Rural Development Scheme.* January 24, 1973.

———. *Development Credit Agreement (Thaba Bosiu Rural Development Scheme) between Kingdom of Lesotho and International Development Association.* March 23, 1973.

———. *Lesotho: A Development Challenge.* Washington, DC: World Bank, 1975.

———. *Report and Recommendation of the President to the Executive Directors on a Proposed Development Credit to the Kingdom of Lesotho for the Thaba Bosiu Rural Development Project.* February 9, 1973.

———. *Staff Appraisal Report. Lesotho Highlands Water Project (Phase 1A).* 1991.

ARTICLES, BOOKS, DISSERTATIONS, REPORTS, AND UNPUBLISHED PAPERS

Aerni-Flessner, John. "Development, Politics, and the Centralization of State Power in Lesotho, 1960–1975." *Journal of African History* 55, no. 3 (2014): 401–21.

———. "Homemakers, Communists, and Refugees: Smuggling Anti-Apartheid Refugees in Rural Lesotho in the 1960s and 1970s." *Wagadu: A Journal of Transnational Women's and Gender Studies* 13 (2015): 183–209.

———. "Self-Help Development Projects and Conceptions of Independence in Lesotho, 1950s–1970s." *International Journal of African Historical Studies* 50, no. 1 (2017): 11–33.

Ahearne, Robert M. "Development and Progress as Historical Phenomenon in Tanzania: 'Maendeleo? We Had That in the Past.'" *African Studies Review* 59, no. 1 (2016): 77–96.

Ahlman, Jeffrey. "A New Type of Citizen: Youth, Gender, and Generation in the Ghanaian Builders Brigade." *Journal of African History* 53, no. 1 (2012): 87–105.

Ajulu, Rok. *South Africa's Strategy of Destabilization: The Case of Lesotho.* Roma, Lesotho: Southern African Research Association, 1983.

Akindele, Femi, and Relebohile Senyane. *The Irony of the "White Gold."* Maseru: Transformation Resource Center, 2004.

Allman, Jean. "The Youngmen and the Porcupine: Class, Nationalism and Asante's Struggle for Self-Determination, 1954–57." *Journal of African History* 31, no. 2 (1990): 263–79.

Ambrose, David. *Maseru: An Illustrated History.* Morija, Lesotho: Morija Museum and Archives, 1993.

———. *Naledi ea Lesotho, the Basutoland Star.* Roma, Lesotho: House 9 Publications, National University of Lesotho, 2007.

Amin, Julius A. *The Peace Corps in Cameroon.* Kent, OH: Kent State University Press, 1992.

Anderson, Benedict. *Imagined Communities: Reflections on the Origin and Spread of Nationalism.* London: Verso, 1983.

Arbousset, Thomas. *Missionary Excursion into the Blue Mountains: Being an Account of King Moshoeshoe's Expedition from Thaba-Bosiu to the Source of the Malibamatso River in the Year 1840.* Morija, Lesotho: Morija Museum and Archives, 1991.

Askew, Kelly Michelle. *Performing the Nation: Swahili Music and Cultural Politics in Tanzania.* Chicago: University of Chicago Press, 2002.

Bailkin, Jordana. "Where Did the Empire Go? Archives and Decolonization in Britain." *American Historical Review* 120, no. 3 (2015): 884–99.

Bank, Leslie. "The Failure of Ethnic Nationalism: Land, Power and the Politics of Clanship on the South African High Veld 1860–1990." *Africa* 65, no. 4 (1995): 565–91.

———. "The Janus-Face of Rural Class Formation: An Economic and Political History of Traders in QwaQwa, 1960–1985." University of Witwatersrand History Workshop, 1990.

Barber, James. *South Africa's Foreign Policy 1945–1970*. New York: Oxford University Press, 1973.

Barber, James, and John Barratt. *South Africa's Foreign Policy: The Search for Status and Security 1945–1988*. New York: Cambridge University Press, 1990.

Bardill, John E. "Destabilization: The Lesotho Case." Collected Seminar Papers. Institute of Commonwealth Studies, 1988.

Bardill, John E., and James Cobbe. *Lesotho: Dilemmas of Dependence in Southern Africa*. Boulder, CO: Westview Press, 1985.

Beinart, William. "Soil Erosion, Conservationism and Ideas about Development: A Southern African Exploration, 1900–1960." *Journal of Southern African Studies* 11, no. 1 (1984): 52–83.

Bender, Matthew V. "'For More and Better Water, Choose Pipes!': Building Water and the Nation on Kilimanjaro, 1961–1985." *Journal of Southern African Studies* 34, no. 4 (2008): 841–59.

Biemanns, J. W. *Lesotho, an Uphill Road*. Maseru: Government Printing, 1968.

Bolnick, Joel. "Potlako Leballo: The Man Who Hurried to Meet His Destiny." *Journal of Modern African Studies* 29, no. 3 (1991): 413–42.

Bonneuil, Christophe. "Development as Experiment: Science and State Building in Late Colonial and Postcolonial Africa, 1930–1970." *Osiris* 15 (2000): 258–81.

———. "Penetrating the Natives: Peanut Breeding, Peasants and the Colonial State in Senegal (1900–1950)." *Science, Technology and Society* 4, no. 2 (1999): 273–302.

Booth, Alan R. "Lord Selborne and the British Protectorates, 1908–1910." *Journal of African History* 10, no. 1 (1969): 133–48.

Bowman, Andrew. "Mass Production or Production by the Masses? Tractors, Cooperatives, and the Politics of Rural Development in Post-Independence Zambia." *Journal of African History* 52, no. 2 (2011): 201–21.

Brown, J. Larry. *Peasants Come Last: A Memoir of the Peace Corps at Fifty*. Sunnyvale, CA: Lucita Publishing, 2011.

Burman, Sandra. *Chiefdom Politics and Alien Law: Basutoland under Cape Rule, 1871–1884*. New York: Africana, 1981.

Casalis, Eugene. *The Basutos, or Twenty-Three Years in Southern Africa*. Morija, Lesotho: Morija Museum and Archives, 1992. Orig. pub. 1861.

Chakela, Mamapele. *The People Always Win*. Florida Hills, South Africa: Vivalia Publishers, 2006.

Cobbe, James. "Economic Aspects of Lesotho's Relations with South Africa." *Journal of Modern African Studies* 26, no. 1 (1988): 71–89.

Coe, Cati. *Dilemmas of Culture in African Schools: Youth, Nationalism, and the Transformation of Knowledge*. Chicago: University of Chicago Press, 2005.

Conz, Chris. "'Wisdom Does Not Live in One House': Compiling Environmental Knowledge in Lesotho, Southern Africa, c. 1885–1965." PhD diss., Boston University, 2017.

Cooper, Frederick. *Africa since 1940: The Presence of the Past*. Cambridge: Cambridge University Press, 2002.

———. *Decolonization and African Society: The Labor Question in French and British Africa*. New York: Cambridge University Press, 1996.

———. "Possibility and Constraint: African Independence in Historical Perspective." *Journal of African History* 49, no. 2 (2008): 167–96.

———. "Writing the History of Development." *Journal of Modern European History* 8, no. 1 (2010): 5–23.

Coplan, David. *In the Time of Cannibals: The Word Music of South Africa's Basotho Migrants*. Chicago: University of Chicago Press, 1994.

———. "A River Runs through It: The Meaning of the Lesotho–Free State Border." *African Affairs* 100, no. 398 (2001): 81–116.

Coplan, David, and Timothy Quinlan. "A Chief by the People: Nation versus State in Lesotho." *Africa: Journal of the International African Institute* 67, no. 1 (1997): 27–60.

Corbridge, Stuart, Glyn Williams, Manoj Srivastava, and Rene Veron. *Seeing the State: Governance and Governmentality in India*. New York: Cambridge University Press, 2005.

Crush, Jonathan, and Belinda Dodson. *Migration, Remittances and "Development" in Lesotho*. Cape Town: Idasa, 2010.

Crush, Jonathan, Alan Jeeves, and David Yudelman. *South Africa's Labor Empire: A History of Black Migrancy to the Mines*. Boulder, CO: Westview Press, 1991.

Cullather, Nick. "Development? It's History." *Diplomatic History* 24, no. 4 (2000): 641–53.

da Corta, Lucia. "The Political Economy of Agrarian Change: Dinosaur or Phoenix?" In *The Comparative Political Economy of Development: Africa and South Asia*, edited by Barbara Harriss-White and Judith Heyer, 18–46. New York: Routledge, 2010.

Darwin, John. *The Empire Project: The Rise and Fall of the British World System, 1830–1970*. New York: Cambridge University Press, 2009.

Davis, James, James J. Acres, William A. Daley, USAID, and US Soil Conservation Service. *An Evaluation of the Thaba Bosiu Rural Development Project in Lesotho*. Maseru: USAID, 1975.

Delius, Peter. *The Land Belongs to Us: The Pedi Polity, the Boers, and the British in the Nineteenth-Century Transvaal*. Berkeley: University of California Press, 1984.

de Wet, C. J. *Moving Together, Drifting Apart: Betterment Planning and Villagisation in a South African Homeland*. Johannesburg: Witwatersrand University Press, 1995.

Duncan, Tyrell, Frank Baffoe, and Karin Metell. *Support against Apartheid: An Evaluation of 28 Years of Development Assistance to Lesotho*. Stockholm: SIDA, 1994.

Easterly, William. *The Tyranny of Experts: Economists, Dictators, and the Forgotten Rights of the Poor*. New York: Basic Books, 2013.

Edgar, Robert. "The Lesotho Coup of 1986." *South African Review* 4 (1988): 373–82.

————. *The Making of an African Communist: Edwin Thabo Mofutsanyana and the Communist Party of South Africa, 1927–1939*. Pretoria: UNISA, 2005.

————. *Prophets with Honour: A Documentary History of Lekhotla la Bafo*. Johannesburg: Ravan Press, 1988.

Eldredge, Elizabeth. *Power in Colonial Africa: Conflict and Discourse in Lesotho, 1870–1960*. Madison: University of Wisconsin Press, 2008.

————. *A South African Kingdom: The Pursuit of Security in Nineteenth-Century Lesotho*. New York: Cambridge University Press, 1993.

Ellenberger, D. F., and J. C. Macgregor. *History of the Basuto: Ancient and Modern*. Morija, Lesotho: Morija Museum and Archives, 1992. Orig. pub. 1912.

Epprecht, Marc. "Domesticity and Piety in Colonial Lesotho: The Private Politics of Basotho Women's Pious Associations." *Journal of Southern African Studies* 19, no. 2 (1993): 202–24.

————. "Women's 'Conservatism' and the Politics of Gender in Late Colonial Lesotho." *Journal of African History* 36, no. 1 (1995): 29–56.

Epprecht, Marc, and Andrea Nattrass. *"This Matter of Women Is Getting Very Bad": Gender, Development and Politics in Colonial Lesotho*. Pietermaritzburg: University of Kwa-Zulu Natal Press, 2000.

Esenjor, Akinagum Fidelis. "A Community Based Conservation Programme for the Management and Conservation of Land Resources in Lesotho." PhD diss., University of the Free State, 2004.

Etherington, Norman. "A Tempest in a Teapot? Nineteenth-Century Contests for Land in South Africa's Caledon Valley and the Invention of the Mfecane." *Journal of African History* 45, no. 2 (2004): 203–19.

Ferguson, James. *The Anti-Politics Machine: "Development," Depoliticization, and Bureaucratic Power in Lesotho*. New York: Cambridge University Press, 1990.

————. "Paradoxes of Sovereignty and Independence: 'Real' and 'Pseudo-' Nation-States and the Depoliticization of Poverty." In *Global Shadows: Africa in the Neoliberal World Order*, edited by James Ferguson, 50–68. Durham, NC: Duke University Press, 2006.

Geiger, Susan. *TANU Women: Gender and Culture in the Making of Tanganyikan Nationalism, 1955–1965*. Portsmouth, NH: Heinemann, 1997.

Germond, R. C. *Chronicles of Basutoland: A Running Commentary on the Events of the Years 1830–1902*. Morija, Lesotho: Morija Sesuto Book Depot, 1967.

Gevisser, Mark. *Thabo Mbeki: The Dream Deferred*. Johannesburg: Jonathan Ball, 2007.

Gill, Stephen J. *A Short History of Lesotho*. Morija, Lesotho: Morija Museum and Archives, 1993.

Glaser, Clive. *The ANC Youth League*. Athens: Ohio University Press, 2012.

———. *Bo-Tsotsi: The Youth Gangs of Soweto, 1935–1976*. Portsmouth, NH: Heinemann, 2000.

Grubbs, Larry. *Secular Missionaries: Americans and African Development in the 1960s*. Boston: University of Massachusetts Press, 2009.

Guy, Jeff, and Motlatsi Thabane. "Technology, Ethnicity and Ideology: Basotho Miners and Shaft Sinking on the South African Gold Mines." *Journal of Southern African Studies* 14, no. 2 (1988): 257–78.

Hailey, Lord. *An African Survey: A Study of Problems Arising in Africa South of the Sahara*. New York: Oxford University Press, 1938.

———. *An Africa Survey Revised 1956: A Survey of Problems Arising in Africa South of the Sahara*. New York: Oxford University Press, 1957.

———. *Native Administration in the British African Territories: Part V, The High Commission Territories: Basutoland, the Bechuanaland Protectorate and Swaziland*. London: Her Majesty's Stationery Office, 1953.

Haliburton, G. M. "Walter Matitta and Josiel Lefela: A Prophet and a Politician in Lesotho." *History of Religion in Africa* 7, no. 2 (1975): 111–31.

Hatchard, John. "Recent Developments in Combating the Bribery of Foreign Public Officials: A Cause for Optimism." *University of Detroit Mercy Law Review* 85 (2007): 1–28.

Havel, Vaclav. "Never Hope against Hope." *Esquire* 120 (October 1993): 68.

Hirschmann, D. *Administration of Planning in Lesotho*. Manchester: University of Manchester Press, 1981.

———. "Changes in Lesotho's Policy toward South Africa." *African Affairs* 78, no. 311 (1979): 177–96.

———. "The Ramabanta-Semonkong Road Project in Lesotho: A Case Study on Community Development and National Planning." *Humanitas* 9, no. 2 (1983): 135–40.

Hodge, Joseph. "British Colonial Expertise, Post-Colonial Careering and the Early History of International Development." *Journal of Modern European History* 8, no. 1 (2010): 24–46.

———. *Triumph of the Expert: Agrarian Doctrines of Development and the Legacies of British Colonialism*. Athens: Ohio University Press, 2007.

Hodge, Joseph, and Gerald Hödl. "Introduction." In *Developing Africa: Concepts and Practices in Twentieth-Century Colonialism*, edited by Joseph Hodge, Gerald Hödl, and Martina Kopf, 1–34. Manchester: Manchester University Press, 2014.

Hoffman, Elizabeth Cobbs. *All You Need Is Love: The Peace Corps and the Spirit of the 1960s*. Cambridge, MA: Harvard University Press, 1998.

Hogendorn, J. S., and K. M. Scott. "The East African Groundnut Scheme: Lessons of a Large-Scale Agricultural Failure." *African Economic History* 10 (1981): 81–115.

Honeck, Mischa, and Gabriel Rosenberg. "Transnational Generations: Organizing Youth in the Cold War." *Diplomatic History* 38, no. 2 (2014): 233–39.

Hunter, Emma. "Dutiful Subjects, Patriotic Citizens, and the Concept of 'Good Citizenship' in Twentieth-Century Tanzania." *Historical Journal* 56, no. 1 (2013): 257–77.

———. "A History of *Maendeleo*: The Concept of 'Development' in Tanganyika's Late Colonial Public Sphere." In *Developing Africa: Concepts and Practices in Twentieth-Century Colonialism*, edited by Joseph Hodge, Gerald Hödl, and Martina Kopf, 87–107. Manchester: Manchester University Press, 2014.

———. "Voluntarism, Virtuous Citizenship, and Nation-Building in Late Colonial and Early Postcolonial Tanzania." *African Studies Review* 58, no. 2 (2015): 43–61.

Iliffe, John. *A Modern History of Tanganyika*. Cambridge: Cambridge University Press, 1979.

Isaacman, Allen F., and Barbara Isaacman. *Dams, Displacement, and the Delusion of Development: Cahora Bassa and Its Legacies in Mozambique, 1965–2007*. Athens: Ohio University Press, 2013.

Jingoes, Stimela Jason, J. G. Perry, and Cassandra Perry. *A Chief Is a Chief by the People: The Autobiography of Stimela Jason Jingoes*. New York: Oxford University Press, 1975.

Jones, Ben. *Beyond the State in Rural Uganda*. Edinburgh: Edinburgh University Press, 2009.

Kalley, Jacqueline Audrey, Elna Schoeman, and Lydia Eve Andor. *Southern African Political History: A Chronology of Key Political Events from Independence to Mid-1997*. Westport, CT: Greenwood Press, 1999.

Kaul, N. *Report on Local Government in Lesotho*. Maseru: Government Printing, 1966.

Kemp, Amanda D., and Robert Vinson. "'Poking Holes in the Sky': Professor James Thaele, American Negroes, and Modernity in 1920s Segregationist South Africa." *African Studies Review* 43, no. 1 (2000): 141–59.

Khaketla, B. M. *Lesotho 1970: An African Coup under the Microscope*. Berkeley: University of California Press, 1972.

Kieh, George K. *Beyond State Failure and Collapse: Making the State Relevant in Africa*. Lanham, MD: Lexington Books, 2007.

Kimble, Judith M. *Migrant Labour and Colonial Rule in Basutoland, 1890–1930*. Grahamstown, South Africa: Institute of Social and Economic Research, 1999.

Konczacki, Z. A., Jane Parpart, and Timothy Shaw, eds. *Studies in the Economic History of Southern Africa*. Vol. 2: *South Africa, Lesotho and Swaziland*. Hoboken, NJ: Routledge, 1990.

Kondlo, Kwandiwe. *In the Twilight of Revolution: The Pan Africanist Congress of Azania (South Africa), 1959–1994*. Basel: Basler Afrika Bibliographien, 2009.

Kotze, D. A. "The Witzieshoek Revolt 1940–1950." *African Studies* 41, no. 1 (1982): 127–41.

Krog, Antjie. *Begging to Be Black*. Cape Town: Random House Struik, 2009.

Kunene, Daniel P. "'Leselinyana la Lesotho' and Sotho Historiography." *History in Africa* 4 (1977): 149–61.

Kynoch, Gary. *We Are Fighting the World: A History of the Marashea Gangs of South Africa, 1947–1999*. Athens: Ohio University Press, 2005.

Lal, Priya. *African Socialism in Postcolonial Tanzania: Between the Village and the World*. New York: Cambridge University Press, 2015.

———. "Militants, Mothers, and the National Family: *Ujamaa*, Gender, and Rural Development in Postcolonial Tanzania." *Journal of African History* 51, no. 1 (2010): 1–20.

———. "Self Reliance and the State: The Multiple Meanings of Development in Early Post-Colonial Tanzania." *Africa* 82, no. 2 (2012): 212–34.

Lancaster, Carol. *Foreign Aid: Diplomacy, Development, Domestic Politics*. Chicago: University of Chicago Press, 2007.

———. *U.S. Aid to Sub-Saharan Africa: Challenges, Constraints, and Choices*. Washington, DC: Center for Strategic and International Studies, 1988.

Latham, Michael E. "Introduction: Modernization, International History and the Cold War World." In *Staging Growth: Modernization, Development, and the Global Cold War*, edited by David C. Engerman, Nils Gilman, Mark H. Haefele, and Michael E. Latham, 1–24. Boston: University of Massachusetts Press, 2003.

Lelimo, Martin Moloantoa. *The Question of Lesotho's Conquered Territory: It's Time for an Answer*. Morija, Lesotho: Morija Museum and Archives, 1998.

Limb, Peter. *The ANC's Early Years: Nation, Class and Place in South Africa before 1940*. Pretoria: UNISA Press, 2010.

Lissoni, Arianna. "The PAC in Basutoland, c. 1962–1965." *South African Historical Journal* 62, no. 1 (2010): 54–77.

Lodge, Tom. *Sharpeville: An Apartheid Massacre and Its Consequences*. New York: Oxford University Press, 2011.

Macartney, W. J. A. "The Lesotho General Election of 1970." *Government and Opposition* 8, no. 4 (1973): 473–94.

———, ed. *Readings in BOLESWA Government: Select Documents on the Government and Politics of Botswana, Lesotho and Swaziland*. Roma: University of Botswana, Lesotho and Swaziland Printing Unit, 1971.

Machobane, J. J., and Robert Berold. *Drive Out Hunger: The Story of J. J. Machobane of Lesotho*. Johannesburg: Jacana Media, 2005.

Machobane, L. B. B. J. *Government and Change in Lesotho, 1800–1966: A Study of Political Institutions*. New York: Cambridge University Press, 1990.

Magaziner, Daniel R. *The Law and the Prophets: Black Consciousness in South Africa, 1968–1977*. Athens: Ohio University Press, 2010.

Maier, Charles. *In Search of Stability: Explorations in Historical Political Economy.* New York: Cambridge University Press, 1987.

Makombe, E. Kushinga. "Developing Rural Africa: Rural Development Discourse in Colonial Zimbabwe, 1944–79." In *Developing Africa: Concepts and Practices in Twentieth-Century Colonialism*, edited by Joseph Hodge, Gerald Hödl, and Martina Kopf, 155–78. Manchester: Manchester University Press, 2014.

Maloka, Eddy Tshidiso. *Basotho and the Mines: A Social History of Labour Migrancy in Lesotho and South Africa, c. 1890–1940.* Dakar: CODESRIA, 2004.

Mamdani, Mahmood. *Citizen and Subject: Contemporary Africa and the Legacy of Late Colonialism.* Princeton, NJ: Princeton University Press, 1996.

Mann, Gregory. *From Empires to NGOs in the West African Sahel: The Road to Nongovernmentality.* New York: Cambridge University Press, 2015.

Mashologu, Mothusi T. *A Broken Reed: The Traumatic Experience of the Last Day of the University of Botswana, Lesotho and Swaziland, and Its Aftermath.* Morija, Lesotho: Phafa Publishers, 2006.

Matlosa, Khabele. "Aid, Development and Democracy in Lesotho, 1966–1996." Unpublished paper, Center for Southern African Studies, University of Western Cape, 1999.

———. "The State, Democracy and Development in Southern Africa." Paper prepared for the 11th General Assembly of CODESRIA, Maputo, Mozambique, December 2005.

Matlosa, Khabele, and Neville Pule. "The Military in Lesotho." *African Security Review* 10, no. 2 (2001): 62–74.

Maundeni, Zibani. "Political Culture as a Source of Political Instability: The Case of Lesotho." *African Journal of Political Science and International Relations* 4, no. 4 (2010): 128–39.

McAllister, P. A. "Resistance to 'Betterment' in the Transkei: A Case Study from Willowvale District." *Journal of Southern African Studies* 15, no. 2 (1989): 346–68.

McCracken, John. *A History of Malawi, 1859–1966.* Rochester, NY: James Currey, 2012.

McGregor, Joann. *Cross the Zambezi: The Politics of Landscape on a Central African Frontier.* Rochester, NY: Boydell & Brewer, 2009.

Mda, Zakes. *Sometimes There Is a Void: Memoirs of an Outsider.* New York: Farrar, Straus and Giroux, 2012.

Mohapeloa, J. M. *Tentative British Imperialism in Lesotho, 1884–1910: A Study in Basotho–Colonial Office Interaction and South Africa's Influence on It.* Morija, Lesotho: Morija Museum and Archives, 2002.

Monson, Jamie. *Africa's Freedom Railway: How a Chinese Development Project Changed Lives and Livelihoods in Tanzania.* Bloomington: Indiana University Press, 2009.

Moodie, T. Dunbar, and Vivienne Ndatshe. *Going for Gold: Men, Mines, and Migration*. Berkeley: University of California Press, 1994.

Moorman, Marissa Jean. *Intonations: A Social History of Music and Nation in Luanda, Angola, from 1945 to Recent Times*. Athens: Ohio University Press, 2008.

Morgan, Eric J. "Our Own Interests: Nixon, South Africa, and Dissent at Home and Abroad." *Diplomacy and Statecraft* 17, no. 3 (2006): 475–95.

Moskowitz, Kara. "'Are You Planting Trees or Are You Planting People?' Squatter Resistance and International Development in the Making of a Kenyan Postcolonial Political Order (c. 1963–78)." *Journal of African History* 56, no. 1 (2015): 99–118.

Mothibe, T. H. "Lesotho: Historical Legacies of Nationalism and Nationhood." In *Southern Africa after Apartheid: Prospects for the Inner Periphery in the 1990s*, edited by Sehoai Santho and Mafa Sejanamane, 188–93. Harare: SAPES Trust, 1991.

———. "The Military and Democratization in Lesotho." *Lesotho Social Science Review* 5, no. 1 (1999): 47–63.

Motloheloa, John. "Lesotho's Road to Independence—The Founding of the Communist Party of Lesotho (Basutoland)." *African Communist* 10 (1962): 21–30.

Mphanya, Ntsukunyane. *A Brief History of the Basutoland Congress Party, Lekhotla la Mahatammoho: 1952–2002*. Morija, Lesotho: Morija Printing Works, 2004.

Muehlenbeck, Philip E. *Betting on the Africans: John F. Kennedy's Courting of African Nationalist Leaders*. New York: Oxford University Press, 2014.

Muiu, Mueni Wa. *The Pitfalls of Liberal Democracy and Late Nationalism in South Africa*. New York: Palgrave Macmillan, 2008.

Murray, Colin. *Families Divided: The Impact of Migrant Labour in Lesotho*. New York: Cambridge University Press, 1981.

Murray, Colin, and Peter Sanders. *Medicine Murder in Colonial Lesotho: The Anatomy of a Moral Crisis*. Edinburgh: Edinburgh University Press, 2005.

Mwangi, Oscar. "Environmental Change and Human Security in Lesotho: The Role of the Lesotho Highlands Water Project in Environmental Degradation." *African Security Review* 17, no. 3 (2008): 58–70.

———. "Hydropolitics, Ecocide, and Human Security in Lesotho: A Case Study of the Lesotho Highlands Water Project." *Journal of Southern African Studies* 33, no. 1 (2007): 3–17.

Ngqaleni, Malijeng. "A Review of Lesotho's Agricultural Policies and Strategies for the 1990s." In *Southern Africa after Apartheid: Prospects for the Inner Periphery in the 1990s*, edited by Sehoai Santho and Mafa Sejanamane, 128–46. Harare: SAPES Trust, 1991.

Ohiorhenuan, John F. E. "Don't Cry for Me Africa." *Transition* 102 (2010): 140–55.

Parsons, Timothy. *Race, Resistance, and the Boy Scout Movement in British Colonial Africa*. Athens: Ohio University Press, 2004.

Peterson, Derek R. *Creative Writing: Translation, Bookkeeping, and the Work of Imagination in Colonial Kenya*. Portsmouth, NH: Heinemann, 2004.

Piot, Charles. *Nostalgia for the Future: West Africa after the Cold War*. Chicago: University of Chicago Press, 2010.

Platteau, Jean-Philippe. "Institutional Obstacles to African Economic Development: State, Ethnicity and Custom." *Journal of Economic Behavior and Organization* 71 (2009): 669–89.

Power, Joey. *Political Culture and Nationalism in Malawi: Building Kwacha*. Rochester, NY: Rochester University Press, 2010.

Ritchie, Donald A. *Doing Oral History*. New York: Twayne Publishers, 1995.

Robertson, A. F. "Popular Scientist: James Jacob Machobane and 'Mantsa Tlala.'" *African Affairs* 93, no. 370 (1994): 99–121.

Rosenberg, Scott. *Promises of Moshoeshoe: Culture, Nationalism, and Identity in Lesotho*. Roma, Lesotho: Institute of Southern African Studies, 2008.

Rostow, Walter. *Stages of Growth: A Non-Communist Manifesto*. New York: Cambridge University Press, 1960.

Rotberg, Robert. *Peacekeeping and Peace Enforcement in Africa: Methods of Conflict Prevention*. Washington, DC: Brookings Institution Press, 2010.

Rwelamira, Medard. *Refugees in a Chess Game: Reflections on Botswana, Lesotho and Swaziland Refugee Policies*. Uppsala: Scandinavian Institute of African Studies, 1990.

Sanders, Peter. *Moshoeshoe, Chief of the Sotho*. London: Heinemann, 1975.

———. *"Throwing Down White Man": Cape Rule and Misrule in Colonial Lesotho, 1871–1884*. Pontypool, Wales: Merlin Press, 2011.

Schneider, Leander. *Government of Development: Peasants and Politicians in Postcolonial Tanzania*. Bloomington: Indiana University Press, 2014.

Scott, James C. *Seeing Like a State: How Certain Schemes to Improve the Human Condition Have Failed*. New Haven, CT: Yale University Press, 1998.

Sekoati, Michael Seeiso. *The History of the Roman Catholic Church in Lesotho: 1862–1989*. Pretoria: UNISA Press, 2001.

Showers, Kate B. *Imperial Gullies: Soil Erosion and Conservation in Lesotho*. Athens: Ohio University Press, 2005.

Smith, Edwin W. *The Mabilles of Basutoland*. Morija, Lesotho: Morija Museum and Archives, 1996. Originally published 1939.

Smith, R. Drew, and Stephanie C. Boddie. "Civic Service in Lesotho: Local Sources and US Connections." CSD Research Report 08-34, 2008, https://csd.wustl.edu/publications/documents/rp08-34.pdf.

Smyth, Rosaleen. "The Roots of Community Development in Colonial Office Policy and Practice in Africa." *Social Policy and Administration* 38, no. 4 (2004): 418–36.

South African Democracy Education Trust. *The Road to Democracy in South Africa*, vol. 2 (1970–80). Pretoria: UNISA Press, 2006.

Straker, Jay. "Youth, Globalisation and Millennial Reflection in a Guinean Forest Town." *Journal of Modern African History* 45, no. 2 (2007): 299–319.

———. *Youth, Nationalism and the Guinean Revolution.* Bloomington: Indiana University Press, 2009.

Ström, Gabriel Winai. *Development and Dependence in Lesotho, the Enclave of South Africa.* Uppsala: Scandinavian Institute of African Studies, 1978.

———. *Migration and Development. Dependence on South Africa: A Study of Lesotho.* Uppsala: Scandinavian Institute of African Studies, 1986.

Tague, Joanna. "Before Asylum and Expert Witness: Mozambican Refugee Settlement and Rural Development in Southern Tanzania, 1964–75." In *African Asylum at a Crossroads: Activism, Expert Testimony, and Refugee Rights*, edited by Iris Berger, Tricia Redeker Hepner, Benjamin N. Lawrance, Joanna T. Tague, and Meredith Terretta, 38–57. Athens: Ohio University Press, 2015.

Tashjian, Victoria, and Jean Allman. *"I Will Not Eat Stone": A Women's History of Colonial Asante.* Portsmouth, NH: Heinemann, 2000.

Thabane, Motlatsi. "Aspects of Colonial Economy and Society, 1868–1966." In *Essays on Aspects of the Political Economy of Lesotho, 1500–2000*, edited by Motlatsi Thabane and Neville Pule, 103–30. Roma, Lesotho: Department of History, 2000.

———. *Individual Diamond Digging in Lesotho, 1955–1970: A Study of an Aspect of the Social and Economic History of Lesotho.* Trondheim Studies in History No. 8. Trondheim, Norway: The University, 1995.

———. *"Liphokojoe* of Kao: A Study of a Diamond Digger Rebel Group in the Lesotho Highlands." *Journal of Southern African Studies* 26, no. 1 (2000): 105–21.

———. *Who Owns the Land in Lesotho? Land Disputes and the Politics of Land Ownership in Lesotho.* Roma, Lesotho: Institute of Southern African Studies, 1998.

Thamae, Mabusetsa Lenka, and Lori Pottinger, eds. *On the Wrong Side of Development: Lessons Learned from the Lesotho Highlands Water Project.* Maseru: Transformation Resource Center, 2006.

Thomas, Martin. "Contrasting Patterns of Decolonization: Belgian and Portuguese Africa." In *Crises of Empire: Decolonization and Europe's Imperial States, 1918–1975*, edited by Martin Thomas, Bob Moore, and L. J. Butler, 385–410. London: Hodder Education, 2008.

Thompson, Leonard. *Survival in Two Worlds: Moshoeshoe of Lesotho, 1786–1870.* Oxford: Clarendon Press, 1975.

Tropp, Jacob. "The Contested Nature of Colonial Landscapes: Historical Perspectives on Livestock and Environments in the Transkei." *Kronos* 30 (2004): 118–37.

Turkon, David. "Commoners and Kings and Subaltern: Political Factionism and Structured Inequality in Lesotho." *Political and Legal Anthropology Review* 31 (2008): 203–23.

Van Allen, Judith. "'Bad Future Things' and Liberatory Moments: Capitalism, Gender and the State in Botswana." *Radical History Review* 76 (2000): 136–68.

van Beusekom, Monica M. *Negotiating Development: African Farmers and Colonial Experts at the Office du Niger, 1920–1960*. Portsmouth, NH: Heinemann, 2002.

van der Wiel, A. C. A. *Migratory Wage Labour: Its Role in the Economy of Lesotho*. Mazenod, Lesotho: Mazenod Book Centre, 1977.

Vinson, Robert. *The Americans Are Coming! Dreams of African American Liberation in Segregationist South Africa*. Athens: Ohio University Press, 2011.

Wainwright, Joel. *Decolonizing Development: Colonial Power and the Maya*. Malden, MA: Wiley-Blackwell, 2008.

Wallman, Sandra. "Lesotho's *Pitso*: Traditional Meetings in a Modern Setting." *Canadian Journal of African Studies* 2, no. 2 (1968): 167–74.

———. *Take Out Hunger: Two Case Studies of Rural Development in Basutoland*. London: Athlone Press, 1969.

Weisfelder, Richard. "The Basotho Nation-State: What Legacy for the Future?" *Journal of Modern African Studies* 19, no. 2 (1981): 221–56.

———. "Early Voices of Protest in Basutoland: The Progressive Association and Lekhotla la Bafo." *African Studies Review* 17, no. 2 (1974): 397–409.

———. *Political Contention in Lesotho, 1952–1965*. Roma, Lesotho: Institute of Southern African Studies, 1999.

———. "Power Struggle in Lesotho." *Africa Report* 12, no. 1 (1967): 5–13.

Westad, Odd Arne. *The Global Cold War: Third World Interventions and the Making of Our Times*. New York: Cambridge University Press, 2005.

Woodward, Calvin. "Not a Complete Solution: Assessing the Long Years of Foreign Aid to Lesotho." *Africa Insight* 12, no. 3 (1982): 167–79.

Young, Crawford. *The African Colonial State in Comparative Perspective*. New Haven, CT: Yale University Press, 1994.

———. "Nation, Ethnicity, and Citizenship: Dilemmas of Democracy and Civil Order in Africa." In *Making Nations, Creating Strangers*, edited by Sara Dorman, Daniel Hammett, and Paul Nugent, 241–64. Boston: Brill, 2007.

———. *The Postcolonial State in Africa: Fifty Years of Independence, 1960–2010*. Madison: University of Wisconsin Press, 2012.

INDEX

Page references in **bold** indicate a table; page references in *italics* indicate a figure.

JOHN AERNI-FLESSNER is an assistant professor in the Residential College in the Arts and Humanities at Michigan State University.

Milton Keynes UK
Ingram Content Group UK Ltd.
UKHW021014240124
436597UK00003B/44